INDIA
An Ancient Exotic Wonderland of Mystic Environment

INDIA

An Ancient Exotic Wonderland of Mystic Environment

P.K. Ray

KALPAZ

ISBN: 978-93-5128-006-4

Price: ₹ 990

First Published 2014

Published by

Kalpaz Publications
C-30, Satyawati Nagar,
Delhi - 110052
E-mail: kalpaz@hotmail.com Ph.: 9212142040

Laser Typesetting : Rajender Vashist, Delhi
Printed at: Printed in India at Artxel, Noida 201 30

Cataloging in Publication Data--DK
Courtesy: D.K. Agencies (P) Ltd. <docinfo@dkagencies.com>

Ray, P. K.

India : an ancient exotic wonderland of mystic environment / P.K. Ray.

p. cm.

Includes index.

ISBN 9789351280064

1. Environmental sciences--India. 2. Pollution--India. 3. Environmental protection--India. I. Title.

DDC 363.700954 23

Contents

Preface

In the present book entitled "India: An Ancient Exotic Wonderland of Mystic Environment", I have attempted to provide some glimpses of India's past glory highlighting the golden periods of India, including its famous scriptures, poets, religious figures and the early Indian culture etc. Information about the Epics of India like Ramayana and Mahabharatha and its great impact on Indian psyche has been detailed. For the benefit of all, especially the present generation, a scenario has been depicted such that one can visualise what India was and can also feel proud of being an Indian. Some major Indian monuments, its architectural beauty, varied but wonderful temple architectures, Indian climatic variations and its environmental beauty, etc., are also discussed and presented with some majestic pictures. Indian family structures, Indian foods, Indian customs, traditional marriages, Indian clothes and uniforms are also discussed.

Some emphasis has been laid on the Environment around India, together with its exotic Ecology and Biological diversities. That Environmental degradation is in increasing order because of the various developmental programmes and people's indifference have also been brought forth. The growing pollution problems and its impact on human health has also been discussed. It has been suggested that, if continues unabated, someday it might appear to be unmanageable. Some pollution control measures have been highlighted as a part of increasing awareness among the students and people at large. It has also been prescribed as to what is needed to be done by us to increase our consciousness regarding pollution problems and what pollution control measures are needed to be practised at all levels. I hope and firmly believe that this book will meet the long-standing need of such a book in the market in order to educate the young and curious minds such that they could know more about the positive aspects of India.

Foreigners, Tourists and Researchers might like to educate them further to know more about India and its mystic Environment. I would consider my efforts a great success if it meets everyone's purpose.

P.K. Ray

Acknowledgements

I am deeply indebted to Wikipedia-the free Encyclopaedia, from which I have drawn substantial information about various issues/matters discussed in this book. I am also indebted to Internet, different Websites, etc., for different pictures and other information about India. I am also very much grateful to M/s Kalpaz Publications, Delhi for taking the responsibility to print, publish and distribute this book.

P.K. Ray

General Introduction

India: An Ancient Exotic Wonderland of Mystic Environment

India is one of the ancient civilisations on earth along with the two other old Civilisations of the World, the Egyptian and Chinese civilisations. Long ago, Indian civilisation flourished in many different directions–arts, science, economics, trade and commerce and also in the area of engineering, sculpture, and architecture. So much so that it drew the attentions of the entire world. People were interested to visit India and learn from India's experiences in various directions.

Indian Philosophy pervaded in almost every sphere of life suggesting how to maintain a good healthy life. There has been a very deep religious fervor in the Indian Philosophy. Naturopathy was practiced. Meditation was followed as a part of uplifting self-consciousness, for better self-control and to go to the state of self-enlightenment.

Many people, traders and businessmen from around the World used to come to India for business purposes and also to get familiarity with its environment and Philosophy. Indian wisdom and philosophy always attracted scores of people from around the world. The Chinese traveler Hiu-en-sung gave a detailed account description about India after he toured every nook and corner of India. The Nalanda Vishwavidyalaya (University) was an ancient and very old University of India where Education flourished in various areas, attracting students from various parts of the World.

The Indians had deep sense of love and respect towards their environment from the very beginning. They used to fear various exotic environmental events, such as lightning in the sky, thunder-storms, heavy rains, floods, earthquakes, epidemic diseases etc. They used to believe that if mother's nature is mistreated and tortured inflicting wounds, Nature would retaliate in the form as above. So they used to respect nature as one's own mother and tried to protect it by all means. They used to worship mother nature. That is the reason we find in ancient scriptures that they conceptualised that about each of the natural objects there is a *God* or

Goddess, and used to revere and worship them such that they are not subjected to their anger and curses. Such deep love and respect towards our environmental objects continued through ages in India. Ancient Indians could realise that if they cannot protect their environment they would simply destroy themselves. They realised long ago that for food they have to depend on nature, for air they have to depend on nature and also for water they have to depend on nature, since food, air and water are the three basic requirements for the sustenance of life. So they did everything possible to protect the environment.

In ancient India, several illustrious poets and writers were born. Among them whose names appear in our mind are—Maharishi Valmiki, Ved Vyas, Mahakabi Kalidasha, Gautama Buddha, Lord Mahavira, Guru Nanak, Shree Chaitanya Mahaprabhu, Shree Ramakrishna, Swami Vivekananda and many others. So far as early India is concerned several names as above, comes in our mind because of their tremendous contributions. Balmiki's Ramayana and Mahabharata by Ved Vyas emerged as two great EPICS attracting attention of the World. So also was Kalidasa's **Meghdoot**. Many years later, Nobel Laureate Rabindranath Tagore created, through his poems and verses, nritya natya and other literatures in the world. Several other writers and poets such as Bankim Chandra Chattopadhya, Saratchandra, Madhusudan Datta, Kazi Nazrul Islam, Tara Shankar Bandyopadhyay, Bibhutibhusan Bandyopadhyay or Manikopadhyay and many others like Kabir also created some astounding literatures which could stand the test of time survived many years. Many of these works were translated in various languages in India and abroad.

Hindi Novelist, such as Munshi Premchand, Mulk Raj Anand, Hindi/ Poet, Mahadevi Verma, Meera, Mirza Ghalib and other also contributed significantly.

Gautama Buddha, Mahavira, Guru Nanak, Chaitanya Mahaprabhu and Shree Ramakrishna were sages and religious preachers of Buddhism, Jainism, Sikhism and Hinduism respectively. But spreading one common thought that all religions are equal and meet at one focal point–that all creatures are created by **God**. Love and respect them all and help them in every possible way. As time passes, such philosophy became stronger and stronger and is now deep-rooted in the Indian psyche.

After passing through thousands of years, India emerged as a country of its own. Indians were very religious and India and its ancient inhabitants were basically Hindus. Later, after the birth of Gautama Buddha and Mahavira, Buddhism and Jainism spread in some part of India. Buddhism also spread in the entire South East Asia, but remained somewhat squeezed in most of India. India was invaded by the foreigners again and again. Muslim rulers from adjacent nations invaded India again and again and ruled over this country for about 300 hundred years gradually they occupied most of the country. There were several Princely states, Nawabs, Rajas and Maharajas, who were fighting among themselves. Ultimately came the British East India Company, initially to do business in India. but later they occupied most part of the country and brought it under the British rule.

For long 200 years, India fought against the British for independence and many stalwarts from India gave the leadership needed to fight out the British. Notable among them are—Mahatma Gandhi, Netaji Subhas Chandra Bose, Pandit Jawaharlal Nehru, Sardar Patel, Abul Kalam Azad Rajendra Prasad, Lala Rajpat Rai, Chittaranjan Das and many others. There were some groups who preferred a revolutionary type of movement against the British. Notable among them were –Rishi Aurobindo Ghosh, Khudiram Das, Master Da, Jatin Das, Bhagat Singh and many others. Ultimately, India got its independence in 1947. Independent sovereign state of India was born, but fully torn apart into India (mostly populated by the Hindus) and Pakistan (mostly populated by the Muslims). Before leaving the country, the British did a permanent damage in this subcontinent. One nation was divided into two. These two nations are still fighting with each other and had shown deep-rooted animosity against each other and even fought three Wars already.

Sovereign India soon dedicated its entire efforts and attention in the area of nation-building—a task which was not so easy. But India could make it within a short period of time. It took some 4-5 decades and India gradually became one of the strongest nations on earth, economically, scientifically, educationally, agriculturally and otherwise. India is now one of the front liners in terms of its agricultural and industrial productivity. In the recent past, its GDP had touched upto 8.5 and aspires for more heights to achieve.

If we look at the environmental side, India's overall environment is full of mystic beauty, wonders, and awesome diversity. India also possesses a vibrant, culturally rich social environment, which are also different in different parts of India. It drew the attentions of foreigners and tourists in millions every year to visit India. In spite of differences, you will see in India a perfect place of Unity in Diversity. In different parts of India, you will see a culturally vibrant group of people living side by side, sharing and caring for each other. This is the uniqueness of India and there lies the real strength of India.

Environmentally, you will also see that the Country is blessed by the creator by placing The mighty Himalayan Range in the North East, exotic scenic breath-taking beauty in Kashmir in the north, the Thar desert in Rajasthan in the North West, and Andaman and Nicober Islands in the extreme South where you may find the Adivasis living still in the Jungle-in one hand, all these are Tourists' delight. On the other, it had also guarded the geographical boundaries of India from foreign adventurism, external invasions and other onslaughts. The mighty Himalayas in the entire North East, and the Arabian Sea, Indian Ocean, and the Bay of Bengal appeared to provide protective barriers guarding the entire North Eastern, Western, Eastern and the extreme southern part of India. The North West is being safeguarded by the Thar Desert. It is a unique geographic character of India.

India's population rapidly grew to 1.28 billion. Many of them are still poor, poverty-stricken and with no education or less education. These are primarily responsible to increase the pollution level in the country. Initially, there were unplanned growth and development which added to the pollution problems so much so, that the environment around us is becoming unlivable gradually because of indifference, negligence, increasing greed, uprising consumerism, unplanned development, indiscriminate industrialisation and above all the failures of containment of pollution by legislation. Environment and Philosophy are responsible for all these? There can be just one answer – it is the people at large. Basically, all of us are responsible for this increasing order of pollution of our environment. Therefore, the responsibility bestows on us to ensure that we do not pollute and also allow others to pollute.

I am sure you will agree with me that the greatest creation of Mother Nature is the creation of *Earth*. It took millions of years to become a habitable place where the living being can live and survive. Several millions of years have passed by to get ultimately the optimum concentration of oxygen in our air, the optimum amount of heat on the surface of earth and also water. After the single cell appeared together with food and nutrients for supporting the cell growth, gradually larger plants and animals appeared in the horizon. Only those which could tolerate the prevailing atmospheric conditions they could only survived and others got extinct.

Gradually human beings were evolved through the long stretch of the evolutionary processes. Lower aquatic animals and plants came of course earlier. Through the intricate process of evolution, surprisingly only one place was created in this planet, our Earth, which is the only suitable place so far known where man and his ecological partners, i.e., animals, birds, plants, insects, parasites, and a large body of microorganisms can survive and thrive. We need all of them for the maintenance of the ecological balance, for maintaining the prey and predator relationship. There is a harmony, a unique balance, music, a tune in the Nature around us that keeps everything bonded together. It's a give and take policy that exists here. If this harmony, this balance, is lost we would face serious repercussions in the form of Nature's fury in one form or another. To day we all must have recognised that Nature's fury is no longer a mysterious thing any more; it is a counter action against man's insults to our mother nature.

Today, we see a tremendous population explosion in our planet! During the past half of the twentieth century (primarily from 1950–2000), there had been a galloping increase in the population of the World. India is the second largest in terms of population load (1.28 Billion), the first being China. It had sounded an alarm that unless population increase can be checked, it itself might be the cause of destruction of the world someday.

Everybody is now realising that Nature has only limited carrying capacity. Its own reserves of land mass, drinking water, and water for irrigation of lands, and mineral resources, etc., might not be always available in an abundant quantity, particularly when the pollution levels will rise further.

Although three parts of the world is full of water, when it comes to the question of drinking water and water for irrigation purposes, it is already in short supply. One should not be surprised if someday water famine take place and people die of shortage of drinking water. Already most of the available water resources are polluted. Cities are crowded with buildings, our sewerage system has become very poor, density of population is very high in urban areas, and air pollutants are increasing day by day. Industries are coming up here and there. Big housing complexes are sprouting up both within and outside the cities. Thus, agricultural land is gradually shrinking. The environmental pollution is now threatening our ambient environment and ecology. It has started affecting both human and animal health, causing also an ecological imbalance. Someday it might go to the extent that the very existence of man might be at risk, say after 300–500 years, it might be the only cause for destruction of this environment, that no life will be possible here anymore!

India is an ancient nation with rich tradition, varied culture, vast wisdom and tremendous philosophical insights. When rest of the world was in its primitive profile, India flourished almost in every respect showing an example before the rest of the world. India's history was full of ups and downs. Still it did exist and has ultimately emerged as a strongest nation on earth. Within its exotic diversity, the country has inherited great wisdom and philosophy that enabled it to go ahead of others within a short period of time after independence.

Love and respect for nature has always been a part of India's culture. There are various religious scriptures and ancient literatures of India where people had been asked to respect nature and its objects and live in a peaceful coexistence with each other and one another. The nature was considered to be a Mother figure which reared everything very affectionately for our benefits, for our existence and the existence of the future. The nature was considered to be like Gods and Goddesses and was even asked to worship them and protect them dearly.

Of course, we all know something or the other about our environment. The entire galaxy, the horizons, stratospheric, ionospheric and atmospheric zones of the environment are composed of terrestrial and extraterrestrial bodies, the sun, the moon, and all the planets including earth with its Biotic and Abiotic bodies. These are all a part of our Environment. Water (aquatic and marine), soil, air, the forests, deserts, grasslands, mountains, the entire flora and fauna, microbes, parasites, both uni-cellular and multi-cellular organisms, virus particles, microscopic plants and animals (both phytoplanktons and zooplanktons), larger animals including man and woman; all are constituent parts of our Natural Environment.

What is Environmental Science?

Today it has become a reality to understand more about the Environment and the science behind it. Environmental science is the study of the science of environment. It studies the interaction among the various units of the environment and its effects on the health of each of the components of the environment. The environmental science also deals with the reasons causing continuous pollution through various man-made activities. It deals with the hazards of various toxic chemicals on man and his environment and attempts to find out how the pollution of the environment can be averted.

What are our Main Environmental Problems Today?

Our main environmental problems basically are—polluted drinking water, polluted air and contaminated or spoiled foods, an abrupt change in our weather conditions due to global warming phenomena, an increasing order of ozone hole transmitting Ultraviolet rays directly on earth's surface, vanishing habitats and ecosystems, increasing numbers of endangered species, eruption of new organisms or resistant species of organisms, and so evolution of new diseases from time to time having no knowledge of any treatment etc. We have to restrict the pollution problems by taking several measures— regular monitoring and strictest legislative measures are required. "Polluters Pay" should not be limited only as a slogan; it should be implemented also sincerely and honestly.

Himalayan Expedition—Human Endeavors to know the unknown mysteries of NATURE had always been a part of human interests, which actually helped man to know the unknowns and discover many facets of our lives and our environment.

First Himalayan Expedition (as shown in the picture above).

Carbon Emission

As has been said above, men always tried to know the unknown mysteries of Nature. He loved and enjoyed adventure. Through such adventure, men discovered many things which increased our knowledge considerably. Adventurism has become a sport these days all over the world. Man has discovered many things which made our lives beautiful and more comfortable. As a result our environment is getting polluted. Global Warming is thc off-shoots of that, threatening the very existence of Nature and its Beauty. Melting of Glaciers in the North Pole has become an unfortunate reality today because of an increasing order of Pollution burden in our environment (primarily due to increasing rate of Carbon emissions in our environment).

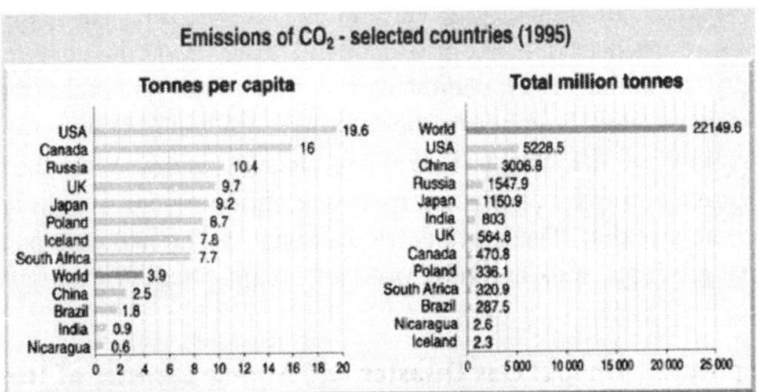

The chart above shows the Emissions of CO_2 by country in 1995. Data: United Nations Environment Programme.

Global Perspectives of Environmental Pollution

The entire world is very much concerned regarding the growing pollution burden of our environment. Pollution has been increasing at such a galloping rate that the people have become very much worried. Environmental pollution has become one such area, which is a matter of great concern for everybody, since pollutants do not rest or get confined within the geographical boundaries of any one country or a region. Through water and air it spreads all over the world; first to the adjacent nations and then gradually to others. Due to increasing global trade and commerce it might reach from one part of the world to another.

Ozone hole have already been spotted over both the north and the south poles. These are believed to be due to the increase in "Greenhouse Gases". They are responsible for "Global Warming Phenomena". Global warming is a great cause of concern as the rate by which the Earth's surface temperature is increasing it will have very adverse effect on our climate. We will discuss this later.

Halogenated gaseous substances, methane (CH_4), other hydrocarbons, nitric Oxide (NO_2), carbon dioxide (CO_2), are the major contributors to cause green house effects. CFCs (chlorofluorocarbons), brominated hydrocarbons and chlorinated hydrocarbons are responsible for causing holes in the protective ozone layers in our upper atmospheres. Normally, the thick ozone layer does not allow the harmful ultraviolet rays to pass through and come all the way to the surface of earth. If ultraviolet light (UV) may pass through the thin ozone layer, it may cause skin cancer, various other skin disorders, such as dermatitis, keratitis etc.

We are surrounded by many harmful or toxic chemicals, such as pesticides, fungicides, rodenticides, herbicides, coloring matters, food additives, food preservatives, various toxic gases, dusts, car exhausts, industrial wastes, municipal and agricultural wastes, etc. Through export-import of various materials (both consumables and non-consumables) from one country to another. Toxic chemicals also move from one place to another. In these days of global economy, there is more trade and commerce among various nations of the world. Therefore, chances of traveling the disease causing germs and toxic chemicals from one region of the world to another have become a reality. These are carried through by human beings, animals and animal products, milk and milk products, plants, both raw and processed foods etc.

Toxic Exposure—Bhopal Gas Disaster and Atomic Disaster of Hiroshima and Nagasaki

It has been the eye-opener of the world as to how dangerous the toxic pollutants could be on man and his environment. An accidental release of very toxic Methyl isocyanite gas (MIC) from the storage tanks at the Union Carbide factory at Bhopal, India, killed more than 3500 people just overnight and more than several thousand people are still suffering after long 20 years from various ailments. Such was the intensity of the health impact of that very toxic gas. This has shown to the world how toxic chemicals could be to human beings and his environment. Several thousand domestic animals died overnight due to exposure to MIC gas. Pond Water in the nearby lake got poisoned killing several thousand fish. Tree leaves were burnt and many trees were burnt completely. Several thousand cattle, goats, and poultry lied dead on the road side in the direction of the wind through which MIC gas was spreading around. These are some of the examples of man-made and accidental disasters in our history. Nothing could of course surpass the devastations caused by dropping of two atom bombs on Hiroshima and Nagasaki of Japan during the Second World War by USA. Several thousand people were spontaneously dead and several thousand people became the victims of exposure to Radiation and had been suffering from Cancer, blood diseases, mental problems, miscarriages, blindness etc.

Nuclear Programmes

Ambitious nuclear programmes adopted in various countries of the world also pose potential threat to man and his environment. It is a major problem as to how to deal with nuclear waste materials. Three miles island in USA, had to release once huge amount of radioactive water to save the entire plant. The infamous Chernobyl disaster in USSR and it's after effects, and nuclear attacks on Hiroshima and Nagasaki are some of the concrete examples as to how dangerous they are.

Consumerism

The psyche of consumerism is becoming a threat to the environment. It is a potential cause for generating an increasing order of garbage and dumping them on agricultural or forest lands. It spoils not only the quality of the soil, but it also kills the soil flora and fauna by covering them up and depriving them of sunlight and food material. Most significant among these are various plastic and polymeric bags and other materials. Those are non-biodegradable. It causes variety of dangers to human health including cancer and also harms the quality of the environment.

What are the Roots of Environmental Pollution?

There are many different reasons for environmental pollution. Some of them are described below:

1. The root of all environmental problems lies in the various bad practices of human beings by themselves. Increasing population burden, poverty, less or no education, superstition, greed, abnormal ambition, etc., are some of the root causes of increasing order of pollution.

2. Human bad habits, such as smoking; living in unsanitary conditions such as in slum areas;
3. Human greed for more income by way of adulterating food materials, using non-permitted colors;
4. To indulge in spending huge amount of money in advertising so as to glamorise various merchandise to attract and spoil the young minds; this causes social pollution;
5. Hankering for more power and attempting to take control of other nations by force or deliberately declaring war or pronounce sanctions and even to go to indulge in dropping Nuclear bombs;
6. Modern life styles such as too much dependence on processed foods, cigarette smoking, taking drugs and various hallucinating medicines, not allowing breast feeding, not to go to bear child at early ages, indulging in abnormal sexual practices etc.;
7. Also, having too ambitious aptitudes and growing attractions toward taking various drugs, steroids, and other stimulators by the athletes, students and sport-persons for better performance, are becoming a common practice of today's society. It's dangerous! It has to be checked by all means; otherwise a whole society may be ruined.

We must recognise that Pollutants are slow poisons. These are produced due to various man-made activities. It kills us bit by bit, without giving us any early signals. Therefore, proper environmental education is a must to make us sufficiently aware as to how to protect our environment. Our present as well as our future generations should have adequate knowledge about our environment, the cause of pollution, its adverse effects and how to mitigate the pollution problems etc.

This book can be used as a general guide book to expand our knowledge about India, regarding the Environment as a whole. In this book Environment has been looked into in a broader perspective. Discussions on the early Universe, evolution of man and his environment containing water, air, soil, forests, etc., have found place in this book. Our how environment is getting polluted because of man-made activities that have found places in the book. Our heritage, environmental contrasts, our needs from the environment, our social and cultural environment, etc., found place also in the book.

Suggestions are put forward for organising or practicing different programmes or activities to increase environmental awareness among people. It has been suggested that local clubs can organise visits to hospitals, reserve forests, water bodies, bird sanctuaries, etc., as a part of the environmental awareness campaign publishing through bulletin boards/ school magazines, etc., on issues related to environment has also been encouraged.

It has also been implicated that Clubs, schools and other social organisations can organise discussions/debates on various topics of the environment. Such topics are— 1. To go to collect data from car-drivers/ owner about various aspects of the car, its maintenance and care etc., 2. To go to collect data from various households about their consciousness regarding the environment. 3. The students can be also oriented about the global environmental issues and concerns, water analysis, water treatment etc., 4. Mass awareness campaign is a major activity that the students must organise. Various teaching and learning strategies should be adopted. The school teachers can organise programmes to encourage the students in these activities as a part of their Environmental Education as per the time and resources available.

I have tried my best to develop the book with utmost efforts so that it becomes suitable for increasing love/affection/interest and respect to our environment. I would consider this effort a great success if it serves that purpose.

I acknowledge with gratitude all the writers and publishers of many different books and articles, the published materials available in the internet for public consumption, and Wikipedia, for using and consulting those sources as resource materials without which this work would not have been possible. I would appreciate receiving suggestions and guidance from the readers / teachers and others to improve upon certain areas if it is found to be inadequate or too exhaustive.

I am grateful to my wife, Khana, for her help in a number of ways. Once again, I am thankful to all the sources, books, journals, Internet, etc., from which information was collected in public interest for the dissemination of knowledge.

DON'T INDULGE IN POLLUTING PRACTICES!!!

Save your Environment, your country and your Heritage. Let us join our hands together in this noble task.

PART-I
INDIA: AN ANCIENT EXOTIC WONDERLAND

1

Our Country–India, Its History, Literature and Culture

(A) India–An Ancient Exotic Wonderland

(a) Historical Perspectives of India–The homeland of 1.28 Billion People of the World

(b) India Our Motherland–The Modern India

(B) Some of India's Architectural Masterpieces

(a) Our Family Structure–
Indian Arts and Literature
Indian Society
Indian Customs
Indian Sports

(b) Our Flora and Fauna.

(C) India's Environmental Contrasts–A Tourists' Delight

(a) The Mighty Himalayas and its Environment and Ecology—Richest in the World

(b) Thor Desert and its Environment and Ecology—A Test of endurance and adaptation

(c) Andaman and Nicober Islands-its Environment and Ecology-Where jungle man still exists

(d) Kashmir Valley–A Heaven on Earth

(A) India–One of the ancient civilisations on earth-an exotic wonderland

(a) Historical Perspectives of Ancient India through different stages.

When we talk about Ancient India, several illustrious names appear in our mind—Maharishi Valmiki, Ved Vyas, Mahakabi Kalidasha, Gautama Buddha, Mahavira, Guru Nanak, Shree Shree Ramakrishna, Swami Vivekananda and many others. So far as early India is concerned several names as above, comes in our mind because of their tremendous contributions. Balmiki's Ramayana and Mahabharata became two great **Epics** attracting attention of the World. So also was Kalidasa's **Meghdoot.** Gautama Buddha, Mahavira, Guru Nanak and Shree Ramakrishna were religious preachers of Buddhism,

Jainism, Sikhism and Hinduism respectively spreading the thought that all religions are equal and meets at one point—all creatures are created by God. Love and respect them all and help them in every possible way. As time passes, such philosophy became stronger and stronger and is now deep-rooted in the Indian psyche

> Mahabharata and Bhagabat Gita have a very high place in the Indian psyche. Bhagabat Gita is considered to be very sacred by all the Hindus, as Quran is considered by the Muslims and Bible is considered by the Christians.

The Epic Mahabharata eternalised the Battle of Kurukshetra, where Bhagwan Srikrishna, along with his close follower cum friend Arjuna, blind Raja Dhritarastra, Senior most Pandava brother Judhistira, Strongman Bhima, their Astra guru Dronacharya, their adversaries like Durjodhana and Dusshasaana, Raja Dhritarastra's two sons, Vishma, Karna, and the central female figure Draupadi found major places in its illustrations and depiction of their lives.

Krishna, Arjuna at Kurukshetra, 18–19th Century Painting.

As has been said above, The *Mahabharata* (Sanskrit *Mahabhārata* महाभारत, IPA: [mahabarata] is one of the two major Sanskrit epics of ancient India, the other being the *Ramayana*.

Besides its epic narrative of the Kurukshetra War and the fates of the Kauravas (Durjodhana, Dusshasanas) and the Pandavas (Judhisthira, Bhima, Arjunamas) princes, the *Mahabharata* contains much philosophical and devotional material, such as a discussion of the four "goals of life" or *purusharthas.* Among the principal works and stories that are a part of the

Mahabharata are the Bhagavad Gita, the story of Damayanti, an abbreviated version of the Ramayana, and the Rishyasringa, often considered as works in their own right.

Traditionally, the authorship of the *Mahabharata* is attributed to Vyasa. There have been many attempts to unravel its historical growth and compositional layers. The oldest preserved parts of the text are not thought to be appreciably older than around 400 BCE, though the origins of the story probably fall between the 8th and 9th centuries BCE. The text probably reached its final form by the early Gupta period (c4th century). The title may be translated as "the great tale of the Bhārata dynasty". According to the *Mahabharata* itself, the tale is extended from a shorter version of 24,000 verses called simply *Bhārata*

The Mahabharata is the longest Sanskrit epic. Its longest version consists of over 100,000 *shloka* or over 200,000 individual verse lines (each shloka is a couplet), and long prose passages. About 1.8 million words in total, the Mahabharata is roughly ten times the length of the *Iliad* and *Odyssey* combined, or about four times the length of the Ramayana. W.J. Johnson has compared the importance of the Mahabharata to world civilisation to that of the Bible, the works of Shakespeare, the works of Homer, Greek drama, or the Qur'an

The epic is traditionally ascribed to the sage Vyasa, who is also a major character in the epic. The first section of the *Mahabharata* states that it was god Ganesha who, at the request of Vyasa, wrote down the text to Vyasa's dictation. Ganesha is said to have agreed to write it only on condition that Vyasa never pause in his recitation. Vyasa agrees on condition that Ganesha takes the time to understand what was said before writing it down.

The epic employs the story within a story structure, otherwise known as frame tales, popular in many Indian religious and non-religious works. It is recited to the King Janamejaya who is the great-grandson of Pandava prince Arjuna, by sage Vaisampayana, a disciple of Vyasa. The recitation of Vaisampayana to Janamejaya is then recited again by a professional storyteller named Ugrasrava Sauti, many years later, to an assemblage of sages performing the 12 year sacrifice for King Saunaka Kulapati in the Naimisha Forest.

Jaya, the core of Mahābhārata is structured in the form of a dialogue between Kuru king Dhritarashtra and Sanjaya, his advisor and chariot driver. Sanjaya narrates each incident of the Kurukshetra War, fought in 18 days, as and when it happened. Dhritarâshtra sometimes asks questions and doubts, and sometimes laments, sensing the imminent destruction that would be caused by the war, to his sons, friends and kinsmen. He also feels guilty about his own role in the war.

In the beginning, Sanjaya gives a description of the continents of the Earth, the other planets, and focuses on the Indian Subcontinent and gives an elaborate list of hundreds of kingdoms, tribes, provinces, cities, towns, villages, rivers, mountains, forests, etc., of the (ancient) Indian Subcontinent (Bhārata Varsha). He also explains about the military formations adopted by each side on each day, the death of each hero and the details of each war-racings. Some 18 chapters of Vyasa's Jaya constitutes the Bhagavad Gita, the sacred text of the Hindus. Thus, this work of Vyasa, called Jaya deals with diverse subjects like geography, history, warfare, religion and morality. According to the *Mahabharata* itself, Vaisampayana's *Bharata* expanded on the story, with Vyasa's Jaya embedded within it. Ugrasrava eventually composed the final *Mahabharata*, with Vyasa's Jaya and Vaisampayana's Bharata embedded in the epic.

The background to the *Mahabharata* suggests the origin of the epic occurs "after the very early Vedic period" and before "the first Indian 'empire' was to rise in the third century B.C." It is generally agreed that "Unlike the Vedas, the epic was a popular work so the earliest 'surviving' components of this dynamic text are believed to be no older than the earliest 'external' references we have to the epic, which may include an allusion in Panini's fourth century BCE grammar *Ashtādhyāyî.*"

The *Mahabharata* itself distinguishes a core portion of 24,000 verses: The oldest surviving Sanskrit text dates to the Kushan Period (200 CE). From this evidence, it is likely that the redaction into 18 books, or parvas, took place in the 1st century. The name *Mahabharata*, later identified Vyasa as the work's author

Historical References

The earliest known references to the *Mahabharata* and its core *Bharata* date to the *Ashtadhyayi* of Panini (fl. 4th century BCE) and in the *Ashvalayana Grhyasutra. This* may suggest that the core 24,000 verses, known as the *Bharata*, as well as an early version of the extended *Mahabharata*, were composed by the 4th century BCE.

Several stories within the Mahabharata took on separate identities of their own in Classical Sanskrit literature. For instance, the great sanskrit poet Kālidāsa (c. 400 CE), believed to have lived in the era of the Gupta dynasty, is based on a story that is the precursor to the Mahabharata. Urubhanga, a Sanskrit play written by Bhāsa who is believed to have lived before Kālidāsa, is based on the slaying of Duryodhana by the splitting of his thighs by Bhima.

The 18 Parvas or Books

The division into 18 parvas is as follows: How the Mahabharata came to be narrated by Sauti to the assembled rishis at Naimisharanya, after having been recited at the sarpasattra of Janamejaya by Vaishampayana at Takcaúilâ. The history and genealogy of the Bharata and Bhrigu races is recalled, as is the birth and early life of the Kuru princes (adi means first).

Maya Danava erects the palace and court (sabha), at Indraprastha. Life at the court, Yudhishthira's Rajasuya Yajna, the game of dice, and the eventual exile of the Pandavas.

The twelve years of exile in the forest (aranya).

The year spent incognito at the court of Virata. Preparations for war and efforts to bring about peace between the Kurus and the Pandavas eventually fail (udyoga means effort or work).

The first part of the great battle, with Bhishma as commander for the Kauravas and his fall on the bed of arrows. (Includes the Bhagavad Gita in chapters 25[22]-42[23]). The battle continues, with Drona as commander. This is the major book of the war. Most of the great warriors on both sides are dead by the end of this book.

The battle again, with Karna as commander. The last day of the battle, with Shalya as commander. Also told in detail is the pilgrimage of Balarama to the fords of the river Saraswati and the mace fight between Bhima and Duryodhana which ends the war, since Bhima kills Duryodhana by smashing him on the thighs with a mace. Ashvattama, Kripa and Kritavarma kill the remaining Pandava army in their sleep. Only seven warriors remain on the Pandava side and three on the Kaurava side. Gandhari, Kunti and the women (stri) of the Kurus and Pandavas lament the dead.

The crowning of Yudhisthira as king of Hastinapura, and instructions from Bhishma for the newly anointed king on society, economics and politics. This is the longest book of the Mahabharata (shanti means peace).

The final instructions (anushasana) from Bhishma.

The royal ceremony of the Ashvamedha (Horse sacrifice) conducted by Yudhisthira. The world conquest by Arjuna. The Anugita is told by Krishna to Arjuna.

The eventual deaths of Dhritarashtra, Gandhari and Kunti in a forest fire when they are living in a hermitage in the Himalayas. Vidura predeceases them and Sanjaya on Dhritarashtra's bidding goes to live in the higher Himalayas.

The infighting between the Yadavas with maces (mausala) and the eventual destruction of the Yadavas. The great journey of Yudhisthira and his brothers across the whole country and finally their ascent of the great Himalayas where each Pandava falls except for Yudhisthira. Yudhisthira's final test and the return of the Pandavas to the spiritual world (svarga).

This is an addendum to the 18 books, and covers those parts of the life of Krishna which is not covered in the 18 parvas of the Mahabharata.

Historical Context

Kurukshetra War

The historicity of the Kurukshetra War is unclear. Many historians estimate the date of the Kurukshetra war to Iron age India of the 10th century BCE. The setting of the epic has a historical precedent in Iron age (Vedic) India, where the Kuru kingdom was the center of political power during roughly 1200 to 800 BCE. A dynastic conflict of the period could have been the inspiration for the *Jaya*, the foundation on which the Mahabharata corpus was built, with a climactic battle eventually coming to be viewed as an epochal event.

Puranic literature presents genealogical lists associated with the Mahabharata narrative. The evidence of the Puranas is of two kinds. Of the first kind, there is the direct statement that there were 1015 (or 1050) years between the birth of Parikshit (Arjuna's grandson) and the accession of Mahapadma Nanda, commonly dated to 382 BCE, which would yield an estimate of about 1400 BCE for the Bharata battle however, this would imply improbably long reigns on average for the kings listed in the genealogies. Of the second kind are analyses of parallel genealogies in the Puranas between the times of Adhisimakrishna (Parikshit's great-grandson) and Mahapadma Nanda. Pargiter accordingly estimated 26 generations by averaging 10 different dynastic lists and, assuming 18 years for the average duration of a reign, arrived at an estimate of 850 BCE for Adhisimakrishna, and thus approximately 950 BCE for the Bharata battle.

The core story of the work is that of a dynastic struggle for the throne of Hastinapura, the kingdom ruled by the Kuru clan. The two collateral branches of the family that participate in the struggle are the Kaurava and the Pandava. Although the Kaurava is the senior branch of the family, Duryodhana, the eldest Kaurava, is younger than Yudhisthira, the eldest Pandava. Both Duryodhana and Yudhisthira claim to be first in line to inherit the throne.

The struggle culminates in the great battle of Kurukshetra, in which the Pandavas are ultimately victorious. The battle produces complex conflicts of kinship and friendship, instances of family loyalty and duty taking precedence over what is right, as well as the converse.

The *Mahabharata* itself ends with the death of Krishna, and the subsequent end of his dynasty and ascent of the Pandava brothers to heaven. It also marks the beginning of the Hindu age of Kali (Kali Yuga), the fourth and final age of mankind, in which great values and noble ideas have crumbled, and man is heading toward the complete dissolution of right action, morality and virtue.

Arshia Sattar states that the central theme of the Mahabharata, as well as the Ramayana, is respectively Krishna's and Rama's hidden divinity and its progressive revelation

The Older Generations

The story goes like this King Janamejaya's ancestor Shantanu, the king of Hastinapura, has a short-lived marriage with the goddess Ganga and has

Shantanu Woos Satyavati, the Fisherwoman.

a son, Devavrata (later to be called Bhishma, a great warrior), who becomes the heir apparent. Many years later, when King Shantanu goes hunting, he sees Satyavati, the daughter of the chief of fisherman, and asks her father for her hand. Her father refuses to consent to the marriage unless Shantanu promises to make any future son of Satyavati the king upon his death. To resolve his father's dilemma, Devavrata agrees to relinquish his right to the throne. As the fisherman is not sure about the prince's children honouring the promise, Devavrata also takes a vow of lifelong celibacy to guarantee his father's promise.

Shantanu has two sons by Satyavati, Chitrāngada and Vichitravirya. Upon Shantanu's death, Chitrangada becomes king. He lives a very short uneventful life and dies. Vichitravirya, the younger son, rules Hastinapura. Meanwhile, the King of Kasi arranges a swayamvara for his three daughters, neglecting to invite the royal family of Hastinapur. In order to arrange the marriage of young Vichitravirya, Bhishma attends the swayamvara of the three princesses Amba, Ambika and Ambalika, uninvited, and proceeds to abduct them. Ambika and Ambalika consent to be married to Vichitravirya.

The oldest princess Amba, however, informs Bhishma that she wishes to marry king of Shalva whom Bhishma defeated at their swayamvara. Bhishma lets her leave to marry king of Shalva, but Shalva refuses to marry her, still smarting at his humiliation at the hands of Bhishma. Amba then returns to marry Bhishma but he refuses due to his vow of celibacy. Amba becomes enraged and becomes Bhishma's bitter enemy, holding him responsible for her plight. Later she is reborn to King Drupada as Shikhandi

The Pandava and Kaurava Princes.

(or Shikhandini) and causes Bhishma's fall, with the help of Arjuna, in the battle of Kurukshetra.

The picture above shows Draupadi with her five husbands—the Pandavas. The central figure is Yudhishthira; the two on the bottom are Bhima and Arjuna. Nakula and Sahadeva, the twins, are standing. Painting by Raja Ravi Varma, c.1900.

When Vichitravirya dies young without any heirs, Satyavati asks her first son Vyasa to father children with the widows. The eldest, Ambika, shuts her eyes when she sees him, and so her son Dhritarashtra is born blind. Ambalika turns pale and bloodless upon seeing him, and thus her son Pandu is born pale and unhealthy (the term Pandu may also mean 'jaundiced'). Due to the physical challenges of the first two children, Satyavati asks Vyasa to try once again. However, Ambika and Ambalika send their maid instead, to Vyasa's room. Vyasa fathers a third son, Vidura, by the maid. He is born healthy and grows up to be one of the wisest characters in the *Mahabharata.* He serves as Prime Minister (Mahamantri or Mahatma) to King Pandu and King Dhritarashtra.

When the princes grow up, Dhritarashtra is about to be crowned king by Bhishma when Vidura intervenes and uses his knowledge of politics to assert that a blind person cannot be king. This is because a blind man cannot control and protect his subjects. The throne is then given to Pandu because of Dhritarashtra's blindness. Pandu marries twice, to Kunti and Madri. Dhritarashtra marries Gandhari, a princess from Gandhara, who blindfolds herself so that she may feel the pain that her husband feels. Her brother Shakuni is enraged by this and vows to take revenge on the Kuru family. One day, when Pandu is relaxing in the forest, he hears the sound of a wild animal. He shoots an arrow in the direction of the sound. However the arrow hits the sage Kindama, who curses him that if he engages in a sexual act, he will die. Pandu then retires to the forest along with his two wives, and his brother Dhritarashtra rules thereafter, despite his blindness.

Pandu's older queen Kunti, however, had been given a boon by Sage Durvasa that she could invoke any god using a special mantra. Kunti uses this boon to ask Dharma the god of justice, Vayu the god of the wind, and Indra the lord of the heavens for sons. She gives birth to three sons, Yudhisthira, Bhima, and Arjuna, through these gods. Kunti shares her mantra with the younger queen Madri, who bears the twins Nakula and Sahadeva through the Ashwini twins. However, Pandu and Madri indulge in sex, and Pandu dies. Madri dies on his funeral pyre out of remorse. Kunti raises the five brothers, who are from then on usually referred to as the Pandava brothers.

Dhritarashtra had hundred sons through Gandhari, all born after the birth of Yudhishtira. These are the Kaurava brothers, the eldest being Duryodhana, and the second Dushasana. Other Kaurava brothers were Vikarna and Sukarna. The rivalry and enmity between them and the Pandava brothers, from their youth and into manhood, leads to the Kurukshetra war.

Lākṣagṛha (The House of Lac)

After the deaths of their mother (Madri) and father (Pandu), the Pandavas and their mother Kunti return to the palace of Hastinapur. Yudhisthira is made Crown Prince by Dhritarashtra, under considerable pressure from his kingdom. Dhritarashtra wanted his own son Duryodhana to become king and lets his ambition get in the way of preserving justice.

Shakuni, Duryodhana and Dusasana plot to get rid of the Pandavas. Shakuni calls the architect Purochana to build a palace out of flammable materials like lac and ghee. He then arranges for the Pandavas and the Queen Mother Kunti to stay there, with the intention of setting it alight. However, the Pandavas are warned by their wise uncle, Vidura, who sends them a miner to dig a tunnel. They are able to escape to safety and go into hiding. Back at Hastinapur, the Pandavas and Kunti are presumed dead.

Marriage to Draupadi

Arjuna piercing the eye of the fish as depicted in Chennakesava Temple built by Hoysala Empire.

During the course of their hiding the Pandavas learn of a swayamvara which is taking place for the hand of the Pāñcāla princess Draupadî. The Pandavas enter the competition in disguise as Brahmins. The task is to string a mighty steel bow and shoot a target on the ceiling, which is the eye of a moving artificial fish, while looking at its reflection in oil below. Most of the princes fail, many being unable to lift the bow. Arjuna succeeds however. The Pandavas return home and inform their mother that Arjuna has won a competition and to look at what they have brought back. Without looking, Kunti asks them to share whatever it is Arjuna has won among themselves. On explaining the previous life of Draupadi, she ends up being the wife of all five brothers.

Indraprastha

After the wedding, the Pandava brothers are invited back to Hastinapura. The Kuru family elders and relatives negotiate and broker a split of the kingdom, with the Pandavas obtaining a new territory. Yudhishtira has a new capital built for this territory at Indraprastha. Neither the Pandava nor Kaurava sides are happy with the arrangement however.

Shortly after this, Arjuna elopes with and then marries Krishna's sister, Subhadra. Yudhishtira wishes to establish his position as king; he seeks Krishna's advice. Krishna advises him, and after due preparation and the elimination of some opposition, Yudhishthira carries out the *rājasûya yagna* ceremony; he is thus recognised as pre-eminent among kings.

The Pandavas have a new palace built for them, by Maya the Danava. They invite their Kaurava cousins to Indraprastha. Duryodhana walks round the palace, and mistakes a glossy floor for water, and will not step in. After being told of his error, he then sees a pond, and assumes it is not water and falls in. Draupadi laughs at him and ridicules him by saying that this is because of his blind father Dire tarastra. He the decides to avenge his humiliation.

The Dice Game (some pictures below)

Shakuni, Duryodhana's uncle, now arranges a dice game, playing against Yudhishtira with loaded dice. Yudhishtira loses all his wealth, then his

A Painting of how Draupadi was humiliated.

kingdom. He then even gambles his brothers, himself, and finally his wife into servitude. The jubilant Kauravas insult the Pandavas in their helpless state and even try to disrobe Draupadi in front of the entire court, but her honor is saved by Krishna who miraculously creates lengths of cloth to replace the ones being removed.

Dhritarashtra, Bhishma, and the other elders are aghast at the situation, but Duryodhana is adamant that there is no place for two crown princes in Hastinapura. Against his wishes Dhritarashtra orders for another dice game. The Pandavas are required to go into exile for 12 years, and in the 13th year must remain hidden. If discovered by the Kauravas, they will be forced into exile for another 12 years.

Pandava's Exile and Return

The Pandavas spend thirteen years in exile; many adventures occur during this time. They also prepare alliances for a possible future conflict. They spend their final year in disguise in the court of Virata, and are discovered just after the end of the year.

At the end of their exile, they try to negotiate a return to Indraprastha. However, this fails, as Duryodhana objects that they were discovered while in hiding, and that no return of their kingdom was agreed. War becomes inevitable.

The Battle at Kurukshetra on Stone Carvings.

A black stone relief depicting a number of men wearing a crown and a dhoti, fighting with spears, swords and bows. A chariot with half the horse out of the frame is seen in the middle.

The two sides summon vast armies to their help and line up at Kurukshetra for a war The kingdoms of Panchala, Dwaraka, Kasi, Kekaya, Magadha, Matsya, Chedi, Pandya, Telinga, and the Yadus of Mathura and some other clans like the Parama Kambojas were allied with the Pandavas. The allies of the Kauravas included the kings of Pragjyotisha, Anga, Kekaya, Sindhudesa (including Sindhus, Sauviras and Sivis), Mahishmati, Avanti in Madhyadesa, Madra, Gandhara, Bahlikas, Kambojas and many others. Before war being declared, Balarama had expressed his unhappiness at the developing conflict and left to go on pilgrimage; thus he does not take part in the battle itself. Krishna takes part in a non-combatant role, as charioteer for Arjuna.

Before the battle, Arjuna, seeing himself facing his great grandfather Bhishma and his teacher Drona on the other side, has doubts about the battle and he fails to lift his Gāndeeva bow. Krishna wakes him up to his call of duty in the famous Bhagavad Gita section of the epic.

Though initially sticking to chivalrous notions of warfare, both sides soon adopt dishonourable tactics. At the end of the 18-day battle, only the Pandavas, Satyaki, Kripa, Ashwatthama, Kritavarma, Yuyutsu and Krishna survive.

The End of the Pandavas

Gandhari, blindfolded, supporting Dhrtarashtra and following Kunti when Dhrtarashtra became old and infirm and retired to the forest. A miniature

painting from a 16th century manuscript of part of the Razmnama, Persian translation of the Mahabharata.

After "seeing" the carnage, Gandhari who had lost all her sons, curses Krishna to be a witness to a similar annihilation of his family, for though divine and capable of stopping the war, he had not done so. Krishna accepts the curse, which bears fruit 36 years later.

The Pandavas who had ruled their kingdom meanwhile, decide to renounce everything Clad in skins and rags they retire to the Himalaya and climb towards heaven in their bodily form. A stray dog travels with them. One by one the brothers and Draupadi fall on their way. As each one stumbles, Yudhisthira gives the rest the reason for their fall (Draupadi was partial to Arjuna, Nakula and Sahadeva were vain and proud of their looks, Bhima and Arjuna were proud of their strength and archery skills, respectively). Only the virtuous Yudhisthira, who had tried everything to prevent the carnage, and the dog remain. The dog reveals himself to be the god Yama (also known as Yama Dharmaraja), and then takes him to the underworld where he sees his siblings and wife. After explaining the nature of the test, Yama takes Yudhishthira back to heaven and explains that it was necessary to expose him to the underworld because (Rajyante narakam dhruvam) any ruler has to visit the underworld at least once. Yama then assures him that his siblings and wife would join him in heaven after they had been exposed to the underworld for measures of time according to their vices.

Arjuna's grandson Parikshit rules after them and dies bitten by a snake. His furious son, Janamejaya, decides to perform a snake sacrifice (*sarpasattra*) in order to destroy the snakes. It is at this sacrifice that the tale of his ancestors is narrated to him.

Just War and Bhagabat Gita

The Mahabharata offers one of the first instances of theorising about "Just war", illustrating many of the standards that would be debated later across the world. In the story, one of five brothers asks if the suffering caused by war can ever be justified. A long discussion ensues between the siblings, establishing criteria like *proportionality* (chariots cannot attack cavalry, only other chariots, no attacking people in distress), *just means* (no poisoned or barbed arrows), *just cause* (no attacking out of rage), and fair treatment of captives and the wounded.

The epic Mahabharata is traditionally ascribed to the Sage Ved Vyasa; the Bhagavad Gita, being a part of the Mahabharata, is also ascribed to him. Theories on the date of composition of the Gita vary considerably. Scholars accept dates from fifth century to second century BCE as the probable range. Professor Jeanine Fowler, in her commentary on the Gita, considers second century BCE to be the likely date of composition. Kashi Nath Upadhyaya, a Gita scholar, on the basis of the estimated dates of Mahabharata, Brahma sutras, and other independent sources, concludes that the Bhagavad Gita was composed between fifth and fourth centuries BCE. The actual dates of composition of the Gita remain unresolved.

Bhagavad Gita–the Sacred Book of the Hindus

Bhagavad Gita comprises 18 chapters (section 25 to 42) in the *Bhishma Parva* of the epic Mahabharata and consists of 700 verses. Because of differences in recensions, the verses of the Gita may be numbered in the full text of the *Mahabharata* as chapters 6.25–42 or as chapters 6.23–40. According to the recension of the Gita commented on by Adi Shankara, a prominent philosopher of the Vedanta school, the number of verses is 700, but there is evidence to show that old manuscripts had 745 verses. The verses themselves, using the range and style of Sanskrit *Anustup* meter (*chhandas*) with similes and metaphors, are written in a poetic form that is traditionally chanted.

Due to its presence in the Mahabharata, Bhagavad Gita is classified as a Smriti text or "that which is remembered" Sruti texts, such as the Upanishads, are believed to be revelations of divine origin, whereas Smritis are authored recollections of tradition and are therefore fallible. As a Smriti, the scriptural authority of the Gita is dependent on the Upanishads (Œruti). However, those branches of Hinduism that give it the status of an Upanishad also consider it to be a Œruti or "revealed text". Even though the Bhagavad Gita is in many respects different from the Upanishads in format and content, it is still taken to represent a summary of the Upanishadic teachings and is thus called "the Upanishad of the Upanishads." Advaita Vedanta (monistic conclusion of the Vedas) school of philosophy uses the Bhagavad Gita in conjunction with the Upanishads and Brahma sutras to arrive at its message of non-duality.

A Manuscript Illustration of the battle of Kurukshetra, fought between the Kauravas and the Pandavas, recorded in the *Mahabharata*.

Background

In the epic Mahabharata, Sanjaya, counselor of the Kuru king Dhritarashtra, after returning from the battlefield to announce the death of Bhisma begins recounting the details of the Mahabharata war. Bhagavad Gita forms the content of this recollection. The Gita begins before the start of the climactic Kurukshetra war, where the Pandava prince Arjuna is filled with doubt on the battlefield. Realising that his enemies are his own relatives, beloved friends, and revered teachers, he turns to his charioteer and guide, Krishna, for advice. Responding to Arjuna's confusion and moral dilemma, Krishna explains to Arjuna his duties as a warrior and prince, elaborating on a variety of philosophical concepts.

Characters

- Arjuna, one of the Pandavas
- Krishna, Arjuna's charioteer and guru
- Sanjaya, counselor of the Kuru king Dhritarashtra
- Dhritarashtra, Kuru king.

Overview of Chapters

The Bhagavad Gita is divided into eighteen chapters. The Sanskrit editions of the Gita name each chapter as a particular form of yoga. However, these chapter titles do not appear in the Sanskrit text of the Mahabharata. Swami Chidbhavananda explains that each of the eighteen chapters is designated as a separate yoga because each chapter, like yoga, "trains the body and the mind". He labels the first chapter "Arjuna Vishada Yogam" or the "Yoga of Arjuna's Dejection".

Gita Dhyanam: (contains 9 verses) The *Gita Dhyanam* is not a part of the main Bhagavad Gita, but it is commonly published with the Gîtā as a prefix. The verses of the *Gita Dhyanam* (also called *Gîtā Dhyāna* or *Dhyāna Úlokas*) offer salutations to a variety of sacred scriptures, figures, and entities, characterise the relationship of the Gîtā to the Upanishads, and affirm the power of divine assistance. It is a common practice to recite these before reading the Gita.

1. *Arjuna–Visada yoga:* (contains 46 verses) Arjuna has requested Krishna to move his chariot between the two armies. His growing dejection is described as he fears losing friends and relatives as a consequence of war.
2. *Sankhya yoga:* (contains 72 verses) After asking Krishna for help, Arjuna is instructed into various subjects such as, Karma yoga, Jnana yoga, Sankhya yoga, Buddhi yoga and the immortal nature of the soul. This chapter is often considered the summary of the entire Bhagavad Gita.

3. *Karma yoga:* (contains 43 verses) Krishna explains how performance of prescribed duties, but without attachment to results, is the appropriate course of action for Arjuna.
4. *Jnana–Karma-Sanyasa yoga:* (contains 42 verses) Krishna reveals that he has lived through many births, always teaching yoga for the protection of the pious and the destruction of the impious and stresses the importance of accepting a guru.
5. *Karma–Sanyasa yoga:* (contains 29 verses) Arjuna asks Krishna if it is better to forgo action or to act ("renunciation or discipline of action"). Krishna answers that both are ways to the same goal, but that acting in Karma yoga is superior.
6. *Dhyan yoga or Atmasanyam yoga:* (contains 47 verses) Krishna describes the Ashtanga yoga. He further elucidates the difficulties of the mind and the techniques by which mastery of the mind might be gained.
7. *Jnana–Vijnana yoga:* (contains 30 verses) Krishna describes the absolute reality and its illusory energy Maya.
8. *Aksara–Brahma yoga:* (contains 28 verses) This chapter contains eschatology of the Bhagavad Gita. Importance of the last thought before death, differences between material and spiritual worlds, and light and dark paths that a soul takes after death are described.
9. *Raja–Vidya–Raja–Guhya yoga:* (contains 34 verses) Krishna explains how His eternal energy pervades, creates, preserves, and destroys the entire universe. According to theologian Christopher Southgate, verses of this chapter of the Gita are pane theistic.
10. *Vibhuti–Vistara–yoga:* (contains 42 verses) Krishna is described as the ultimate cause of all material and spiritual existence. Arjuna accepts Krishna as the Supreme Being, quoting great sages who have also done so.

Krishna displays his Vishvarupa (Universal Form) to Arjuna on the battlefield of Kurukshetra, described in Visvarupa–Darsana yoga, Chapter 11.

11. *Visvarupa–Darsana yoga:* (contains 55 verses) On Arjuna's request, Krishna displays his "universal form" (*Viúvarûpa*), a theophany of a being facing every way and emitting the radiance of a thousand suns, containing all other beings and material in existence.
12. *Bhakti yoga:* (contains 20 verses) In this chapter Krishna glorifies the path of devotion to God. Krishna describes the process of devotional service (Bhakti yoga). He also explains different forms of spiritual disciplines.
13. *Ksetra–Ksetrajna Vibhaga yoga:* (contains 35 verses) The difference between transient perishable physical body and the immutable eternal soul is described. The difference between individual consciousness and universal consciousness is also made clear.
14. *Gunatraya–Vibhaga yoga:* (contains 27 verses) Krishna explains the three modes (gunas) of material nature pertaining to goodness, passion, and nescience. Their causes, characteristics, and influence on a living entity are also described.
15. *Purusottama yoga:* (contains 20 verses) Krishna identifies the transcendental characteristics of God such as, omnipotence, omniscience, and omnipresence. Krishna also describes a symbolic tree (representing material existence), which has its roots in the heavens and its foliage on earth. Krishna explains that this tree should be felled with the "axe of detachment", after which one can go beyond to his *supreme abode*.
16. *Daivasura–Sampad–Vibhaga yoga:* (contains 24 verses) Krishna identifies the human traits of the divine and the demonic natures. He counsels that to attain the supreme destination one must give up lust, anger, greed, and discern between right and wrong action by discernment through Buddhi and evidence from the scriptures.
17. *Sraddhatraya-Vibhaga yoga:* (contains 28 verses) Krishna qualifies the three divisions of faith, thoughts, deeds, and even eating habits corresponding to the three modes (gunas).
18. *Moksha–Sanyasa yoga:* (contains 78 verses) In this chapter, the conclusions of previous seventeen chapters are summed up. Krishna asks Arjuna to abandon all forms of dharma and simply surrender unto him and describes this as the ultimate perfection of life.

Dharma

The first reference to *dharma* in the Bhagavad Gita occurs in its first verse, where Dhritarashtra refers to the Kurukshetra as the 'Field of *dharma'*. Fowler believes, that *dharma* in this verse refers to the *sanatana dharma* or the eternal order which pervades the whole cosmos and is ultimately true and right. Therefore, 'Field of action' implies the field of righteousness, where truth will eventually triumph. However, both Sri Aurobindo, a freedom fighter and philosopher, and Sarvapalli Radhakrishnan, a philosopher and the second president of India, see the 'Field of action' as the world, which is a "battleground for moral struggle". Early in the text, responding to Arjuna's despondency, Krishna asks him to follow his *swadharma*. *Swadharma* literally means work born out of one's nature and in this verse, is often interpreted as the *varna dharma* or in the case of Arjuna, the duty of a warrior. Eighteenth chapter of the Gita examines the relationship between *swadharma* and *swabhava* or essential nature. In this chapter, the *swadharma* of an individual is linked with the *gunnas* or tendencies arising out of one's *swabhava*. The idea that an individual's *dharma* was based on their essential nature allowed Aurobindo to deduce his doctrine that "the functions of a man ought to be determined by his natural turn, gift, and capacities". Gandhi found in the concept of *swadharma*, the basis for his idea of *swadeshi*. To him, *swadeshi* was "*swadharma* applied to one's immediate environment.

Moksha: Liberation

Liberation or *moksha* in Vedanta philosophy is not something that can be acquired or reached. *Ātman* (Self), the goal of *moksha*, is something that is always present as the essence of the self, and can be revealed by deep intuitive knowledge. While the Upanishads largely uphold such a monistic viewpoint of liberation, the Bhagavad Gita also accommodates the dualistic and theistic aspects of *Moksha*. The Gita, while occasionally hinting at impersonal *Brahman* as the goal, revolves around the relationship between the Self and a personal God or *Saguna Brahman*. A synthesis of knowledge, devotion, and desireless action is given as a prescription for Arjuna's despondence; the same combination is suggested as a way to moksha. Winthrop Sargeant further explains, "In the model presented by the *Bhagavad Gītā*, every aspect of life is in fact a way of salvation."

Unlike any other religious scripture, the Bhagavad Gita broadcasts its message in the centre of the battlefield. The choice of such an unholy ambience for the delivery of a philosophical discourse has been an enigma to many commentators. Eknath Easwaran writes that the Gita's subject is "the war within, the struggle for self-mastery that every human being must wage if he or she is to emerge from life victorious", and "The language of battle is often found in the scriptures, for it conveys the strenuous, long, drawn-out campaign we must wage to free ourselves from the tyranny of the ego, the cause of all our suffering and sorrow." Swami Nikhilananda, takes Arjuna as an allegory of Ātman, Krishna as an allegory of *Brahman*, Arjuna's chariot as the body, and Dhritarashtra as the ignorance filled mind. Mohandas Karamchand Gandhi, in his commentary on the Gita, interprets the battle as "an allegory in which the battlefield is the soul and Arjuna, man's higher impulses struggling against evil".

Yoga

Yoga in the Bhagavad Gita refers to the skill of union with the ultimate reality or the Absolute. In his commentary, Zaehner says that the root meaning of yoga is "yoking" or "preparation"; he proposes the basic meaning "spiritual exercise", which conveys the various nuances in the best way. Sivananda's commentary regards the eighteen chapters of the Bhagavad Gita as having a progressive order, by which Krishna leads "Arjuna up the ladder of Yoga from one rung to another." The influential commentator Madhusudana Sarasvati divided the Gita's eighteen chapters into three sections of six chapters each. Swami Gambhirananda characterises Madhusudana Sarasvati's system as a successive approach in which Karma yoga leads to Bhakti yoga, which in turn leads to Jnana yoga.

Karma Yoga

According to Fowler, since it is impossible for living beings to avoid action all together, the Bhagavad Gita therefore offers a practical approach to liberation in the form of Karma yoga. The path of Karma yoga upholds the necessity of action. However, this action is to be undertaken without any attachment to the work or desire for results. Bhagavad Gita terms this "inaction in action and action in inaction (4.18)". The concept of such detached action is also called *Nishkam Karma*, a term not used in the Gita. Krishna, in the following verses, elaborates on the role actions, performed without desire and attachment, play in attaining freedom from material bondage and transmigration:

To action alone hast thou a right and never at all to its fruits; let not the fruits of action be thy motive; neither let there be in thee any attachment to inaction Fixed in yoga, do thy work, O Winner of wealth (Arjuna), abandoning attachment, with an even mind in success and failure, for evenness of mind is called yoga. (2.47-8) With the body, with the mind, with the intellect, even merely with the senses, the Yogis perform action toward self-purification, having abandoned attachment. He who is disciplined in Yoga, having abandoned the fruit of action, attains steady peace. (5.11)

Mohandas Karamchand Gandhi writes, "The object of the Gita appears to me to be that of showing the most excellent way to attain self-realisation", and this can be achieved by selfless action, "By desireless action; by renouncing fruits of action; by dedicating all activities to God, i.e., by surrendering oneself to Him body and soul." Gandhi called Gita, *The Gospel of Selfless Action*. In order to achieve true liberation, it is important to control all mental desires and tendencies to enjoy sense pleasures. The following verses illustrate this:

When a man dwells in his mind on the object of sense, attachment to them is produced. From attachment springs desire and from desire comes anger. From anger arises bewilderment, from bewilderment loss of memory; and from loss of memory, the destruction of intelligence and from the destruction of intelligence he perishes. (2.62-3)

Bhakti Yoga

The introduction to chapter seven of the Bhagavad Gita explains *bhakti* as a mode of worship which consists of unceasing and loving remembrance of God. Faith (*Úraddhā*) and total surrender to a chosen God (*Ishta-deva*) are considered to be important aspects of *bhakti*. Theologian Catherine Cornille writes, "The text [of the Gita] offers a survey of the different possible disciplines for attaining liberation through knowledge (*jnana*), action (*karma*), and loving devotion to God (*bhakti*), focusing on the latter as both the easiest and the highest path to salvation." M.R. Sampatkumaran, a Bhagavad Gita scholar, explains in his overview of Ramanuja's commentary on the Gita, "The point is that mere knowledge of the scriptures cannot lead to final release. Devotion, meditation, and worship are essential."Ramakrishna believed that the essential message of the Gita could be obtained by repeating the word *Gita* several times, "'Gita, Gita, Gita', you begin, but then find yourself saying 'ta-Gi, ta-Gi, ta-Gi'. *Tagi* means one who has renounced everything for God." In the following verses, Krishna elucidates the importance of bhakti:

And of all yogins, he who full of faith worships Me, with his inner self abiding in Me, him, I hold to be the most attuned (to me in Yoga).

> ... those who, renouncing all actions in Me, and regarding Me as the Supreme, worship Me... For those whose thoughts have entered into Me, I am soon the deliverer from the ocean of death and transmigration, Arjuna. Keep your mind on Me alone, your intellect on Me. Thus you shall dwell in Me hereafter.

He who does work for Me, he who looks upon Me as his goal, he who worships Me, free from attachment, who is free from enmity to all creatures, he goes to Me, O Pandava.

Jnana Yoga

Jnana yoga is the path of wisdom, knowledge, and direct experience of *Brahman* as the ultimate reality. The path renounces both desires and actions, and is therefore depicted as being steep and very difficult in the

Adi Shankara with Disciples, *by Raja Ravi Varma (1904), propounding knowledge of absolute as of primary importance.*

Bhagavad Gita. This path is often associated with the non-dualistic Vedantic belief of the identity of the *Ātman* with the *Brahman*. For the followers of this path, the realisation of the identity of *Ātman* and *Brahman* is held as the key to liberation. When a sensible man ceases to see different identities due to different material bodies and he sees how beings are expanded everywhere, he attains to the *Brahman* conception. Those who see with eyes of knowledge the difference between the body and the knower of the body, and can also understand the process of liberation from bondage in material nature, attain to the supreme goal.

Influence of Bhagavad Gita

The Bhagavad Gita has been highly praised not only by prominent Indians such as Mohandas Karamchand Gandhi but also by Aldous Huxley,

Henry David Thoreau, Albert Einstein, J. Robert Oppenheimer, Ralph Waldo Emerson, Carl Jung, and Herman Hesse. The Gita's emphasis on selfless service was a prime source of inspiration for Gandhi, who said "When doubts haunt me, when disappointments stare me in the face, and I see not one ray of hope on the horizon, I turn to Bhagavad Gita and find a verse to comfort me; and I immediately begin to smile in the midst of overwhelming sorrow. My life has been full of external tragedies and if they have not left any visible or invisible effect on me, I owe it to the teaching of the Bhagavad Gita." Jawaharlal Nehru, the first Prime Minister of independent India, commented on the Gita, "The Bhagavad-Gita deals essentially with the spiritual foundation of human existence. It is a call of action to meet the obligations and duties of life; yet keeping in view the spiritual nature and grander purpose of the universe." J. Robert Oppenheimer, American physicist and director of the Manhattan Project, learned Sanskrit in 1933 and read the Bhagavad Gita in the original, citing it later as one of the most influential books to shape his philosophy of life. Upon witnessing the world's first nuclear test in 1945, he later said he had thought of the quotation "Now I am become Death, the destroyer of worlds", verse 32 from chapter 11 of the Bhagavad Gita. A 2006 report suggests that the Gita is replacing the influence of *The Art of War* (ascendant in the 1980s and 1990s) in the Western business community.

Classical Commentaries

Bhagavad Gita integrates various schools of thought like Vedanta, Samkhya, Yoga, and other theistic schools. Therefore, it remains a popular text for commentators belonging to various philosophical schools. However, its composite nature also leads to varying interpretations of the text. In the words of Mysore Hiriyanna, "[The Gita] is one of the hardest books to interpret, which accounts for the numerous commentaries on it–each differing from the rest in one essential point or the other." Different translators and commentators have widely differing views on what multi-layered Sanskrit words and passages signify, and their presentation in English depending on the sampradaya they are affiliated to. The oldest and most influential medieval commentary was that of the founder of the Vedanta school of extreme "non-dualism", Adi Shankara (788 A.D.), also known as Shankaracharya (Sanskrit: Sankarācārya). Shankara's commentary was based on a recension of the Gita containing 700 verses, and that recension has been widely adopted by others. Ramanujacharya's commentary chiefly seeks to show that the discipline of devotion to God (Bhakti yoga) is the way of salvation. Madhva, a commentator of the Vedanta school, whose dates are given either as (1199 CE) or as (1238 CE), also known as Madhvacharya (Sanskrit: Madhvācārya), wrote a commentary on the Bhagavad Gita, which exemplifies the thinking of the "dualist" school. Winthrop Sargeant quotes a dualistic assertion of the Madhva's school that there is "an eternal and complete distinction between the Supreme, the many souls, and matter and its divisions". His commentary on the Gita is called Gita Bhāshya. It has been annotated on by many ancient pontiffs of Dvaita Vedanta school like Padmanabha Tirtha, Jayatirtha, and Raghavendra Tirtha.

Every Indian must be acquainted with both Mahabharata and Bhagwat Gita.

Independence Movement in India

At a time when Indian nationalists were seeking an indigenous basis for social and political action, Bhagavad Gita provided them with a rationale for their activism and fight against injustice. Among nationalists, notable commentaries were written by Bal Gangadhar Tilak and Mahatma Gandhi, who used the text to help inspire the Indian independence movement. Tilak wrote his commentary while in jail during the period 1910–1911 serving a six-year sentence imposed by the British colonial government in India for sedition. While noting that the Gita teaches possible paths to liberation, his commentary places most emphasis on Karma yoga. No book was more central to Gandhi's life and thought than the Bhagavad-Gita, which he referred to as his "spiritual dictionary". During his stay in Yeravda jail in 1929, Gandhi wrote a commentary on the *Bhagavad Gita* in Gujarati. The Gujarati manuscript was translated into English by Mahadev Desai, who provided an additional introduction and commentary. It was published with a foreword by Gandhi in 1946. Mahatma Gandhi expressed his love for the Gita in these words:

> "I find a solace in the *Bhagavadgîtā* that I miss even in the Sermon on the Mount. When disappointment stares me in the face and all alone I see not one ray of light, I go back to the *Bhagavadgîtā*. I find a verse here and a verse there and I immediately begin to smile in the midst of overwhelming tragedies–and my life has been full of external tragedies–and if they have left no visible, no indelible scar on me, I owe it all to the teaching of *Bhagavadgîtā*."

Other Modern Commentaries

Among notable modern commentators of the Bhagavad Gita are Aurobindo, Sarvepalli Radhakrishnan, and Chinmayananda who took a syncretistic approach to the text. Paramahansa Yogananda's commentary on the Gita called *God Talks with Arjuna: The Bhagavad Gita* was released 1993. Eknath Easwaran has also written a commentary on the Bhagavad Gita. It examines the applicability of the principles of Gita, to the problems of modern life. Other notable commentators include Jeaneane Fowler and Ithamar Theodor.

Three translations: *Bhagavad Gita as it is*, a Gujarati translation by Gita Press, and another English one published by Barnes and Noble.

Although Vivekananda did not write any commentaries on the Bhagavad Gita, his works contained numerous references to the Gita, such as his lectures on the four yogas–Bhakti, Jnana, Karma, and Raja. Through the message of the Gita, Vivekananda sought to energise the people of India to claim their own dormant but strong identity

The Gita has also been translated into other European languages. In 1808, passages from the Gita were part of the first direct translation of Sanskrit into German, appearing in a book through which Friedrich Schlegel became known as the founder of Indian philology in Germany. Swami Rambhadracharya released the first Braille version of the scripture, with the original Sanskrit text and a Hindi commentary, on 30 November 2007.

Mahakavi Kalidasa and his Works (Abhigñānaúākuntalam)

Kālidāsa (Devanāgarî: कालीदास "servant of Kali") was a renowned Classical Sanskrit writer, widely regarded as the greatest poet and dramatist in the Sanskrit language. His *floruit* cannot be dated with precision, but most likely falls within the 5th century CE. His plays and poetry are primarily based on the Hindu Puranas and Hindu philosophy. A short account about him is given below.

Location

Scholars have speculated that Kālidāsa may have lived either near the Himalayas, or in the vicinity of Nagpur, central India, where the Kalidas University is situated now, or in Kalinga. The three speculations are based respectively on Kālidāsa's detailed description of the Himalayas in his *Kumrasambhava*, the display of his love for Ujjain in *Meghadta*, and his highly eulogistic descriptions of Kalingan emperor Hemāngada in *Raghuvamsa* (sixth *Kalidasa*).

Works/Plays

Kālidāsa wrote three plays. Among them, *Abhigñānaúākuntalam* ("Of Shakuntala recognised by a token") is generally regarded as a masterpiece. It was among the first Sanskrit works to be translated into English, and has since been translated into many languages.

The picture above shows Shakuntala stops to look back at Dushyanta, Raja Ravi Varma (1848–1906).

- Mālavikāgnimitram ("Mālavikā and Agnimitra") tells the story of King Agnimitra, who falls in love with the picture of an exiled servant girl named Mālavikā. When the queen discovers her husband's passion for this girl, she becomes infuriated and has Mālavikā imprisoned, but as fate would have it, Mālavikā is in fact a true-born princess, thus legitimising the affair.

- Abhignaúākuntalam ("Of Shakuntala recognised by a token") tells the story of King Dushyanta who, while on a hunting trip, meets Shakuntal, the adopted daughter of a sage, and marries her. A mishap befalls them when he is summoned back to court: Shakuntala, pregnant with their child, inadvertently offends a visiting sage and incurs a curse, by which Dushyanta will forget her completely until he sees the ring he has left with her. On her trip to Dushyanta's court in an advanced state of pregnancy, she loses the ring, and has to come away unrecognised. The ring is found by a fisherman who recognises the royal seal and returns it to Dushyanta, who regains his memory of Shakuntala and sets out to find her. After more travails, they are finally reunited.
- Vikramôrvaúîyam ("Pertaining to Vikrama and Urvashi") tells the story of mortal King Pururavas and celestial nymph Urvashi who fall in love. As an immortal, she has to return to the heavens, where an unfortunate accident causes her to be sent back to the earth as a mortal with the curse that she will die (and thus return to heaven) the moment her lover lays his eyes on the child which she will bear him. After a series of mishaps, including Urvashi's temporary transformation into a vine, the curse is lifted, and the lovers are allowed to remain together on the earth.

Kālidāsa is the author of two epic poems, *Raghuvaa* ("Dynasty of Raghu") and *Kumarasambhava* (Birth of 'Kumara' or Subrahmanya).

- Raghuvamsa is an epic poem about the kings of the Raghu dynasty.
- Kumarasambhava describes the birth and adolescence of the goddess Parvati, and her marriage to Lord Shiva.

He has also written two Khanda Kayvas:

- Rtusamhra describes the six seasons by narrating the experiences of two lovers in each of the seasons.
- Meghadûta or Meghasāndesa is the story of a Yaksha trying to send a message to his lover through a cloud. Kalidasa set this poem to the 'mandākrānta' meter known for its lyrical sweetness. It is one of Kalidasa's most popular poems and numerous commentaries on the work have been written. It has been said that Meghaduta was written in the region of Maharashtra near Nagpur. Now the Kavikulguru Kalidas Sanskrit University is situated at Ramtek, Nagpur.

Style

Kālidāsa's poetry is celebrated for its beautiful imagery and use of similes. The following are some specimen verses from his works.

One celebrated example occurs in the *Kumārasambhava*. Umā (Parvati) has been meditating throughout the summer, and as the monsoon arrives, the first raindrop falls on her:

— Kumârasambhava: Still sat Umâ though scorched by various flame of solar fire and fires of kindled birth, until at summer's end the waters came. Steam rose from her body as it rose from earth. With momentary pause the first drops rest upon her lash then strike her nether lip, fracture upon the highland of her breast, across the ladder of her waist then trip and slowly at her navel come to rest. — translation by Ingalls

The beauty of this verse is held to result from "the association through suggestion of numerous harmonious ideas". Firstly (as described in Mallinatha's commentary), the description suggests signs of her physical beauty: long eyelashes, pouting lower lip, deep navel, and so on. Secondly (as described in Appayya Dikshita's commentary), it suggests her pose as a perfect *yoginî*: her motionlessness through pain and pleasure, her posture, and so on. Finally, and more subtly, in comparing the mother goddess to the mother earth, and the rain coursing down her as it courses over the surface of the earth, it suggests earthly fertility. Thus the verse harmoniously brings to mind beauty, self-restraint, and fertility.

In another work, King Aja grieves over the death of Indumati and is consoled by a hermit:

—Raghuvamsa: O king! you are the finest among men with self-control. It is not fit of you to be struck by sorrow like the ordinary folk. If a great wind can move a tree and a mountain equally, how is the mountain better?

Dushyanta describes Shakuntala to his friend:

— Abhijñānaúākuntalam: She seems a flower whose fragrance none has tasted, A gem uncut by workman's tool, A branch no desecrating hands have wasted, Fresh honey, beautifully cool. No man on earth deserves to taste her beauty, Her blameless loveliness and worth, Unless he has fulfilled man's perfect duty—And is there such a one on earth? —translation by Arthur W. Ryder.

At Indumati's swayamvara, princes are downcast as she passes by without showing interest:

— Raghuvamsa as Indumati walked past each king and went to the next king (in a ceremony of choosing her husband), the king's face would turn bright and then pale. It was like watching a line of houses in the night as a dazzling lamp passed by—literal translation. And every prince rejected while she sought a husband, darkly frowned, as turrets, bright one moment with the flame from torches caught, Frown gloomily again and sink in night.

—Ryder

Dasharatha's hunt:

—Raghuvamsa: Dasaratha saw many beasts as he was hunting. Although he saw a peacock fly very close to his chariot, he did not shoot his arrow. For, as the peacock spread its tail feathers before him, it reminded him of his wife's hair adorned with flowers of different kinds and how it would become disarranged during their lovemaking.

Rama's coronation is announced:

— Raghuvamsa: The news of the beloved Rama being crowned as king gave special joy to every citizen, like a stream that wets every tree in a garden.

One of the loveliest verses in Meghadûta is as follows:

Meaning: when I try to draw your picture and show in it that I am bowing at your feet, with a 'kawa-a type of chalk', on the rock; due to emotional outbreak, my eyes get wet. The 'Krutāntā or Yama' himself does not wish to have our meet in the picture itself.

Similarly, a woman's beauty has been artfully depicted in a verse of Kalidasa's Meghadûta as follows:

Meaning: This verse's meaning can best be understood when translated word-by-word:

1. tanvi - slim;
2. shyamā—an adult woman who has not yet enjoyed sex with a male and thus has no experience of pregnancy and the like;
3. shikhari dashanā—a woman having, well-arranged, clean, white teeth;
4. pakwabimbādharóshthi—having lips the color of a morning reddish sun;
5. kshāmā—short-waisted;
6. chakithariniprekshanā—with the look of a frightened deer;
7. nimnanābhi—having a deep navel;
8. shronibhārāt alasagamanā—a slow walker, due to heavy hips;
9. stoknamrā stanābhyām—slightly bent forward, due to the weight of her breasts;

10. and for the last line the meaning is: such a woman is the idol of beauty for any woman.

Later Culture

Many scholars have written commentaries on the works of Kālidāsa. Among the most studied commentaries are those by Kolāchala Mallinātha Suri, which were written in the 15th century during the reign of the Vijayanagar king, Deva Rya II. The earliest surviving commentaries appear to be those of the 10th-century Kashmirian scholar Vallabhadeva. Eminent Sanskrit poets like Bānabhatta, Jayadeva and Rajasekhara have lavished praise on Kālidāsa in their tributes. A well-known Sanskrit verse ("Upamā Kālidāsasya...") praises his skill at *upamā*, or similes. Anandavardhana, a highly revered critic, considered Kālidāsa to be one of the greatest Sanskrit poets ever. Of the hundreds of pre-modern Sanskrit commentaries on Kālidāsa's works, only a fraction have been contemporarily published. Such commentaries show signs of Kālidāsa's poetry being changed from its original state through centuries of manual copying, and possibly through competing oral traditions which ran alongside the written tradition.

Kālidāsa's *Abhijñānaúākuntalam* was one of the first works of Indian literature to become known in Europe. It was first translated to English and then from English to German, where it was received with wonder and fascination by a group of eminent poets, which included Herder and Goethe.

Ramayana–the Epic

The *Rāmāyana*, originally written by Vālmîki, consists of 24,000 *lokas* in seven cantos (some say six, i.e., excluding the Uttara Rāmāyana). The Rāmāyana tells the story of a prince, Rāma of Ayodhy, whose wife St is abducted by the Demon-King (*Raksasa*) of Lanka, Ravana. The Vālmîki's Rāmāyana is dated variously from 500 BC to 100 BC. As with many traditional epics, it has gone through a long process of interpolations and redactions, making it impossible to date accurately.

Notwithstanding the aforesaid, it is pertinent to note that Vālmîki is also quoted to be the contemporary of Úrî Rāma. Úrî Rāma met Vālmîki during his period of exile and had interacted with him. Vālmîki had Sîtā in his hermitage where Kuúa and Lava were born to Sîtā. Vālmîki taught Rāmāyana to Kuúa and Lava, who later sang the divine story in Ayodhyā during the Aœvamedha yajña congregation, to the pleasure of the audience, whereupon, King Úrî Rāma summoned them to his royal palace. Kuúa and Lava sang the story of Úrî Rāma there, and Úrî Rāma confirmed that whatever had been sung by these two children was entirely true.

The First Sloka

As the story goes, Vālmîki was going to the river Ganges for his daily ablutions. A disciple by the name Bharadvja was carrying his clothes. On

The Killing of Krouncha Heron.

the way, they came across the Tamasa Stream. Looking at the stream, Vālmîki said to his disciple, "Look, how clear is this water, like the mind of a good man! I will bathe here today." When he was looking for a suitable place to step into the stream, he saw a Crane (bird) couple mating. Vālmîki felt very pleased on seeing the happy birds. Suddenly, hit by an arrow; the male bird died on the spot. Filled by sorrow its mate screamed in agony and died of shock. Vālmîki's heart melted at this pitiful sight. He looked around to find out who had shot the bird. He saw a hunter with a bow and arrows, nearby. Vālmîki became very angry. His lips opened and he uttered the following words:

Page 72

mā nicāda praticmhā tvamagama úāúvatî samā

yat krauñcamithunādekam avadhî kāmamohitam

You will find no rest for the long years of Eternity

For you killed a bird in love and unsuspecting

Emerging spontaneously from his rage and grief, this was the first œloka in Sanskrit literature. Later Vālmîki Muni composed the entire Rāmāyana with the blessings of Lord Brahm in the same meter that issued forth from him as the œloka. Thus this œloka is revered as the "first œloka" in Hindu literature. Vālmîki Muni is revered as the first poet, or *Ādi Kavi*, and the Rāmāyana, the first Kvya.

His first disciples to whom he taught the Rāmāyana were Kuúa and Lava, the sons of Úrî Rama.

Early Life

Valmiki was born in a family of hunters and was hunter himself in his youth, he would ruthlessly take the lives of animals in the forests and he has taken the lives of so many animals that he had earned the displeasure of the Gods. One day a group of rishis were gathering in the forest to perform a yagna and then they witnessed valmiki kill a deer, being brahmins killing of animals or any living creature was forbidden and so they approached valmiki and told him that he has almost wiped all the animal species in the forest and they told him that the gods will curse him and he will be shunned by all. Valmiki was shocked and so he asked the rishis for a way out of the gods' wrath. The rishis told him to sit under a sal tree with his eyes shut and keep on reciting the syllables "maraam" (if recited repeatedly it makes the sound "Rama") repeatedly until they return after finishing the yagna. And so they left valmiki there and finished their yagna and returned home without waking up valmiki,months later narada saw valmiki who (still devotedly reciting "maraam" and was covered with anthills because he did not move at all he was so perfectly still) woke up valmiki that he had earned a lot of merit and his bhakti had pleased Rama and was no less than a rishi. And from that day on he was devoted to rama for the rest of his life and camed to be known as Rishi Valmiki. And was the first person to compose the entire Ramayana. Brahma once told Valmiki that "As long as mountains stand and as long as rivers flow, so long will your Ramayana be read by man"

Ram and Ramayana

Ram is the seventh avatar of the god Vishnu in Hinduism, and a king of Ayodhya in Hindu scriptures. In few Ram-centric sects, Ram is considered the Supreme being, rather than an avatar. Ram was born in Suryavansha (Ikshvaku Vansh) later known as Raghuvansha after king Raghu.

The Archaeological Survey of India had found ancient remains of a temple in the Ram Janmabhoomi in a survey conducted in 1992, indicating the existence of pre ancient Rama worship. Rama is one of the many popular figures and deities in Hinduism, specifically Vaishnavism and Vaishnava religious scriptures in South and Southeast Asia. In Ayodhya, the Indian city believed to be the birthplace of Ram, he is also worshipped as an infant or Ram Lalla. Most of the details of Ram's life come from the Ramayana, one of the two great epics of India. Born as the eldest son of Kausalya and Dasharatha, king of Ayodhya, Ram is referred to within Hinduism as *Maryada Purushottama*, literally *the Perfect Man* or *Lord of Self-Control* or *Lord of Virtue*. Ram is the husband of Sita, whom Hindus consider to be an Avatar of Lakshmi and the embodiment of perfect womanhood.

Ram's life and journey is one of perfect adherence to dharma despite harsh tests of life and time. He is pictured as the ideal man and the perfect human. For the sake of his father's honor, Ram abandons his claim to Kosala's throne to serve an exile of fourteen years in the forest. His wife Sita and brother Lakshmana, unable to live without Ram, decide to join him, and all three spend the fourteen years in exile together. While in exile, Sita is kidnapped by Ravana, the Rakshasa (Asura) monarch of Lanka. After a long and arduous search that tests his personal strength and virtue, Ram fights a colossal war against Ravana's armies. In a war of powerful and magical beings, greatly destructive weaponry and battles, Ram slays Ravana in battle and liberates his wife. Having completed his exile, Ram returns to be crowned king in Ayodhya (the capital of his kingdom) and eventually becomes emperor, rules with happiness, peace, prosperity and justice—a period known as *Ram Rajya*. Rama is consider as the greatest Avatar of Vishnu.

Ram's courage in searching for Sita and fighting a terrible war to rescue his wife and their honor is complemented by Sita's absolute devotion to her husband's love, and perfect chastity despite being Ravana's captive. Ram's younger brothers, namely Lakshmana, Shatrughna and Bharata strongly complement his piety, virtue and strength, and they are believed by many to belong to the *Maryada Purushottama* and the Seventh Avatara, mainly embodied by Ram. Ram's piety and virtue attract powerful and devoted allies such as Hanuman and the Vanaras of Kishkindha, with whose help he rescues Sita. The legend of Rama is deeply influential and popular in the societies of the Indian subcontinent and across South East Asia. Ram is revered for his unending compassion, courage and devotion to religious values and duty by all the Hindus.

Ramayana was also written by TULSIDAS that is worth reading.

Buddhism in India and Lord Buddha

Apart from Hinduism, Buddhism also spread in India and later in the entire South East Asia. Gautama Buddha or Siddhārtha Gautama Buddha

Famous painting of Gautama Buddha.

(Sanskrit: Pali: Siddhattha Gotama), also called Sakyamuni, was a sage. from the ancient Shakya republic, on whose teachings Buddhism was founded. He is also referred to as "the Buddha" or simply as "Buddha." Buddha means "awakened one" or "the enlightened one." "Buddha" is also used as a title for the first awakened being in an era. In most Buddhist traditions, Siddhartha Gautama is regarded as the Supreme Buddha of our age. Gautama taught a Middle Way compared to the severe asceticism found in the Sramana (renunciation) movement common in his region. He later taught throughout regions of eastern India such as Magadha and Kośala. The time of Gautama's birth and death is uncertain: Most historians in the early 20th century dated his lifetime as circa 563 BCE to 483 BCE, but more recent opinion dates his death to between 486 and 483 BCE or, according to some, between 411 and 400 BCE. However, at a specialist symposium on this question held in 1988 in Göttingen, the majority of those scholars who presented definite opinions gave dates within 20 years either side of 400 BCE for the Buddha's death, with others supporting earlier or later dates. These alternative chronologies, however, havauddhaism e not yet been accepted by all other historians. Gautama is the primary figure in Buddhism, and accounts of his life, discourses, and monastic rules are believed by

Buddhists to have been summarised after his death and memorised by hi s followers. Various collections of teachings attributed to him were passed down by oral tradition, and first committed to writing about 400 years later.

Queen Māyā miraculously giving birth to Prince Siddhārtha; Sanskrit manuscript; Nālandā; Bihar, India; Pāla period. Traditional biographies of Gautama generally include numerous miracles, omens, and supernatural events. The character of the Buddha in these traditional biographies is often that of a fully transcendent (Skt. lokottara) and perfected being who is unencumbered by the mundane world. In the Mahāvastu, over the course of many lives, Gautama is said to have developed supramundane abilities including: a painless birth conceived without intercourse; no need for sleep, food, medicine, or bathing, although engaging in such "in conformity with the world"; omniscience, and the ability to "suppress karma". Nevertheless, some of the more ordinary details of his life have been gathered from these traditional sources. In modern times there has been an attempt to form a secular understanding of Siddhārtha Gautama's life by omitting the traditional supernatural elements of his early biographies. It is important to stress that, despite modern Theravada teachings to the contrary (often a sop to skeptical Western pupils), he was never seen as being merely human. For instance, he is often described as having the thirty-two major and eighty minor marks or signs of a mahāpurusa, "superman"; the Buddha himself denied that he was either a man or a god; and in the Mahāparinibbāna Sutta he states that he could live for an aeon were he asked to do so. The ancient Indians were generally unconcerned with chronologies, being more focused o n phil osophy. Buddhist texts reflect this tendency, providing a clearer picture of what Gautama may have taught than of the dates of the events in his life. These texts contain descriptions of the culture and daily life of ancient India which can be corroborated from the Jain scriptures, and make the Buddha's time the earliest period in Indian history for which significant accounts exist. British author Karen Armstrong writes that although there is very little information that can be considered historically sound, we can be reasonably confident that Siddhārtha Gautama did exist as a historical figure. Michael Carrithers goes a bit further by stating that the most general outline of "birth, maturity, renunciation, search, awakening and liberation, teaching, death" must be true.

Basic Teachings of Buddha

Buddha Preached that there are **three universal truths**

Years later the scientific world discovered many hidden truths of Nature as were preached and revealed by Gautama Buddha and others many many years ago here in India. Such was the wisdom of these great men.

One day, the Buddha sat down in the shade of a tree and noticed how beautiful the countryside was. Flowers were blooming and trees were putting on bright new leaves, but among all this beauty, he saw much unhappiness. A farmer beat his ox in the field. A bird pecked at an earthworm, and then an eagle swooped down on the bird. Deeply troubled, he asked, "Why does the farmer beat his ox? Why must one creature eat another to live?"

During his enlightenment, the Buddha found the answer to these questions. He discovered three great truths. He explained these truths in a simple way so that everyone could understand them.

1. Nothing is Lost in the Universe: The first truth is that nothing is lost in the universe. Matter turns into energy, energy turns into matter. A dead leaf turns into soil. A seed sprouts and becomes a new plant. Old solar systems disintegrate and turn into cosmic rays. We are born of our parents, our children are born of us.

We are the same as plants, as trees, as other people, as the rain that falls. We consist of that which is around us, we are the same as everything. If we destroy something around us, we destroy ourselves. If we cheat another, we cheat ourselves. Understanding this truth, the Buddha and his disciples never killed any animal.

2. Everything Changes: The second universal truth of the Buddha is that everything is continuously changing. Life is like a river flowing on and on, ever-changing. Sometimes it flows slowly and sometimes swiftly. It is smooth and gentle in some places, but later on snags and rocks crop up out of nowhere. As soon as we think we are safe, something unexpected happens.

Once dinosaurs, mammoths, and saber-toothed tigers roamed this earth. They all died out, yet this was not the end of life. Other life forms like smaller mammals appeared, and eventually humans, too. Now we can even see the Earth from space and understand the changes that have taken place on this planet. Our ideas about life also change. People once believed that the world was flat, but now we know that it is round.

3. Law of Cause and Effect: The third universal truth explained by the Buddha is that there is continuous changes due to the law of cause and effect. This is the same law of cause and effect found in every modern science textbook. In this way, science and Buddhism are alike.

The law of cause and effect is known as karma. Nothing ever happens to us unless we deserve it. We receive exactly what we earn, whether it is good or bad. We are the way we are now due to the things we have done in the past. Our thoughts and actions determine the kind of life we can have. If we do good things, in the future good things will happen to us. If we do bad things, in the future bad things will happen to us. Every moment we create new karma by what we say, do, and think. If we understand this, we do not need to fear karma. It becomes our friend. It teaches us to create a bright future.

The Buddha said,

"The kind of seed sown
will produce that kind of fruit.
Those who do good will reap good results.
Those who do evil will reap evil results.
If you carefully plant a good seed,
You will joyfully gather good fruit."

It is amasing that Gautama Buddha, through his spiritual insights, wisdom and understanding could realise such basic truths of life such a long time ago.

Lord Mahavira's Philosophy–The Birth of Jainism

The philosophies of Lord Mahavira are based on the sole purpose of improving the quality of life. The basic idea is to attain spiritual excellence by maintaining ethical dhuur and following proper code of conduct. Mahavira philosophy primarily consists of metaphysics and ethics. The metaphysics comprise of three main principles, namely, Anekantavada, Syadvada and Karma. The five ethical principles underlying the philosophy of Lord Mahavira are Satya, Ahimsa, Brahmacharya, Asteya, and Aparigraha.

Philosophy of Mahavira

Mahavira's philosophy has eight cardinal principles–three metaphysical and five ethical. The objective is to elevate the quality of life. Page text.

Mahavira preached that from eternity, every living being (soul) is in bondage to karmic atoms accumulated by good or bad deeds. In a state of karmic delusion, the individual seeks temporary and illusory plea sure in material possessions, which are the root causes of self-centered violent thoughts and deeds as well as anger, hatred, greed, and other vices. These result in further accumulation of karma.

To liberate one's self, Mahavira taught the necessity of right faith (samyak-darshana), right knowledge (samyak-gyana), and right conduct (samyak-charitra'). At the heart of right conduct for Jains lie the five great vows:

Nonviolence (Ahimsa)–to cause no harm to living beings;

Truthfulness (Satya)–to speak the harmless truth only;

Non-stealing (Asteya)–to take nothing not properly given;

Chastity (Bramacharya)–to indulge in no sensual pleasure;

Non-possession/Non-attachment (Aparigraha)–to detach completely from people, places, and material things.

These vows cannot be fully implemented without accepting the philosophy of non-absolutism (anekantavada) and the theory of relativity (syādvāda, also translated "qualified prediction"). Monks and nuns adhere strictly to these vows, while the laypeople observe them as best they can.

Mahavira taught that men and women are spiritual equals and that both may renounce the world in search of moksha or ultimate happiness.

Mahavira organised his followers into a fourfold order; monk (dhu), nun (sādhvî), layman (Úrāvaka), and laywoman (Úrāvikā). This order is known as Chaturvidh Jain Sangha.

Mahavira's sermons were preserved orally by his immediate disciples known as Ganadharas in the Jain Agamas. Through time Agama Sutras have been lost, destroyed, or modified. About one thousand years after Mahavira's time the Agama Sutras were recorded on palm leaf paper. Svetambaras accept these sutras as authentic teachings while Digambaras use them as a reference.

Jainism existed before Mahavira, and his teachings were based on those of his predecessors. Thus Mahavira was a reformer and propagator of an existing religion, rather than the founder of a new faith. He followed the well established creed of his predecessor Tirthankara Parshva. However, Mahavira did reorganise the philosophical tenets of Jainism to correspond to his times.

Mahavira in Meditation.

A few centuries after Mahavira's Nirvana, the religious order grew more and more complex. There were schisms on minor points, although they did not affect Mahavira's original doctrines. Later generations saw the introduction of rituals and complexities that is criticised as placing Mahavira and other Tirthankaras on the throne similar to those of Hindu deities.

Mahavir Jayanti

Mahavir Jayanti has a lot of religious significance for people belonging to the Jain religion. It is observed to celebrate the birthday of the great Lord Mahavira, who was born at Kshatriyakund near modern Patna in Bihar in 599 BC. According to the Gregorian calendar, the Mahavir Jayanti festival falls during the period between March and April. As a part of Mahavir Jayanthi celebrations, the Jain temples are beautifully adorned with flags.

Guru Nanak and Sikhism

Guru Nanak Dev (Punjabi: ; Hindi: गुरुनानक, Urdu: *Gurû Nānak*) (15 April 1469–22 September 1539) was the founder of the religion of Sikhism and the first of the eleven Sikh Gurus, the eleventh being the *living Guru*, Guru Granth Sahib. His birth is celebrated world-wide on Kartik Puranmashi, the full-moon day which falls on different dates each year in the month of Katak, October-November.

Guru Nanak traveled to places far and wide teaching people the message of One God who dwells in every one of His creations and constitutes the Eternal Truth.

It is part of Sikh religious belief that the spirit of Guru Nanak's sanctity, divinity and religious authority descended upon each of the nine subsequent Gurus when the Guru ship was devolved on to them.

Family and Early Life

Nanak was born on 15 April 1469, now celebrated as Prakash Divas of Guru Nanak Dev, at Rāi Bhoi Kî Talvandi, now called Nankana Sahib, near

Gurdwara Janam Asthan.

Lahore, Pakistan. Today, his birthplace is marked by Gurdwara Janam Asthan. His parents were Kalyan Chand Das Bedi, popularly shortened to Kalu Mehta, and Mata Tripta. His father was a *patwari* (accountant) for crop revenue in the village of Talwandi, employed by a Muslim landlord of that area, Rai Bular Bhatti.

He had one sister, Bibi Nanaki, who was five years older than him and became a spiritual figure in her own right. In 1475 she married Jai Ram and went to his town of Sultanpur, where he was the steward (modi) to Daulat Khan Lodi, the eventual governor of Lahore. Nanak was attached to his older sister, and, in traditional Indian fashion, he followed her to Sultanpur to live with her and her husband. Nanak also found work with Daulat Khan, when he was around 16 years old. This was a formative time for Nanak, as the Puratan Janam Sakhi suggests, and in his numerous allusions to governmental structure in his hymns, most likely gained at this time.

Picture above shows Guru Nanak and his disciples.

Commentaries on his life give details of his blossoming awareness from a young age. At the age of five, Nanak is said to have voiced interest in divine subjects. At age seven, his father, Kalu Mehta, enrolled him at the village school as was the custom. Notable lore recounts that as a child Nanak astonished his teacher by describing the implicit symbolism of the first letter of the alphabet, which is an almost straight stroke in Persian or Arabic, resembling the mathematical version of one, as denoting the unity or oneness of God. Other childhood accounts refer to strange and miraculous events about Nanak, such as one witnessed by Rai Bular, in which the sleeping child's head was shaded from the harsh sunlight, in one account, by the stationary shadow of a tree or, in another, by a poisonous cobra.

On 24 September 1487 Nanak married Mata Sulakkhani, daughter of Mûl Chand and Chando Rānî, in the town of Batala. The couple had two sons, Sri Chand (8 September 1494–13 January 1629) and Lakhmi Chand (12 February 1497–9 April 1555).

The earliest biographical sources on Nanak's life recognised today are the *Janamsākhîs* (life accounts) and the *vārs* (expounding verses) of the scribe Bhai Gurdas. The most popular Janamsākhî were allegedly written by a close companion of the Guru, Bhai Bala. However, the writing style and language employed have left scholars, such as Max Arthur Macauliffe, certain that they were composed after his death.

Gurdas, a purported scribe of the Gur Granth Sahib, also wrote about Nanak's life in his *vārs*. Although these too were compiled some time after Nanak's time, they are less detailed than the Janamsākhîs. The Janamsākhîs recount in minute detail the circumstances of the birth of the guru. The Janamsākhîs state that, at his birth an astrologer, who came to write his horoscope, insisted on seeing the child. On seeing the infant, he is said to have worshipped him with clasped hands and remarked that, "I regret that I shall never live to see young Nanak as an adult."

Rai Bular, the local landlord and Nanak's sister Bibi Nanaki were the first people who recognised divine qualities in the boy. They encouraged and supported him to study and travel. Sikh tradition states that at around 1499, at the age of 30, he had a vision. After he failed to return from his ablutions, his clothes were found on the bank of a local stream called the Kali Bein. The townspeople assumed he had drowned in the river; Daulat Khan had the river dragged, but no body was found. Three days after disappearing, Nanak reappeared, staying silent. The next day, he spoke to pronounce:

"There is neither Hindu nor Mussulman (Muslim) so whose path shall I follow? I shall follow God's path. God is neither Hindu nor Mussulman and the path which I follow is God's."

Nanak said that he had been taken to God's court. There, he was offered a cup filled with amrita (nectar) and given the command,

> "This is the cup of the adoration of God's name. Drink it. I am with you. I bless you and raise you up. Whoever remembers you will enjoy my favour. Go, rejoice of my name and teach others to do so. I have bestowed the gift of my name upon you. Let this be your calling."

From this point onwards, Nanak is described in accounts as a Guru, and Sikhism was born.

Although the exact account of his itinerary is disputed, he is widely acknowledged to have made four major journeys, spanning thousands of kilometres, the first tour being east towards Bengal and Assam, the second south towards Sri Lanka, the third north towards Kashmir, Ladakh, and Tibet, and the final tour west towards Baghdad, Mecca and Medina on the Arabian Peninsula.

Nanak crossed into Arunachal Pradesh and visited most of the part. First while going to Lhasa (Tibet) he passed through Tawang after crossing from Bhutan and entered Tibet from Samdurang Chu. He returned from Lhasa and went to the famous monastery Samye and entered Pemoshubu Menchukha in Arunachal Pradesh. He meditated for some time at this location. From Menchukha he went back to Tibet, brought the residents of Southern Tibet and got them settled in Menchukha. Thereafter through Gelling and Tuiting he proceeded to Saidya and Braham-Kund, before entering the state of Assam again. Nanak is the founder of the Sikh religion.

Nanak's Teachings

Guru Nanak's teachings can be found in the Sikh scripture Guru Granth Sahib, as a vast collection of revelatory verses recorded in Gurmukhi.

From these some common principles seem discernible. Firstly a supreme Godhead who although incomprehensible, manifests in all major religions, the Singular "Doer" and formless. It is described as the indestructible (undying) form.

Nanak describes the dangers of Egotism (haumai-"I am") and calls upon devotees to engage in worship through the word of God. *Naam*, implies God, the Reality, mystical word or formula to recite or meditate upon (shabad in Gurbani), divine order (hukam) and at places divine teacher (guru) and guru's instructions) and singing of God's qualities, discarding doubt in the process. However, such worship must be selfless (sewa). The word of God, cleanses the individual to make such worship possible. This is related to the revelation that God is the Doer and without God there is no other. Nanak warned against hypocrisy and falsehood saying that these are pervasive in humanity and that religious actions can also be in vain. It may also be said that ascetic practices are disfavoured by Nanak, who suggests remaining inwardly detached whilst living as a householder.

Through popular tradition, Nanak's teaching is understood to be practised in three ways:

- *VaGChakk*: Sharing with others, helping those with less who are in need.
- *Kirat Karô*: Earning/making a living honestly, without exploitation or fraud.
- *Naam Japna*: Chanting the Holy Name and thus remembering God at all times (ceaseless devotion to God).

Nanak put the greatest emphasis on the worship of the Word of God (Naam Japna). One should follow the direction of awakened individuals (Gurmukh or God willed) rather than the mind (state of Manmukh-being led by Self will)-the latter being perilous and leading only to frustration.

Reforms that occurred in the institution and both Godhead and Devotion, are seen as transcending any religious consideration or divide, as God is not separate from any individual.

Guru Nanak's Divine Journeys

Nanak was moved by the plight of the people of world and wanted to tell them about the "real message of God". The people of the world were confused by the conflicting message given by priests, pundits, qazis, mullahs, etc., He was determined to bring his message to the masses; so in 1499, he decided to set out on his sacred mission to spread the holy message of peace and compassion to all of mankind.

Most of his journeys were made on foot with his companion Bhai Mardana. He travelled in all four directions–North, East, West and South. The founder Sikh Guru is believed to have travelled more than 28,000 km in five major tours of the world during the period from 1500 to 1524.

Nanak saw the world suffering out of hatred, fanaticism, falsehood and hypocrisy. The world had sunk in wickedness and sin. So he decided that he had to travel and educate and press home the message of Almighty Lord. So he set out in 1499 on his mission for the regeneration of humanity on this earth. He carried the torch of truth, heavenly love, peace and joy for mankind. For one year he spread his message of .peace, compassion, righteousness and truth to the people in and around his home.

Then in 1500, he embarked on his Divine Mission and went towards east, west, north and south and visited various centers of Hindus, Muslims, Buddhists, Jainis, Sufis, Yogis and Sidhas. He met people of different religions, tribes, cultures and races. He travelled on foot with his Muslim companion named Bhai Mardana, a minstrel. His travels are called Udasis. In his first Udasi (travel), Nanak covered east of India and returned home after spending about 6 years. He started from Sultanpur in 1500 and went to his village Talwandi to meet and inform his parents about his long journey. His parents wanted their young son to provide comfort and protection for them in their old age and so they told him they would prefer it if he did not go. But he told them that the world was burning in the fire of Kalyug and that thousands and thousands were waiting for the Divine message of the Almighty for comfort, love and salvation. The Guru, therefore, told his parents, "There is a call from Heaven, I must go whither He directs me to go." Upon hearing these words, his parents agreed and gave their blessings. So Nanak started his mission and the roots of Sikhism were laid down first towards the east of India.

According to the Puratan Janamsakhi, which is one of the oldest accounts of the life history of Guru Nanak, the Guru undertook five missionary journeys (udasiya) to the far away places of Ceylon (Sri Lanka), Mecca, Baghdad, Kamroop (Assam), Tashkand and many more. Guru ji travelled far and wide to spread the word of Gurbani and covered most of India, present day Bangladesh, Pakistan, Tibet, Nepal, Bhutan, South West China, Afghanistan, Iran, Iraq, Saudi Arabia, Egypt, Israel, Jordan, Syria, Kazakhstan, Turkmenistan, Uzbekistan, Tajikistan, and Kyrgyzstan.

The Five Journeys

Below is a brief summary of the confirmed places visited by Nanak:

- First Udasi: (1500-1506 AD) Lasted about seven years and covered the following towns and regions: Sultanpur, Tulamba (modern Makhdumpur, zila Multan), Panipat, Delhi, Banaras (Varanasi), Nanakmata (Zila Nainital, U.P.), Tanda Vanjara (Zila Rampur), Kamrup (Assam), Asa Desh (Assam), Saidpur (modern Eminabad, Pakistan), Pasrur (Pakistan), Sialkot (Pakistan).
- Second Udasi: (1506-1513 AD) Lasted about seven years and covered the following towns and regions: Dhanasri Valley, Sangladip (Ceylon).
- Third Udasi: (1514-1518 AD) Lasted about five years and covered the following towns and regions: Kashmir, Sumer Parbat, Nepal, Tashkand, Sikkim, Tibet.
- Fourth Udasi: (1519-1521 AD) Lasted about three years and covered the following towns and regions: Mecca and the Arab countries.
- Fifth Udasi: (1523-1524 AD) Lasted about two years and covered the following towns and regions: Places within the Punjab.

To spread his knowledge, Nanak traveled widely throughout Asia. To this end he undertook four Udasis (Tours). The first udasi (1500-1505) was to the central and eastern parts of India. Second udasi (1506-1509) took him to important towns and religious centers of south India, including Sri Lanka. During the third Udasi (1514–1516) Nanak traveled to the Gangetic plains, Bihar, Nepal, Lahsa, Leh, as far as Tashkand and then back to Punjab via the Kashmir valley. The fourth Udasi (1518–1521) took him to various Arab countries.

Chaitanya Mahaprabhu.

The birth of Baisnab Dharma Chaitanya Mahaprabhu.

Born: Vishvambar 1486 Nabadwip, present day Nadia, West Bengal, India.

Died: 1534 (aged 47–48) Puri, Odisha, India.

Titles/honours Followers of Gaudiya Vaishnavism believe him to be the full incarnation of Lord Krishna.

Philosophy: Bhakti yoga.

Chaitanya Mahaprabhu (also transliterated Caitanya, IAST *caitanya mahāprabhu*) (1486–1534) was a social reformer in eastern India (specifically present-day Bangladesh and states of West Bengal, Bihar, Jharkhand, Manipur, Assam, and Odisha of India) in the 16th century, worshipped by followers of Gaudiya Vaishnavism as the full incarnation of Lord Krishna. Sri Krishna Chaitanya was a notable proponent for the Vaishnava school of Bhakti yoga (meaning loving devotion to Krishna), based on the philosophy of the Bhagavata Purana and Bhagavad Gita. Specifically, he worshipped the forms of Krishna, popularised the chanting of the Hare Krishna maha mantra and composed the Siksastakam (eight devotional prayers) in Sanskrit. His line of followers, known as Gaudiya Vaishnavas, revere him as an Avatar of Krishna in the mood of Radharani who was prophesied to appear in the later verses of the Bhagavata Purana.

He was also sometimes referred to by the names Gaura (Sanskrit for 'golden'), due to his fair complexion, and Nimai due to his being born underneath a Neem tree. There are numerous biographies available from the time giving details of Chaitanya's life, the most prominent ones being the Chaitanya Charitamrita of Krishnadasa Kaviraja Goswami, the earlier Chaitanya Bhagavata of Vrindavana Dasa (both originally written in Bengali but now widely available in English and other languages), and the Chaitanya Mangala, written by Lochana Dasa. These works are in Bengali with some Sanskrit verses interspersed. In addition to these there are other Sanskrit biographies composed by his contemporaries. Chief among them are the literary masterpiece, Sri Chaitanya Charitamritam Mahakavyam (written in 20 sargas and 1911 shlokas) by Kavi Karnapura and Sri Krishna Chaitanya Charitamritam by Murari Gupta. Chaitanya's life.

Chaitanya Mahaprabhu is revered by devotees as an incarnation of Krishna and Radharani as avatars of the Parmatma, or Supreme Godhead. He was born in a Odia Brahmin family. According to *Chaitanya Charitamrita*, Nimäi was born on the full moon night of 18 February 1486, at the time of a lunar eclipse. His parents named him 'Vishvambhar'. Sri Chaitanya was the second son of Jagannath Mishra and his wife Sachi Devi who lived in the town of Nabadwip in Nadia, West Bengal. Chaitanya's ancestry is a contentious issue between the people of Odisha and West Bengal with Shree Chaitanya having family roots in Jajpur, Odisha, from where his grandfather, Madhukar Mishra had emigrated to nearby Bengal.

Birthplace of Chaitanya Mahaprabhu in Pracheen Mayapur area, Nabadwip, West Bengal, India.

In his youth, Chaitanya Mahäprabhu was primarily known as an erudite scholar, whose learning and skills in argumentation in his locality were second to none. Kashinath Mukhopadhyay was his private tutor during those days. A number of stories also exist telling of Chaitanya's apparent attraction to the chanting and singing of Krishna's names from a very young age, but largely this was perceived as being secondary to his interest in acquiring knowledge and studying Sanskrit. When travelling to Gaya to perform the shraddha ceremony for his departed father Chaitanya met his guru, the ascetic Ishvara Puri, from whom he received initiation with the Gopala Krishna mantra. This meeting was to mark a significant change in Mahäprabhu's outlook and upon his return to Bengal the local Vaishnavas, headed by Advaita Āchrya, were stunned at his external sudden 'change of heart' (from 'scholar' to 'devotee') and soon Chaitanya became the eminent leader of their Vaishnava group within Nadia.

After leaving Bengal and receiving entrance into the sannyasa order by Keshava Bharati, Chaitanya journeyed throughout the length and breadth of India for several years, chanting the divine Names of Krishna constantly. He spent the last 24 years of his life in Puri, Odisha, the great temple city of Jagannth. The Suryavanshi Hindu emperor of Odisha, Gajapati Maharaja Prataparudra Dev, regarded the Lord as Krishna's incarnation and was an enthusiastic patron and devotee of Chaitanya's sankeertan party. It was during these years that Lord Chaitanya is believed by His followers to have sank deep into various Divine-Love (samādhi) and performed pastimes of divine ecstasy (bhakti).

Identity

Sri Chaitanya and Nityananda, is shown performing a 'kirtan' in the streets of Nabadwip, Bengal.

According to beliefs of orthodox followers Caitanya Mahaprabhu united in himself two aspects: Ecstatic devotee of Krishna and Krishna himself in inseparable union with Radha. According to the hagiographies of 16th-century authors he has exhibited his Universal Form identical to that of Krishna on a number of occasions, notably to Advaita Ācārya and Nityānanda Prabhu.

Teachings

Chaitanya has left one written record in Sanskrit called Siksastakam. Chaitanya's epistemological, theological and ontological teachings are summarised as ten roots or maxims (dasa mula). The statements of amnaya (scripture) are the chief proof. By these statements the following ten topics are taught.

1. Krishna is the Supreme Absolute Truth.
2. Krishna is endowed with all energies.
3. Krishna is the ocean of rasa (theology).
4. The jivas (individual souls) are all separated parts of the Lord.
5. In bound state the jivas are under the influence of matter, due to their tatastha nature.
6. In the liberated state the jivas are free from the influence of matter, due to their tatastha nature.
7. The jivas and the material world are both different from and identical to the Lord.

8. Pure devotion is the practice of the jivas.
9. Pure love of Krishna is the ultimate goal.
10. Krishna is the only lovable blessing to be received.

Shree Shree Ramakrishna Paramahamsa

Ramakrishna (Bengali: *Ramkico Pôromôhongœo*), (18 February 1836–16 August 1886), born Gadadhar Chattopadhyay (Bengali: *Gôdadhor Chôṭṭopaddhae*), was a famous mystic of 19th-century India. His religious school of thought led to the formation of the Ramakrishna Mission by his chief disciple Swami Vivekananda–both were influential figures in the Bengali Renaissance as well as the Hindu renaissance during the 19th and 20th centuries. Many of his disciples and devotees believe he was an *Avatar* or incarnation of God. He is also referred to as "Paramahamsa" by his devotees, as such he is popularly known as Ramakrishna Paramahamsa.

Ramakrishna was born in a poor Brahmin Vaishnava family in rural Bengal. He became a priest of the Dakshineswar Kali Temple, dedicated to the goddess Kali, which had the influence of the main strands of Bengali *bhakti* tradition. The most widely known amongst his first spiritual teachers was an ascetic woman, called Bhairavi Brahmani skilled in Tantra and Vaishnava *bhakti*. Later an *Advaita Vedantin* ascetic taught him non-dual meditation, and according to Ramakrishna, he experienced *nirvikalpa samadhi* under his guidance. Ramakrishna also experimented with other religions, notably Islam and Christianity, and said that they all lead to the same God. Though he quit conventional education, he attracted the attention of the middle class, upper middle class and numerous Bengali intellectuals.

Birth and Childhood

Ramakrishna was born on 13 March, 1836, in the village of Kamarpukur, in the Hooghly district of West Bengal, into a very poor but pious, orthodox brahmin family. Kamarpukur was untouched by the glamour of the city and contained rice fields, tall palms, royal banyans, a few lakes, and two cremation grounds. His parents were Kshudiram Chattopādhyāya and Chandramani Devî. According to his followers, Ramakrishna's parents experienced supernatural incidents, visions before his birth. His father Khudiram had a dream in Gaya in which Lord Gadadhara (a form of Vishnu), said that he would be born as his son. Chandramani Devi is said to have had a vision of light entering her womb from Shiva's temple.

The small house at Kamarpukur where Ramakrishna lived (centre). The family shrine is on the left, birthplace temple on the right.

Ramakrishna attended a village school with some regularity for 12 years, he later rejected the traditional schooling saying that he was not interested in a "bread-winning education". Kamarpukur, being a transit-point in well-established pilgrimage routes to Puri, brought him into contact with renunciates and holy men. He became well-versed in the *Puranas*, the *Ramayana*, the *Mahabharata*, and the *Bhagavata Purana*, hearing them from wandering monks and the *Kathaks*—a class of men in ancient India who preached and sang the *Purānas*. He could read and write in Bengali. While the official biographies write that the name Ramakrishna was given by Mathura Biswas—chief patron at Dakshineswar Kali Temple, it has also been suggested that this name was given by his own parents. Ramakrishna describes his first spiritual ecstasy at the age of six: while walking along the paddy fields, a flock of white cranes flying against a backdrop of dark thunder clouds caught his vision. He reportedly became so absorbed by this scene that he lost outward consciousness and experienced indescribable joy in that state. Ramakrishna reportedly had experiences of similar nature a few other times in his childhood—while worshipping the goddess *Vishalakshi*, and portraying god Shiva in a drama during *Shivaratri* festival. From his tenth or eleventh year on, the trances became common, and by the final years of his life, Ramakrishna's *samdhi* periods occurred almost daily. Ramakrishna's father died in 1843, after which time family responsibilities fell on his elder brother Ramkumar. This loss drew him closer to his mother, and he spent his time in household activities and daily worship of the household deities and became more involved in contemplative activities such as reading the sacred epics. When Ramakrishna was in his teens, the family's financial position worsened. Ramkumar started a Sanskrit school in Calcutta and also served as a priest. Ramakrishna moved to Calcutta in 1852 with Ramkumar to assist in the priestly work.

Dakshineswar Kali Temple

Dakshineswar Kāli Temple, where Ramakrishna spent a major portion of his adult life.

In 1855 Ramkumar was appointed as the priest of Dakshineswar Kali Temple, built by Rani Rashmoni—a rich woman of Calcutta who belonged to the *kaivarta* community. Ramakrishna, along with his nephew Hriday, became assistants to Ramkumar, with Ramakrishna given the task of decorating the deity. When Ramkumar died in 1856, Ramakrishṇa took his place as the priest of the Kali temple.

After Ramkumar's death Ramakrishna became more contemplative. He began to look upon the image of the goddess Kali as his mother and the mother of the universe. Ramakrishna reportedly had a vision of the goddess Kali as the universal Mother, which he described as "...houses, doors, temples and everything else vanished altogether; as if there was nothing anywhere! And what I saw was an infinite shoreless sea of light; a sea that was consciousness. However far and in whatever direction I looked, I saw shining waves, one after another, coming towards me."

Marriage

Rumors spread to Kamarpukur that Ramakrishna had become unstable as a result of his spiritual exercises at Dakshineswar. Ramakrishna's mother

Sarada Devi (1853–1920), wife and spiritual counterpart of Ramakrishna.

and his elder brother Rameswar decided to get Ramakrishna married, thinking that marriage would be a good steadying influence upon him—by forcing him to accept responsibility and to keep his attention on normal affairs rather than his spiritual practices and visions. Ramakrishna reportedly mentioned that they could find the bride at the house of Ramchandra Mukherjee in Jayrambati, three miles to the north-west of Kamarpukur. The five-year-old bride, Saradamani Mukhopadhyaya (later known as Sarada Devi) was found and the marriage was duly solemnised in 1859. Ramakrishna was 23 at this point, but the age difference was typical for 19th century rural Bengal. They later spent three months together in Kamarpukur. Sarada Devi was fourteen while Ramakrishna was thirty-two. Ramakrishna became a very influential figure in Sarada's life, and she became a strong follower of his teachings.

After the marriage, Sarada stayed at Jayrambati and joined Ramakrishna in Dakshineswar at the age of 18.

By the time his bride joined him, Ramakrishna had already embraced the monastic life of a sannyasi; as a result, the marriage was never consummated. As a priest Ramakrishna performed the ritual ceremony—the *Shodashi Puja*–where Sarada Devi was made to sit in the seat of goddess Kali, and worshiped as the Divine mother. Ramakrishna regarded Sarada as the Divine Mother in person, addressing her as the Holy Mother, and it was by this name that she was known to Ramakrishna's disciples. Sarada Devi outlived Ramakrishna by 34 years and played an important role in the nascent religious movement.

Religious Practices and Teachers

After his marriage Ramakrishna returned to Calcutta and resumed the charges of the temple again, and continued his *sadhana*. According to his official biographers, he continued his *sadhana* under teachers of Tantra, Vedanta and Vaishnava.

In 1861, Ramakrishna accepted Bhairavi Brahmani, an orange-robed, middle-aged female ascetic, as a teacher. She carried with her the *Raghuvir Shila*, a stone icon representing Ram and all Vaishnava deities. She was thoroughly conversant with the texts of Gaudiya Vaishnavism and practiced Tantra. According to the Bhairavi, Ramakrishna was experiencing phenomena that accompany *mahabhava*—the supreme attitude of loving devotion towards the divine–and quoting from the *bhakti shastras*, she said that other religious figures like Radha and Chaitanya had similar experiences.

The Bhairavi initiated Ramakrishna into Tantra. Tantrism focuses on the worship of *shakti* and the object of Tantric training is to transcend the barriers between the holy and unholy as a means of achieving liberation and to see all aspects of the natural world as manifestations of the divine *shakti*. Under her guidance, Ramakrishna went through sixty four major tantric sadhanas which were completed in 1863. He began with mantra rituals such as japa and purascarana and many other rituals designed to purify the mind and establish self-control. He later proceeded towards tantric sadhanas, which generally include a set of heterodox practices called *vamachara* (left-hand path), which utilise as a means of liberation, activities like eating of parched grain, fish and meat along with drinking of wine and sexual intercourse. According to Ramakrishna and his biographers, Ramakrishna did not directly participate in the last two of those activities, all that he needed was a suggestion of them to produce the desired result. Ramakrishna acknowledged the left-hand tantric path, though it had "undesirable features", as one of the "valid roads to God-realisation", he consistently cautioned his devotees and disciples against associating with it. The Bhairavi also taught Ramakrishna the *kumari-puja*, a form of ritual in which the Virgin Goddess is worshiped symbolically in the form of a young girl. Under the tutelage of the Bhairavi, Ramakrishna also learnt Kundalini Yoga. The Bhairavi, with the yogic techniques and the tantra played an important part in the initial spiritual development of Ramakrishna.

Vaishnava Bhakti

The Vaishnava Bhakti traditions speak of five different moods, referred to as *bhāvas*—different attitudes that a devotee can take up to express his love for God. They are: *úānta*, the "peaceful attitude"; *dāsya*, the attitude of a servant; *sakhya*, the attitude of a friend; *vātsalya*, the attitude of a mother toward her child; and *madhura*, the attitude of a woman towards her lover.

At some point in the period between his vision of Kali and his marriage, Ramakrishna practiced *dāsya bhāva*, during which he worshiped Rama with the attitude of Hanuman, the monkey-god, who is considered to be the ideal devotee and servant of Rama. According to Ramakrishna, towards the end of this *sadhana*, he had a vision of Sita, the consort of Rama, merging into his body.

In 1864, Ramakrishna practiced *vātsalya bhāva* under a Vaishnava guru Jatadhari. During this period, he worshipped a metal image of Ramlālā (Rama as a child) in the attitude of a mother. According to Ramakrishna, he could feel the presence of child Rama as a living God in the metal image.

Ramakrishna later engaged in the practice of *madhura bhāva*— the attitude of the Gopis and Radha towards Krishna. During the practise of this *bhava*, Ramakrishna dressed himself in women's attire for several days and regarded himself as one of the Gopis of Vrindavan. According to Sri Ramakrishna, *madhura bhava* is practised to root out the idea of sex, which is seen as an impediment in spiritual life. According to Ramakrishna, towards the end of this *sadhana*, he attained *savikalpa samadhi*—vision and union with Krishna.

Ramakrishna visited Nadia, the home of Chaitanya and Nityananda, the 15th-century founders of Bengali Gaudiya Vaishnava bhakti. According to Ramakrishna, he had an intense vision of two young boys merging into his body. Earlier, after his vision of Kali, he is said to have cultivated the *Santa bhava*—the child attitude—towards Kali.

Totapuri and Vedanta

The Panchavati and the hut where Ramakrishna performed his advaitic sadhana. The mud hut has been replaced by a brick one.

In 1865, Ramakrishna was initiated into *sannyasa* by Tota Puri, an itinerant monk who trained Ramakrishna in *Advaita Vedanta*, the Hindu philosophy which emphasises non-dualism.

Totapuri first guided Ramakrishna through the rites of *sannyasa*—renunciation of all ties to the world. Then he instructed him in the teaching

of *advaita*—that "Brahman alone is real, and the world is illusory; I have no separate existence; I am that Brahman alone." Under the guidance of Totapuri, Ramakrishna reportedly experienced *nirvikalpa samadhi*, which is considered to be the highest state in spiritual realisation.

Totapuri stayed with Ramakrishna for nearly eleven months and instructed him further in the teachings of *advaita*. Ramakrishna said that this period of *nirvikalpa samadhi* came to an end when he received a command from the Mother Kali to "remain in *Bhavamukha*; for the enlightenment of the people". *Bhavamukha* being a state of existence intermediate between *samādhi* and normal consciousness.

Islam and Christianity

In 1866, Govinda Roy, a Hindu guru who practiced Sufism, initiated Ramakrishna into Islam. Ramakrishna said that he "devoutly repeated the name of Allah, wore a cloth like the Arab Moslems, said their prayer five times daily, and felt disinclined even to see images of the Hindu gods and goddesses, much less worship them—for the Hindu way of thinking had disappeared altogether from my mind." According to Ramakrishna, after three days of practice he had a vision of a "radiant personage with grave countenance and white beard resembling the Prophet and merging with his body".

At the end of 1873 he started the practice of Christianity, when his devotee Shambu Charan Mallik read the Bible to him. Ramakrishna said that for several days he was filled with Christian thoughts and no longer thought of going to the Kali temple. Ramakrishna describes of a vision in which the picture of Madonna and Child Jesus became alive and had a vision in which Jesus merged with his body. In his own room amongst other divine pictures was one of Christ, and he burnt incense before it morning and evening.

There was also a picture showing Jesus Christ saving St Peter from drowning in the water.

Arrival of Followers

Ramakrishna in Bhava Samadhi at the house of Keshab Chandra Sen. He is seen supported by his nephew Hriday and surrounded by Brahmo Devotees.

In 1875, Ramakrishna met the influential Brahmo Samaj leader Keshab Chandra Sen. Keshab had accepted Christianity, and had separated from the Adi Brahmo Samaj. Formerly, Keshab had rejected idolatry, but under the influence of Ramakrishna he accepted Hindu polytheism and established the "New Dispensation" (*Nava Vidhan*) religious movement, based on Ramakrishna's principles—"Worship of God as Mother", "All religions as true" and "Assimilation of Hindu polytheism into Brahmoism". Keshab also publicised Ramakrishna's teachings in the journals of *New Dispensation* over a period of several years, which was instrumental in bringing Ramakrishna to the attention of a wider audience, especially the Bhadralok (English-educated classes of Bengal) and the Europeans residing in India.

Following Keshab, other Brahmos such as Vijaykrishna Goswami started to admire Ramakrishna, propagate his ideals and reorient their socio-religious outlook. Many prominent people of Calcutta—Pratap Chandra Mazumdar, Shivanath Shastri and Trailokyanath Sanyal—began visiting him during this time (1871–1885). Mozoomdar wrote the first English biography of Ramakrishna, entitled *The Hindu Saint* in the *Theistic Quarterly Review* (1879), which played a vital role in introducing Ramakrishna to Westerners like the German indologist Max Muller. Newspapers reported that Ramakrishna was spreading "Love" and "Devotion" among the educated classes of Calcutta and that he had succeeded in reforming the character of some youths whose morals had been corrupt.

Ramakrishna also had interactions with Debendranath Tagore, the father of Rabindranath Tagore, and Ishwar Chandra Vidyasagar, a renowned social worker. He had also met Swami Dayananda. Ramakrishna is considered as one of the main contributors to the Bengali Renaissance. However, some Brahmos like Upadhyay Brahmabandhab disapproved of his avatarahood and ascetic renunciation and considered Ramakrishna's samadhi as a nervous malady.

Among the Europeans who were influenced by Ramakrishna was Principal Dr. W.W. Hastie of the Scottish Church College, Calcutta. In the course of explaining the word *trance* in the poem *The Excursion* by William Wordsworth, Hastie told his students that if they wanted to know its "real meaning", they should go to "Ramakrishna of Dakshineswar." This prompted some of his students, including Narendranath Dutta (later Swami Vivekananda), to visit Ramakrishna.

Devotees and Disciples

Disciples of Ramakrishna and Swami Vivekananda

Some Monastic Disciples (L to R): Trigunatitananda, Shivananda, Swami Vivekananda, Turiyananda, Brahmananda. Below Saradananda.

Most of Ramakrishna's prominent disciples came between 1879–1885, and were influenced by his style of preaching and instruction.

His chief disciples consisted of:

- *Grihastas* or *The householders*—Mahendranath Gupta, Girish Chandra Ghosh, Akshay Kumar Sen and others.
- *Monastic disciples* who renounced their family and became the earliest monks of the Ramakrishna order—Narendranath Dutta (Swami Vivekananda), Rakhal Chandra Ghosh (Swami Brahmananda), Kaliprasad Chandra (Swami Abhedananda), Taraknath Ghoshal (Swami Shivananda), Sashibhushan Chakravarty (Swami Ramakrishnananda), Saratchandra Chakravarty (Swami Saradananda), Tulasi Charan Dutta (Swami Nirmalananda), Gangadhar Ghatak (Swami Akhandananda), Hari Prasana (Swami Vijnanananda) and others.
- A small group of women disciples including *Gauri Ma* and *Yogin Ma*. A few of them were initiated into *sanyasa* through *mantra deeksha*. Among the women, Ramakrishna emphasised service to other women rather than *tapasya* (practice of austerities). Gauri Ma founded the Saradesvari Ashrama at Barrackpur, which was dedicated to the education and uplift of women.

As his name spread, an ever-shifting crowd of all classes and castes visited Ramakrishna. According to *Kathamrita* it included, childless widows, young school-boys, aged pensioners, Hindu scholars and religious figures, men betrayed by lovers, people with suicidal tendencies, small-time businessmen, and people "dreading the grind of samsaric life". Ramakrishna's primary biographers, describe him as talkative. According to the biographers, for hours Ramakrishna would reminisce about his own eventful spiritual life, tell tales, explain Vedantic doctrines with extremely mundane illustrations, raise questions and answer them himself, crack jokes, sing songs, and mimic the ways of all types of worldly people, keeping the visitors enthralled. In preparation for monastic life, Ramakrishna ordered his monastic disciples to beg their food from door to door without distinction of caste. He gave them the saffron robe, the sign of the Sanyasi, and initiated them with *Mantra Deeksha*.

In the beginning of 1885 Ramakrishna suffered from clergyman's throat, which gradually developed into throat cancer. He was moved to Shyampukur near Calcutta, where some of the best physicians of the time, including Dr. Mahendralal Sarkar, were engaged. When his condition aggravated he was relocated to a large garden house at Cossipore on December 11, 1885. During his last days, he was looked after by his monastic disciples and

Sarada Devi. Ramakrishna was advised by the doctors to keep the strictest silence, but ignoring their advice, he incessantly conversed with visitors. According to traditional accounts, before his death, Ramakrishna transferred his spiritual powers to Vivekananda and reassured Vivekananda of his avataric status. Ramakrishna asked Vivekananda to look after the welfare of the disciples, saying, "keep my boys together" and asked him to "teach them". Ramakrishna also asked other monastic disciples to look upon Vivekananda as their leader. Ramakrishna's condition gradually worsened and he expired in the early morning hours of August 16, 1886 at the Cossipore garden house. According to his disciples, this was *mahasamadhi*. After the death of their master, the monastic disciples led by Vivekananda formed a fellowship at a half-ruined house at Baranagar near the river Ganges, with the financial assistance of the householder disciples. This became the first Math or monastery of the disciples who constituted the first Ramakrishna Order.

Teachings of Ramakrishna

Ramakrishna's teachings were imparted in rustic Bengali, using stories and parables. These teachings made a powerful impact on Calcutta's intellectuals, despite the fact that his preachings were far removed from issues of modernism or national independence. His spiritual movement indirectly aided nationalism, as it rejected caste distinctions and religious prejudices.

In the Calcutta scene of the mid to late nineteenth century, Ramakrishna was opinionated on the subject of Chakri. Chakri can be described as a type of low-paying servitude done by educated men—typically government or commerce-related clerical positions. On a basic level, Ramakrishna saw this system as a corrupt form of European social organisation that forced educated men to be servants not only to their bosses at the office but also to their wives at home. What Ramakrishna saw as the primary detriment of Chakri, however, was that it forced workers into a rigid, impersonal clock-based time structure. He saw the imposition of strict adherence to each second on the watch as a roadblock to spirituality. Despite this, however, Ramakrishna demonstrated that Bhakti could be practiced as an inner retreat to experience solace in the face of Western-style discipline and often discrimination in the workplace.

Ramakrishna emphasised God-realisation as the supreme goal of all living beings. Ramakrishna taught that *kamini-kanchana* is an obstacle to God-realisation. *Kamini-kanchan* literally translates to "woman and gold."

Carl T. Jackson interprets *kamini-kanchana* to refer to the idea of sex and the idea of money as delusions which prevent people from realising God.

Ramakrishna also cautioned his women disciples against *purusa-*

kanchana ("man and gold") and Tyagananda writes that Ramakrishna used *Kamini-Kanchana* as "cautionary words" instructing his disciples to conquer the "lust *inside* the mind."

Ramakrishna looked upon the world as Maya and he explained that *avidya maya* represents dark forces of creation (e.g. sensual desire, evil passions, greed, lust and cruelty), which keep people on lower planes of consciousness. These forces are responsible for human entrapment in the cycle of birth and death, and they must be fought and vanquished. *Vidya maya*, on the other hand, represents higher forces of creation (e.g. spiritual virtues, enlightening qualities, kindness, purity, love, and devotion), which elevate human beings to the higher planes of consciousness.

Ramakrishna practised several religions, including Islam and Christianity, and taught that in spite of the differences, all religions are valid and true and they lead to the same ultimate goal—God. Ramakrishna's taught that *jatra jiv tatra Shiv* (wherever there is a living being, there is Shiva). His teaching, "*Jive daya noy, Shiv gyane jiv seba*" (not kindness to living beings, but serving the living being as Shiva Himself) is considered as the inspiration for the philanthropic work carried out by his chief disciple Vivekananda.

Ramakrishna used rustic colloquial Bengali in his conversations. According to contemporary reports, Ramakrishna's linguistic style was unique, even to those who spoke Bengali. It contained obscure local words and idioms from village Bengali, interspersed with philosophical Sanskrit terms and references to the Vedas, Puranas, Tantras. For that reason, according to philosopher Lex Hixon, his speeches cannot be literally translated into English or any other language.

Ramakrishna was skilled with words and had an extraordinary style of preaching and instructing, which may have helped convey his ideas to even the most skeptical temple visitors. His speeches reportedly revealed a sense of joy and fun, but he was not at a loss when debating with intellectual philosophers. Philosopher Arindam Chakrabarti contrasted Ramakrishna's talkativeness with Buddha's legendary reticence, and compared his teaching style to that of Socrates.

Ramakrishna's explicitly sexual language shocked 19th-century Westerners, even scholars Max Mller who were otherwise his admirers. Müller wrote that his language was at times "*abominably filthy*". He admitted however that such direct speech was natural to contemporary Hindus, "where certain classes of men walk stark naked", and should not be considered intentional filthiness or obscenity. Citing examples of classical poems like *Bhartrihari*, the Bible, Homer, and Shakespeare, Müller felt that few of the sayings would have to be bowdlerised.

Reception and Legacy

Ramakrishna's Influence and Ramakrishna Mission

Several organisations have been established in the name of Ramakrishna. The Ramakrishna Math and Mission is one of the main organisations founded

The Marble Statue of Ramakrishna at Belur Math, the Headquarters of the Ramakrishna Mission.

by Swami Vivekananda in 1897. The Mission conducts extensive work in health care, disaster relief, rural management, tribal welfare, elementary and higher education. The movement is considered as one of the revitalisation movements of India. Other organisations include the Ramakrishna Vedanta Society founded by Swami Abhedananda in 1923, the Ramakrishna Sarada Math founded by a rebel group in 1929,the Ramakrishna Vivekananda Mission formed by Swami Nityananda in 1976, and the Sri Sarada Math and Ramakrishna Sarada Mission founded in 1959 as a sister organisation by the Ramakrishna Math and Mission. Ramakrishna is considered as an important figure in Bengali Renaissance of 19th-20th Century. Max Müller, Mahatma Gandhi, Jawaharlal Nehru, Sri Aurobindo, and Leo Tolstoy have acknowledged Ramakrishna's contribution to humanity. Ramakrishna's influence is also seen in the works of artists such as Franz Dvorak (1862–1927) and Philip Glass.

On Swami Vivekananda's guru, Ramakrishna, Rabindranath Tagore wrote a poem: "To the Ramakrishna Paramahamsa Ramakrishna Deva".

> "Diverse courses of worship from varied springs of fulfillment have mingled in your meditation.The manifold revelation of the joy of the Infinite has given form to a shrine of unity in your life where from far and near arrive salutations to which I join my own."

Tagore was the chief guest on the occasion of birth centenary celebration of Ramakrishna by the Ramakrishna Mission and paid rich tribute to Ramakrishna. During the 1937 Parliament of Religions, which was held at the Ramakrishna Mission in Calcutta, Tagore acknowledged Ramakrishna, whose birth centenary was being celebrated, as a great saint because "the largeness of his spirit could comprehend seemingly antagonistic modes of sadhana, and because the simplicity of his soul shames for all time the pomp and pedantry of pontiffs and pundits."

Religious School of Thought

Several scholars have tried to associate Ramakrishna with a particular religious school of thought—*Bhakti*, Tantra and Vedanta.

In his influential 1896 essay "A real mahatma: Sri Ramakrishna Paramahansa Dev" and his 1899 book *Rāmakrishna: His Life and Sayings*, the German philologist and Orientalist Max Müller portrayed Ramakrishna as "a wonderful mixture of God and man" and as "... a Bhakta, a worshipper or lover of the deity, much more than a Gñānin or a knower."

In London and New York in 1896, Swami Vivekananda delivered his famous address on Ramakrishna entitled "My Master." He said of his master: "this great intellect never learnt even to write his own name, but the most brilliant graduates of our university found in him an intellectual giant." Vivekananda criticised his followers for "brazenly" projecting Ramakrishna as an *avatara* and miracle-worker. Narasingha Sil has argued that Vivekananda revised and mythologised Ramakrishna's image after Ramakrishna's death. In a 1997 book review of a book by Jeffrey Kripal, Malcolm McLean of Otago University supported Kripal's view and argued that the Movement presents "a particular kind of explanation of Ramakrishna, that he was some kind of neo-Vedantist who taught that all religions are the same". Carl Olson argued that in his presentation of his master, Vivekananda had hid much of Ramakrishna's embarrassing sexual oddities from the public, because he feared that Ramakrishna would be misunderstood. Tyagananda and Vrajaprana argue that Oslon makes his "astonishing claim" based on Kripal's speculations in *Kali's Child*, which are unsupported by any of the source texts. Amiya Sen writes that that Vivekananda's "social service gospel" stemmed from direct inspiration from Ramakrishna and rests substantially on the "liminal quality" of the Master's message.

Indologist Heinrich Zimmer was the first Western scholar to interpret Ramakrishna's worship of the Divine Mother as containing specifically Tantric elements. Neeval also argued that tantra played a main role in Ramakrishna's spiritual development.

Philosopher Lex Hixon writes Ramakrishna was an *Advaita Vedantin*. Postcolonial literary theorist Gayatri Chakravorty Spivak wrote that Ramakrishna was a "Bengali *bhakta* visionary" and that as a *bhakta*, "he turned chiefly towards Kali." Amiya Prosad Sen writes that "it is really difficult to separate the Tantrik Ramakrishna from the Vedantic", since Vedanta and Tantra "may appear to be differ in some respects", but they also "share some important postulates between them".

Postcolonial Studies

Postcolonial studies try to locate Ramakrishna in the historical background of Calcutta during the mid-19th Century.

In 1999, postcolonial historian Sumit Sarkar argued that he found in the *Kathamrita* traces of a binary opposition between unlearned oral wisdom and learned literate knowledge. He argues that all of our information about Ramakrishna, a rustic near-illiterate Brahmin, comes from urban *bhadralok* devotees, "...whose texts simultaneously illuminate and transform."

India–this ancient nation had given birth to several religious personalities which also influenced the life and activities of our people.The above illustrations and depictions would justify that. Such great personalities adnd their preachings shaped the life and psyche of our people in India

(a) Historical Perspectives of India–The Homeland of 1.28 Billion People of the World

In India, early human activity of *Homo sapiens* (meaning the early Humans) started as long as 75,000 years ago, or with earlier hominids including *Homo erectus* from about 500,000 years ago. The Indus Valley Civilisation, which spread and flourished in the northwestern part of the Indian subcontinent from c. 3300 to 1300 BCE in present-day Pakistan and northwest of India, was the first major civilisation in South Asia. A sophisticated and technologically advanced urban culture developed in the Mature Harappan period, from 2600 to 1900 BCE. This Bronze Age civilisation collapsed before the end of the second millennium BCE and was followed by the Iron Age Vedic Civilisation, which extended over much of the Indo-Gangetic plain and which witnessed the rise of major polities known as the

Mahajanapadas. In one of these kingdoms, Magadha, Mahavira and Gautama Buddha were born in the 6th or 5th century BCE and propagated their *ramanic* philosophies.

Maurya Empire

Most of the subcontinent was conquered by the Maurya Empire during the 4th and 3rd centuries BCE. It became fragmented, with various parts ruled by numerous Middle kingdoms for the next 1,500 years. This is known as the classical period of Indian history, during which time India has sometimes been estimated to have had the largest economy of the ancient and medieval world, with its huge population generating between one fourth and one third of the world's income up to the 18th century.

Much of northern and central India was united in the 4th century CE, and remained so for two centuries, under the Gupta Empire. This period, witnessing a Hindu religious and intellectual resurgence, is known as the "Golden Age of India". From this time, and for several centuries afterwards, southern India, under the rule of the Chalukyas, Cholas, Pallavas, and Pandyas, experienced its own golden age. During this period, aspects of Indian civilisation, administration, culture, and religion (Hinduism and Buddhism) spread to much of Asia.

Muslim Rule

Kingdoms in southern India had maritime business links with the Roman Empire from around 77 CE. Muslim rule in the subcontinent began in 8th century CE when the Arab general Muhammad bin Qasim conquered Sindh and Multan in southern Punjab in modern day Pakistan, setting the stage for several successive invasions from Central Asia between the 10th and 15th centuries CE, leading to the formation of Muslim empires in the Indian subcontinent such as the Delhi Sultanate and the Mughal Empire. Mughal rule came from Central Asia to cover most of the northern parts of the subcontinent. Mughal rulers introduced Central Asian art and architecture to India. In addition to the Mughals and various Rajput kingdoms, several independent Hindu states, such as the Vijayanagara Empire, the Maratha Empire, Eastern Ganga Empire and the Ahom Kingdom, flourished contemporaneously in southern, western, eastern and gained ascendancy over South Asia, Northeastern India respectively. The Mughal Empire suffered a gradual decline in the early 18th century, which provided opportunities for the Afghans, Balochis, Sikhs, and Marathas to exercise control over large areas in the northwest of the subcontinent until the British East India Company. British East India Company: Beginning in the mid-18th century and over the next century, large areas of India were annexed by the British East India Company. Dissatisfaction with Company rule led to the Indian Rebellion of 1857, after which the British provinces of India were directly administered by the British Crown and witnessed a period of both rapid development of infrastructure and economic decline. During the first half of the 20th century, a nationwide struggle for independence was launched by the Indian National Congress and later joined by the Muslim League. The subcontinent gained independence from the United Kingdom in 1947, after the British provinces were partitioned into the dominions of India and Pakistan and the princely states all acceded to one of the new states.

Prehistoric Era

Kingdoms in southern India had maritime business links with the Roman Empire from around 77 CE. Muslim rule in the subcontinent began in 8th century CE when the Arab general Muhammad bin Qasim conquered Sindh and Multan in southern Punjab in modern day Pakistan, setting the stage for several successive invasions from Central Asia between the 10th and 15th centuries CE, leading to the formation of Muslim empires in the Indian subcontinent such as the Delhi Sultanate and the Mughal Empire. Mughal rule came from Central Asia to cover most of the northern parts of the subcontinent. Mughal rulers introduced Central Asian art and architecture to India. In addition to the Mughals and various Rajput kingdoms, several independent Hindu states, such as the Vijayanagara Empire, the Maratha Empire, Eastern Ganga Empire and the Ahom Kingdom, flourished contemporaneously in southern, western, eastern and gained ascendancy over South Asia, northeastern India respectively. The Mughal Empire suffered a gradual decline in the early 18th century, which provided opportunities for the Afghans, Balochis, Sikhs, and Marathas to exercise control over large areas in the northwest of the subcontinent until the British East India Company. British East India Company : Beginning in the mid-18th century and over the next century, large areas of India were annexed by the British East India Company. Dissatisfaction with Company rule led to the Indian Rebellion of 1857, after which the British provinces of India were directly administered by the British Crown and witnessed a period of both rapid development of infrastructure and economic decline. During the first half of the 20th century, a nationwide struggle for independence was launched by the Indian National Congress and later joined by the Muslim League. The subcontinent gained independence from the United Kingdom in 1947, after the British provinces were partitioned into the dominions of India and Pakistan and the princely states all acceded to one of the new states.

Stone Age

Isolated remains of *Homo erectus* in Hathnora in the Narmada Valley in central India indicate that India might have been inhabited since at least the

Stone age (5000 BC) writings of Edakkal Caves in Kerala, India.

Middle Pleistocene era, somewhere between 500,000 and 200,000 years ago. Tools crafted by proto-humans that have been dated back two million years have been discovered in the northwestern part of the subcontinent. The ancient history of the region includes some of South Asia's oldest settlements and some of its major civilisations. The earliest archaeological site in the subcontinent is the palaeolithic hominid site in the Soan River valley. Soanian sites are found in the Sivalik region across what are now India, Pakistan, and Nepal. The Mesolithic period in the Indian subcontinent was followed by the Neolithic period, when more extensive settlement of the subcontinent occurred after the end of the last Ice Age approximately 12,000 years ago. The first confirmed semipermanent settlements appeared 9,000 years ago in the Bhimbetka rock shelters in modern Madhya Pradesh, India. Early Neolithic culture in South Asia is represented by the Bhirrana findings (7500 BCE)in Haryana, India and Mehrgarh findings (7000 BCE onwards) in Balochistan, Pakistan. Traces of a Neolithic culture have been alleged to be submerged in the Gulf of Khambat in India, radiocarbon dated to 7500 BCE. However, the one dredged piece of wood in question was found in an area of strong ocean currents. Neolithic agriculture cultures sprang up in the Indus Valley region around 5000 BCE, in the lower Gangetic valley around 3000 BCE, and in later South India, spreading southwards and also northwards into Malwa around 1800 BCE. The first urban civilisation of the region began with the Indus Valley Civilisation.

Bronze Age

"Priest King" of Indus Valley Civilisation

The Bronze Age in the Indian subcontinent began around 3300 BCE with the early Indus Valley Civilisation. It was centered on the Indus River

Ancient Lothal as they appear today.

and its tributaries which extended into the Ghaggar-Hakra River valley, the Ganges-Yamuna Doab, Gujarat, and southeastern Afghanistan. The civilisation is primarily located in modern-day India (Gujarat, Haryana, Punjab and Rajasthan provinces) and Pakistan (Sindh, Punjab, and Balochistan provinces). Historically part of Ancient India, it is one of the world's earliest urban civilisations, along with Mesopotamia and Ancient Egypt.

Inhabitants of the ancient Indus river valley, the Harappans, developed new techniques in metallurgy and handicraft (carneol products, seal carving), and produced copper, bronze, lead, and tin.

The Mature Indus civilisation flourished from about 2600 to 1900 BCE, marking the beginning of urban civilisation on the subcontinent. The civilisation included urban centers such as Dholavira, Kalibangan, Rupar, Rakhigarhi, and Lothal in modernday India, and Harappa, Ganeriwala, and Mohenjo-daro in modern day Pakistan. The civilisation is noted for its cities built of brick, roadside drainage system, and multistoried houses.

Early Historic Period

(a) Vedic Period

Vedic Period and the Foundation of Hinduism

The Vedic period is characterised by Indo-Aryan culture associated with the texts of Vedas, sacred to Hindus, which were orally composed in

Vedic Sanskrit. The Vedas are some of the oldest extant texts in India and next to some writings in Egypt and Mesopotamia are the oldest in the world. The Vedic period lasted from about 1500 to 500 BCE.

laying the foundations of Hinduism and other cultural aspects of early Indian society. In terms of culture, many regions of the subcontinent transitioned from the Chalcolithic to the Iron Age in this period. Historians have analysed the Vedas to posit a Vedic culture in the Punjab region and the upper Gangetic Plain.

Most historians also consider this period to have encompassed several ways of Indo-Aryan migration into the subcontinent from the north-west. Vedic people believed in the transmigration of the soul, and the peepal tree and cow were sanctified by the time of the Atharva Veda. Many of the concepts of Indian philosophy espoused later like Dharma, Karma, etc., trace their root to the Vedas.

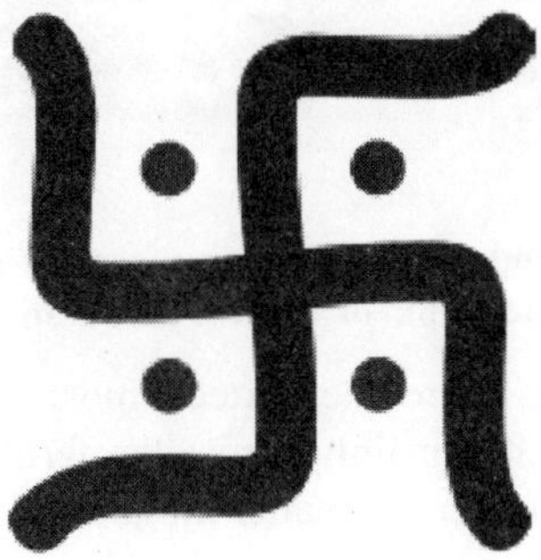

The swastika is a major element of Hindu iconography.

Early Vedic society consisted of largely pastoral groups, with late Harappan urbanisation having been abandoned. After the time of the Rigveda, Aryan society became increasingly agricultural and was socially organised around the four *varnas*, or social classes. In addition to the Vedas, the principal texts of Hinduism, the core themes of the Sanskrit epics *Ramayana* and *Mahabharata* are said to have their ultimate origins during this period. The Mahabharata remains, today, the longest single poem in the world. The events described in the *Ramayana* are from a later period of history than the events of the *Mahabharata.*

The early Indo-Aryan presence probably corresponds, in part, to the Ochre Coloured Pottery culture in archaeological contexts. The Kuru kingdom corresponds to the Black and Red Ware and Painted Grey Ware cultures and to the beginning of the Iron Age in northwestern India, around 1000 BCE, as well as with the composition of the Atharvaveda, the first Indian text to mention iron, as úyāma ayas, literally "black metal." The Painted Grey Ware culture spanned much of northern India from about 1100 to 600 BCE.

The Vedic Period also established republics such as Vaishali, which existed as early as the 6th century BCE and persisted in some areas until the 4th century CE. The later part of this period corresponds with an increasing movement away from the previous tribal system towards the establishment of kingdoms, called *mahajanapadas*.

Gautama Buddha undertaking extreme ascetic practices before his enlightenment on the bank of river Phalgu in Bodh Gaya, Bihar.

The Mahajanapadas were the sixteen most powerful kingdoms and republics of the era, located mainly across the fertile Indo-Gangetic plains, however there were a number of smaller kingdoms stretching the length and breadth of Ancient India.

Nalanda Universty-India's Ancient Pride

Nālandā was an ancient center of higher learning in Bihar, India. The site is located about 88 kilometres south east of Patna, and was a religious center of learning from the fifth century CE to 1197 CE. Nalanda flourished between the reign of the Úakrāditya (whose identity is uncertain and who might have been either Kumara Gupta I or Kumara Gupta II) and 1197 CE, supported by patronage from the Hindu Gupta rulers as well as Buddhist emperors like Harsha and later emperors from the Pala Empire. The complex was built with red bricks and its ruins occupy an area of 14 hectares. At its peak, the university attracted scholars and students from as far away as Tibet, China, Greece, and Persia. Nalanda was ransacked and destroyed by an army under Bakhtiyar Khilji in 1193. The great library of Nalanda University was so vast that it is reported to have burned for three months after the invaders set fire to it, ransacked and destroyed the monasteries, and drove the monks from the site. In 2006, Singapore, China, India, Japan, and other nations, announced a proposed plan to restore and revive the ancient site as Nalanda International University.

Nalanda is considered one of the first great universities in recorded history. It was the center of Buddhist learning and research in the world from 450 to 1193 CE.

The Chinese pilgrim-monk Xuanzang gives several explanations of the name Nālandā. One is that it was named after the Nāga who lived in a tank in the middle of the mango grove. Another, the one he accepted, is that Shakyamuni Buddha once had his capital here and gave "alms without intermission", hence the name.

History of Jainism

In the later Vedic Age, a number of small kingdoms or city states had covered the subcontinent, many mentioned in Vedic, early Buddhist and Jaina literature as far back as 1000 BCE. By 500 BCE, sixteen monarchies and "republics" known as the Mahajanapadas—Kasi, Kosala, Anga, Magadha, Vajji (or Vriji), Malla, Chedi, Vatsa (or Vamsa), Kuru, Panchala, Matsya (or Machcha), Surasena, Assaka, Avanti, Gandhara, and Kamboja—stretched across the Indo-Gangetic Plain from modern-day Afghanistan to Bengal and Maharastra. This period saw the second major rise of urbanism in India after the Indus Valley Civilisation. Many smaller clans mentioned within early literature seem to have been present across the rest of the subcontinent. Some of these kings were hereditary; other states elected their rulers. The educated speech at that time was Sanskrit, while the languages of the general population of northern India are referred to as Prakrits. Many of the sixteen kingdoms had coalesced to four major ones by 500/400 BCE, by the time of Gautama Buddha. These four were Vatsa, Avanti, Kosala, and Magadha. The 9th and 8th centuries BCE witnessed the composition of the earliest Upanishads. Upanishads form the theoretical basis of classical Hinduism and are known as Vedanta (conclusion of the Vedas).

The older Upanishads launched attacks of increasing intensity on the ritual. Anyone who worships a divinity other than the self is called a domestic animal of the gods in the Brihadaranyaka Upanishad. The Mundaka launches the most scathing attack on the ritual by comparing those who value sacrifice with an unsafe boat that is endlessly overtaken by old age and death. Increasing urbanisation of India in 7th and 6th centuries BCE led to the rise of new ascetic or shramana movements which challenged the orthodoxy of rituals.

Mahavira (c. 549–477 BCE), proponent of Jainism, and Buddha (c. 563-483), founder of Buddhism were the most prominent icons of this movement. Shramana gave rise to the concept of the cycle of birth and death, the concept of samsara, and the concept of liberation.

Buddha found a Middle Way that ameliorated the extreme asceticism found in the Sramana religions. Around the same time, Mahavira (the 24th Tirthankara in Jainism) propagated a theology that was to later become Jainism. However, Jain orthodoxy believes the teachings of the Tirthankaras predates all known time and scholars believe Parshva, accorded status as the 23rd Tirthankara, was a historical figure. The Vedas are believed to have documented a few Tirthankaras and an ascetic order similar to the shramana movement. Persian and Greek conquests.

In 530 BCE Cyrus, King of the Persian Achaemenid Empire crossed the Hindu-Kush mountains to seek tribute from the tribes of Kamboja, Gandhara and the trans-India region. By 520 BCE, during the reign of Darius I of Persia, much of the northwestern subcontinent (present day eastern Afghanistan and Pakistan) came under the rule of the Persian Achaemenid Empire. The area remained under Persian control for two centuries. During this time India supplied mercenaries to the Persian army then fighting in Greece. Under Persian rule the famous city of Takshashila became a center where both Vedic and Iranian learning were mingled.

The impact of Persian ideas was felt in many areas of Indian life. Persian coinage and rock inscriptions were copied by India. However, Persian ascendency in northern India ended with Alexander the Great's conquest of Persia in 327 BCE. By 326 BCE, Alexander the Great had conquered Asia Minor and the Achaemenid Empire and had reached the northwest frontiers of the Indian subcontinent. There he defeated King Porus in the Battle of the Hydaspes (near modern day Jhelum, Pakistan) and conquered much of the Punjab. Alexander's march east put him in confrontation with the Nanda Empire of Magadha and the Gangaridai Empire of Bengal. His army, exhausted and frightened by the prospect of facing larger Indian armies at the Ganges River, mutinied at the Hyphasis (modern Beas River) and refused to march further East. Alexander, after the meeting with his officer, Coenus, and learning about the might of Nanda Empire, was convinced that it was better to return.

The Persian and Greek invasions had important repercussions on Indian civilisation. The political systems of the Persians were to influence future forms of governance on the subcontinent, including the administration of the Mauryan dynasty. In addition, the region of Gandhara, or presentday eastern Afghanistan and northwest Pakistan, became a melting pot of Indian, Persian, Central Asian, and Greek cultures and gave rise to a hybrid culture, Greco-Buddhism, which lasted until the 5th century CE and influenced the artistic development of Mahayana Buddhism.

Maurya Empire

Maurya Empire under Ashoka the Great Ashokan Pillar at Vaishali, 3rd Century BCE.

The Maurya Empire (322–185 BCE), ruled by the Mauryan dynasty, was a geographically extensive and powerful political and military empire in ancient India. The empire was established by Chandragupta Maurya in Magadha.

The empire flourished under the reign of Ashoka the Great. At its greatest extent, it stretched to the north to the natural boundaries of the Himalayas and to the east into what is now Assam. To the west, it reached beyond modern Pakistan, annexing Balochistan and much of what is now Afghanistan, including the modern Herat and Kandahar provinces. The empire was expanded into India's central and southern regions by the emperors Chandragupta and Bindusara, but it excluded extensive unexplored tribal and forested regions near Kalinga which were subsequently taken by Ashoka. Like every state, the Maurya Empire needed to have a unified administrative apparatus. Ashoka ruled the Maurya Empire for 37 years from 268 BCE until he died in 232 BCE.

During that time, Ashoka pursued an active foreign policy aimed at setting up a unified state. However, Ashoka became involved in a war with the state of Kalinga which is located on the western shore of the Bay of Bengal. This war forced Ashoka to abandon his attempt at a foreign policy which would unify the Maurya Empire. During the Mauryan Empire slavery developed rapidly and significant amount of written records on slavery are found.

The Mauryan Empire was based on a modern and efficient economy and society. However, the sale of merchandise was closely regulated by the government. Although there was no banking in the Mauryan society, usury was customary with loans made at the recognised interest rate of 15 per cent per annum.

Ashoka's reign propagated Buddhism. In this regard Ashoka established many Buddhist monuments. Indeed, Ashoka put a strain on the economy and the government by his strong support of Buddhism. towards the end of his reign he "bled the state coffers white with his generous gifts to promote the promulation of Buddha's teaching. As might be expected, this policy caused considerable opposition within the government. This opposition rallied around Sampadi, Ashoka's grandson and heir to the throne. Religious opposition to Ashoka also arose among the orthodox Brahmanists and the adherents of Jainism. Chandragupta's minister Chanakya wrote the *Arthashastra*, one of the greatest treatises on economics, politics, foreign affairs, administration, military arts, war, and religion produced in Asia. Archaeologically, the period of Mauryan rule in South Asia falls into the era of Northern Black Polished Ware (NBPW). The *Arthashastra* and the Edicts of Ashoka are primary written records of the Mauryan times. The *Lion Capital of Asoka* at Sarnath, is the national emblem of India.

Early Middle Kingdoms—The Golden Age

Gupta Empire

The middle period was a time of cultural development. The Satavahana dynasty, also known as the Andhras, ruled in southern and central India after around 230 BCE. Satakarni, the sixth ruler of the Satvahana dynasty, defeated the Sunga Empire of north India. Afterwards, Kharavela, the warrior king of Kalinga, ruled a vast empire and was responsible for the propagation of Jainism in the Indian subcontinent. The Kharavelan Jain empire included a maritime empire with trading routes linking it to Sri Lanka, Burma, Thailand, Vietnam, Cambodia, Borneo, Bali, Sumatra, and Java. Colonists from Kalinga settled in Sri Lanka, Burma, as well as the Maldives and Maritime Southeast Asia. The Kuninda Kingdom was a small Himalayan state that survived from around the 2nd century BCE to the 3rd century CE. The Kushanas migrated from Central Asia into northwestern India in the middle of the 1st century

CE and founded an empire that stretched from Tajikistan to the middle Ganges. The Western Satraps (35–405 CE) were Saka rulers of the western and central part of India. They were the successors of the Indo-Scythians and contemporaries of the Kushans who ruled the northern part of the Indian subcontinent and the Satavahana (Andhra) who ruled in central and southern India. Different dynasties such as the Pandyans, Cholas, Cheras, Kadambas, Western Gangas, Pallavas, and Chalukyas, dominated the southern part of the Indian peninsula at different periods of time. Several southern kingdoms formed overseas empires that stretched into Southeast Asia. The kingdoms warred with each other and the Deccan states for domination of the south. The Kalabras, a Buddhist dynasty, briefly interrupted the usual domination of the Cholas, Cheras, and Pandyas in the South.

Northwestern Hybrid Cultures

The northwestern hybrid cultures of the subcontinent included the *Indo-Greeks*, the *Indo-Scythians*, the *Indo-Parthians*, and the *Indo-Sassinids*.

The founder of the Indo-Greek Kingdom, Demetrius I "the Invincible" (205–171 BCE).

The first of these, the Indo-Greek Kingdom, was founded when the Greco-Bactrian king Demetrius invaded the region in 180 BCE, extending his rule over various parts of present-day Afghanistan and Pakistan. Lasting for almost two centuries, the kingdom was ruled by a succession of more than 30 Greek kings, who were often in conflict with each other. The Indo-Scythians were a branch of the Indo-European Sakas (Scythians) who migrated from southern Siberia, first into Bactria, subsequently into Sogdiana, Kashmir, Arachosia, and Gandhara, and finally into India. Their kingdom lasted from the middle of the 2nd century BCE to the 1st century BCE. Yet another kingdom, the Indo-Parthians (also known as the Pahlavas), came to control most of present day Afghanistan and northern Pakistan, after fighting many local rulers such as the Kushan ruler Kujula Kadphises, in the Gandhara region. The Sassanid empire of Persia, who was contemporaneous with the Gupta Empire, expanded into the region of present day Balochistan in Pakistan, where the mingling of Indian culture and the culture of Iran gave birth to a hybrid culture under the Indo-Sassanids.

Kushan Empire

The Kushan Empire expanded out of what is now Afghanistan into the northwest of the subcontinent under the leadership of their first emperor, Kujula Kadphises, about the middle of the 1st century CE. By the time of his grandson, Kanishka, (whose era is thought to have begun c. 127 CE), they had conquered most of northern India, at least as far as Saketa and Pataliputra, in the middle Ganges Valley, and probably as far as the Bay of Bengal. They played an important role in the establishment of Buddhism in India and its spread to Central Asia and China. By the 3rd century, their empire in India was disintegrating; their last known great emperor being Vasudeva I (c. 190-225 CE).

Roman Trade with India

Roman trade with India started around 1 CE, during the reign of Augustus and following his conquest of Egypt, which had been India's biggest trade partner in the West.

Coin of the Roman Emperor Augustus found at the Pudukottai, South India.

The trade started by Eudoxus of Cyzicus in 130 BCE kept increasing, and according to Strabo (II.5.12.), by the time of Augustus, up to 120 ships set sail every year from Myos Hormos on the Red Sea to India. So much gold was used for this trade, and apparently recycled by the Kushans for their own coinage, that Pliny the Elder (NH VI.101) complained about the drain of specie to India:

"India, China and the Arabian peninsula take one hundred million sesterces from our empire per annum at a conservative estimate: that is what our luxuries and women cost us. For what percentage of these imports is intended for sacrifices to the gods or the spirits of the dead?"

The maritime (but not the overland) trade routes, harbours, and trade items are described in detail in the 1st century CE Periplus of the Erythraean Sea.

Gupta Rule

The Classical Age refers to the period when much of the Indian subcontinent was reunited under the Gupta Empire (c. 320–550 CE). This period has been called the Golden Age of India and was marked by extensive

Queen Kumaradevi and King Chandragupta I, depicted on a coin of their son Samudragupta, 335–380 CE.

achievements in science, technology, engineering, art, dialectic, literature, logic, mathematics, astronomy, religion, and philosophy that crystallised the elements of what is generally known as Hindu culture. The decimal numeral system, including the concept of zero, was invented in India during this period. The peace and prosperity created under leadership of Guptas enabled the pursuit of scientific and artistic endeavors in India. The high points of this cultural creativity are magnificent architecture, sculpture, and painting. The Gupta period produced scholars such as Kalidasa, Aryabhata, Varahamihira, Vishnu Sharma, and Vatsyayana who made great advancements in many academic fields. Science and political administration reached new heights during the Gupta era. Strong trade ties also made the region an important cultural center and established it as a base that would influence nearby kingdoms and regions in Burma, Sri Lanka, Maritime Southeast Asia, and Indochina.

The Gupta period marked a watershed of Indian culture: the Guptas performed Vedic sacrifices to legitimise their rule, but they also patronised Buddhism, which continued to provide an alternative to Brahmanical orthodoxy. The military exploits of the first three rulers—Chandragupta I (c. 319–335), Samudragupta (c. 335–376), and Chandragupta II (c. 376–415) — brought much of India under their leadership. They successfully resisted the northwestern kingdoms until the arrival of the Hunas, who established themselves in Afghanistan by the first half of the 5th century, with their capital at Bamiyan. However, much of the Deccan and southern India were largely unaffected by these events in the north.

(b) India Our Homeland—Modern India

India, officially the Republic of India (Hindi: भारत गणराज्य, *Bhārat Ganrarājya*), is the seventh largest country in the world by geographical area. It is the second-most populous country having over 1.28 billion people according to 2012 Census. It is also the most populous Democracy in the world. India is a country in South Asia. As has been said earlier that India is bounded by the Indian Ocean on the south, the Arabian Sea on the South-west, and on the South West is the Bay of Bengal. India shares land borders with Pakistan to the west; China, Nepal, and Bhutan to the north-east; and Burma and Bangladesh to the east. In the Indian Ocean, India is in the vicinity of Sri Lanka and the Maldives; in addition, India's Andaman and Nicobar Islands share a maritime border with Thailand and Indonesia.

Home to the ancient Indus Valley Civilisation and a region of historic trade routes and vast empires, the Indian subcontinent was identified with its commercial and cultural wealth for much of its long history. Four of the world's major religions—Hinduism, Buddhism, Jainism, and Sikhism—originated here in India, whereas Christianity, and Islam arrived in the 1st millennium CE and also helped shape the region's diverse culture. Gradually annexed by and brought under the administration of the British East India Company from the early 18th century and administered directly by the United Kingdom from the mid-19th century, India became an independent nation in 1947 after a struggle for independence that was marked principally by non-violent resistance and led by Mahatma Gandhi, the Father of the Nation.

The Indian economy is the world's tenth-largest economy by nominal GDP and third-largest economy by purchasing power parity (PPP). Following market-based economic reforms in 1991, India became one of the fastest-growing major economies; it is considered a newly industrialised country. Its GDP has been growing at a rate of 7.0 to about 8.5. However, it continues to face the challenges of poverty, illiteracy, corruption, and inadequate public healthcare. A nuclear weapons state and a regional power, it has the third-largest standing army in the world and ranks tenth in military expenditure among nations.

India is a federal constitutional republic governed under a parliamentary system consisting of 28 states and 7 union territories. India is a pluralistic, multilingual, and multiethnic society. It is also home to a diversity of wildlife in a variety of protected habitats.

The name *India* is derived from *Indus*, which is derived from the Old Persian word *Hindu*, from Sanskrit *Sindhu* the historic local appellation for the Indus River. The ancient Greeks referred to the Indians as *Indoi*, the people of the Indus. The Constitution of India and usage in many Indian languages also recognises *Bharat* as an official name of equal status. The name Bharat is derived from the name of the legendary king Bharata in Hindu scriptures. *Hindustan*, originally a Persian word for "Land of the Hindus" and referring to North India and Pakistan before 1947, is also occasionally used as a synonym for all of India.

1. Ancient India

Around 7000 BCE, the first known neolithic settlements appeared on the subcontinent in Mehrgarh and other sites in western Pakistan. These gradually developed into the Indus Valley Civilisation, the first urban culture in South Asia, which flourished during 2500–1900 BCE in Pakistan and western India. Centered around cities such as Mohenjo-daro, Harappa, Dholavira, and Kalibangan, and relying on varied forms of subsistence, the civilisation engaged robustly in crafts production and wide-ranging trade. During the period 2000–500 BCE, many regions of the subcontinent evolved from copper age to Iron Age cultures. The Vedas, the oldest scriptures of Hinduism, were composed during this period. The historians have analysed and described the presence of a Vedic culture in the Punjab region and the upper Ganges Plain. Most historians also consider this period to have encompassed several waves of Indo-Aryan migration into the subcontinent from the north-west.

The caste system, which created a hierarchy of priests, warriors, and free peasants, but which excluded indigenous peoples by labeling their occupations impure, arose during this period. The emerging urbanisation as well as the orthodoxies of the late Vedic age created the religious reform movements of Buddhism and Jainism. Buddhism, based on the teachings of India's first historical figure, Gautam Buddha, attracted followers from all social classes excepting the middle; Jainism came into prominence around the same time during the life of its exemplar, Mahavira. In an age of increasing urban wealth, both religions held up renunciation as an ideal, and both established long-lasting monasteries.

Politically, by the 3rd century BCE, the kingdom of Magadha had annexed or reduced other states to emerge as the Mauryan Empire. The empire was once thought to have controlled most of the subcontinent excepting the far south, but its core regions are now thought to have been separated by large autonomous areas. The Maurya kings are known as much for their empire building and determined management of public life as for Ashoka the Great's renunciation of militarism and far-flung advocacy of the Buddhist *dhamma*. Hinduism asserted patriarchal control within the family leading to increased subordination of women. By the 4th and 5th centuries, the Gupta Empire had created a complex administrative and taxation system in the greater Ganges Plain that became a model for later Indian kingdoms. Under the Guptas, a renewed Hinduism based on devotion rather than the management of ritual began to assert itself. The renewal was reflected in a flowering of sculpture and architecture, which found patrons among the urban elite. Classical Sanskrit literature flowered as well, and Indian science, astronomy, medicine, and mathematics made significant advances.

2. Medieval India

The Indian early medieval age, 600 CE to 1200 CE, is defined by regional kingdoms and cultural diversity. When Harsha of Kannauj, who ruled much of the Ganges plain from 606 to 647 CE, attempted to expand southwards,

The Granite Tower of Brihadeeswarara Temple in Thanjavur was completed in 1010 CE by Raja Chola I.

he was defeated by the Chalukya ruler of the Deccan. When his successor attempted to expand eastwards, he was defeated by the Pala king of Bengal. When the Chalukyas attempted to expand southwards, they were defeated by the Pallavas from farther south, who in turn were opposed by the Pandyas and the Cholas from still farther south. No ruler of this period was able to create an empire and consistently control lands much beyond his core region. In the 6th and 7th centuries, the first devotional hymns were created in the Tamil language. They were imitated all over India and led to both the resurgence of Hinduism and the development of all modern languages of the subcontinent. Indian royalty, big and small, and the temples they patronised, drew citizens in great numbers to the capital cities, which became economic hubs as well. Indian culture and political systems were exported to what today are Thailand, Laos, Cambodia, Vietnam, Malaysia, and Java. Indian merchants, scholars, and sometimes armies were involved in this transmission; South-East Asians took the initiative as well with many sojourning in Indian seminaries and translating Buddhist and Hindu texts into their languages. After the 10th century, Muslim Central Asian nomadic clans, using swift-horse cavalry and raising vast armies united by ethnicity and religion, repeatedly overran South Asia's north-western plains, leading eventually to the establishment of the Islamic Delhi Sultanate in 1206. The Sultanate was to control much of North India, and to make many forays into South India. The Sultanate's raiding and weakening of the regional kingdoms of South India paved the way for the indigenous Vijayanagara Empire. Embracing a strong Shaivite tradition and building upon the military technology of the Sultanate, the empire came to control much of peninsular India, and was to influence South Indian society for long afterwards.

3. Early Modern India

In the early 16th century, northern India, being then under mainly Muslim rulers, fell again to the superior mobility and firepower of a new generation of Central Asian warriors. The resulting Mughal Empire did not stamp out the local societies it came to rule, but rather balanced and pacified them through new administrative practices and diverse and inclusive ruling elites. Especially under Akbar, the Mughals united their far-flung realms through loyalty, expressed through a personalised culture, to an emperor who had near divine status. Newly coherent social groups in northern and western India, such as the Marathas, the Rajputs, and the Sikhs, gained military and governing ambitions during Mughal rule, which, through collaboration or adversity, gave them both recognition and military experience. Expanding commerce during Mughal rule gave rise to new Indian commercial and political elites along the coasts of southern and eastern India. As the empire disintegrated, many among these elites were able to seek and control their own affairs. By the early 18th century, with the lines between commercial and political dominance being increasingly blurred, a number of European trading companies, including the English East India Company, had established outposts on the coast of India. The East India Company's control of the seas, greater resources, and more advanced military training and technology led it to increasingly flex its military muscle and caused it to become attractive to a portion of the Indian elite; both these factors were crucial in allowing the Company to gain control over the Bengal region by 1765 and sideline the other European companies. By the 1820s. India was now no longer exporting manufactured goods as it long had, but was instead supplying the British Empire with raw materials, and many historians consider this to be the onset of India's colonial period. By this time, with its economic power severely curtailed by the British parliament and itself effectively made an arm of British administration, the Company began to more consciously enter non-economic arenas such as education, social reform, and culture.

4. Modern India and British East India Company

According to the Historians, India's modern age have begun sometime between 1848 and 1885. The appointment in 1848 of Lord Dalhousie as Governor General of the East India Company rule in India set the stage for changes essential to a modern state. These included the consolidation and demarcation of sovereignty, the surveillance of the population, and the education of citizens. Technological changes—among them, railways, canals, and the telegraph—were introduced not long after their introduction in Europe. However, disaffection with the Company also grew during this time, and set off the Indian Rebellion of 1857. Fed by diverse resentments and perceptions, including invasive British-style social reforms, harsh land taxes, and summary treatment of some rich landowners and princes, the rebellion rocked many regions of northern and central India and shook the foundations of Company rule. Although the rebellion was suppressed by 1858, it led to the dissolution of the East India Company and to the direct administration of India by the British government. Proclaiming a unitary state and a gradual but limited British-style parliamentary system, the new rulers also protected princes and landed gentry as a feudal safeguard against future unrest. In the decades following, public life gradually emerged all over India, leading eventually to the founding of the Indian National Congress in 1885.

The 19th century was marked by economic setbacks in India because of wrong agricultural policy. There were an increased number of large-scale famines, and little industrial employment was generated for Indians. After World War I, the period was marked by British reforms but also repressive legislation. That was the beginnings of a non-violent movement of non-cooperation, of which Mohandas Karamchand Gandhi would become the leader. During the 1930s, slow legislative reform was enacted by the British; the Indian National Congress won victories in the resulting elections. The next decade was beset with crises: Indian participation in World War II, the Congress's final push for non-cooperation, and an upsurge of Muslim nationalism. All were capped by the independence of India in 1947.

(A) The Republic of India

Jawaharlal Nehru (left) became India's first Prime Minister in 1947. Mahatma Gandhi (right) led the independence movement and attracted the attention of the World. His non-violence movement was the inspiration of

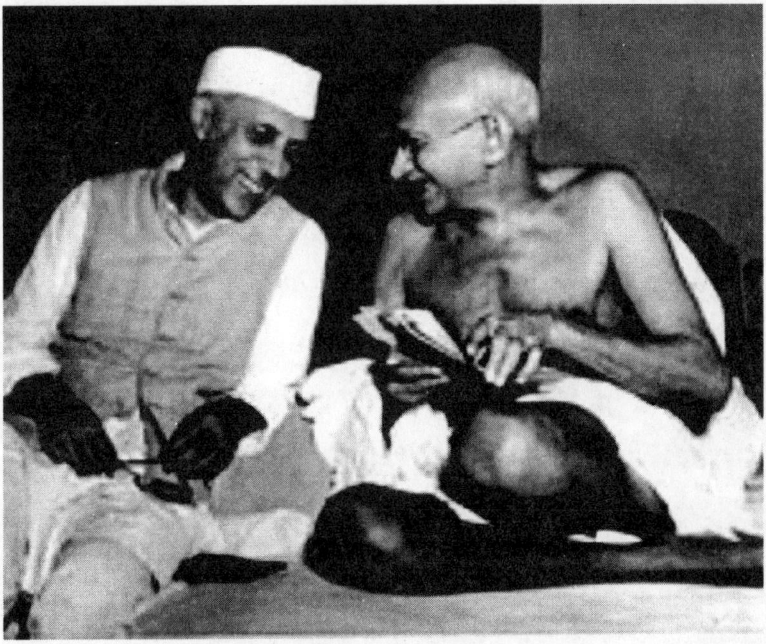

many all over the World, Noted among them are–Martin Luther King of USA and Michael Mandela of South Africa.

India got its independence in 1947. India's constitution was made in 1950, which put in place a sovereign, secular, and democratic republic. In the next 60 years, India had gone through both successes and failures. It has remained a democracy, an activist supreme court, and an independent press. Economic liberalisation, which started in the 1990s, has created a large urban middle class, and transformed India into one of the world's fastest-growing economies. Indian movies, music, and spiritual teachings played an increasing role in creating the republic of India global culture. Yet, India has suffered a great deal due to religious and caste-related violence; by Maoist-inspired Naxalite insurgencies and by separatist agitation in Jammu and Kashmir, and several other places. Territorial disputes with China continued, which escalated into the Sino-Indian War of 1962. India fought several wars with Pakistan in 1947, 1965, 1971, and 1999. The India–Pakistan nuclear rivalry started in 1998. India's sustained democratic freedoms were very unique among the world's new nations; however, in spite of its recent economic successes, various goals remain to be achieved.

India comprises the bulk of the Indian subcontinent. India's geological processes commenced 75 million years ago. As a result of the subcontinent's

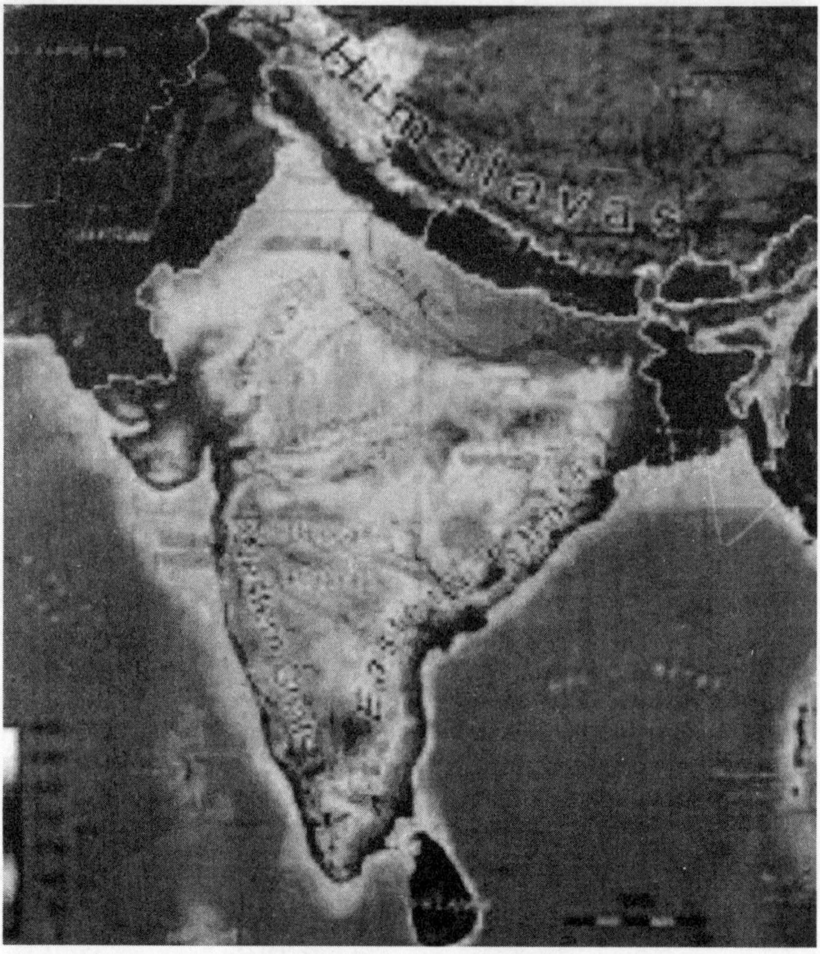

Geographical Map of India.

subsequent collision with the Eurasian Plate bore aloft the planet's highest mountains, the Himalayas. Later plate movement created a vast trough gradually filled with river-borne sediment. It now forms the Indo-Gangetic Plain. To the west lies the Thar Desert, which is cut off by the Aravalli Range. The Deccan Plateau is flanked on the west and east by the coastal ranges, the Western and Eastern Ghats respectively. The plateau contains the nation's oldest rock formations, some over one billion years old. Constituted in such fashion, India lies to the north of the equator between 6°44' and 35°30' north latitude and 68°7' and 97°25' east longitude.

India's coast is 7,517 kilometers (4,700 mi) long; of this distance, 5,423 kilometers (3,400 mi) belong to peninsular India and 2,094 kilometers (1,300 mi) to the Andaman, Nicobar, and Lakshadweep Islands. Major Himalayan-

The Kedar Range of the Greater Himalayas rises behind Kedarnath Temple, one of the twelve *jyotirlinga* shrines.

origin rivers include the Ganges (Ganga) and the Brahmaputra, both of which drain into the Bay of Bengal. Important tributaries of the Ganges include the Yamuna and the Kosi. Major peninsular rivers include the Godavari, the Mahanadi, the Kaveri, and the Krishna, which also drain into the Bay of Bengal; and the Narmada and the Tapti, which drain into the Arabian Sea. Among notable coastal features of India are the marshy Rann of Kutch in western India, and the alluvial Sundarbans delta, which India shares with Bangladesh.

India's Climate

The Indian climate is strongly influenced by the Himalayas and the Thar Desert. The Himalayas prevent cold Central Asian winds from blowing in, keeping the bulk of the Indian subcontinent warmer than most locations at similar latitudes. The Thar Desert plays a crucial role in attracting the moisture-laden south-west summer monsoon winds that, between June and October, provide the majority of India's rainfall. Four major climatic groupings predominate in India: More will be discussed later.

Politics in India

With a multi-party system, India has six recognised national parties, including the Indian National Congress and the Bharatiya Janata Party (BJP), and more than 40 regional parties. For most of the period between 1950—when India first became a republic—and the late 1980s, the Congress held a majority in the parliament. Since then, however, it has increasingly shared the political stage with the BJP, as well as with powerful regional parties which have often forced the creation of multi-party coalitions at the centre. In the Republic of India's first three general elections, in 1951, 1957, and 1962, the Jawaharlal Nehru led Congress won easy victories. On Nehru's death in 1964, Lal Bahadur Shastri briefly became Prime Minister; he was succeeded, after his own unexpected death in 1966, by Indira Gandhi, who went on to lead the Congress to election victories in 1967 and 1971. Following public discontent with the state of emergency she declared in 1975, the Congress was voted out of power in 1977; the just created Janata Party, which had opposed the emergency, was voted in. Its government lasted just over three years. Voted back into power in 1980, the Congress saw a change in leadership in 1984, when Indira Gandhi was assassinated; she was succeeded by her son Rajiv Gandhi, who won an easy victory in the general elections later that year. The Congress was voted out again in 1989 when a National Front coalition, led by the newly formed Janata Dal in alliance with the Left Front, won the elections; that government too proved relatively short-lived: it lasted just under two years. Elections were held again in 1991; no party won an absolute majority. But the Congress, as the largest single party, was able to form a minority government led by P.V. Narasimha Rao.

The two years after the general election of 1996 were marked by political turmoil. Several short-lived alliances shared power at the Centre. The BJP formed a government briefly in 1996; it was followed by two comparatively long-lasting United Front coalitions, which depended on external support. In 1998, the BJP was able to form a successful coalition, the National Democratic Alliance (NDA), which under the leadership of Atal Bihari Vajpayee, became the first non-Congress government to complete a full five-year term. In the 2004 Indian general elections, again no party won an absolute majority, but the Congress emerged as the largest single party, forming a successful coalition: the United Progressive Alliance (UPA). It had the support of left-leaning parties and MPs opposed to the BJP. The UPA coalition was returned to power in the 2009 general election with increased numbers, and it no longer required external support from India's Communist parties. That year, Manmohan Singh became the first prime minister since Jawaharlal Nehru in 1957 and 1962 to be re-elected to a second consecutive five-year term.

Government

India is a federation with a parliamentary system governed under the Constitution of India, which serves as the country's supreme legal document. It is a constitutional republic and representative democracy, in which "majority rule is tempered by minority rights protected by law". Federalism in India defines the power distribution between the federal government and the states. The government abides by constitutional checks and balances. The Constitution of India, which came into effect on 26 January, 1950, states in its preamble that India is a sovereign, socialist, secular, democratic republic. India's form of government, traditionally described as "quasi-federal" with a strong centre and weak states, has grown increasingly federal since the late 1990s as a result of political, economic, and social changes.

The federal government of India comprises three branches:

- **Executive Branch:** The President of India is the head of state who is elected indirectly by a national electoral college for a five-year term. The Prime Minister of India is the head of government and exercises most executive power. Appointed by the President, the Prime Minister is by convention supported by the party or political alliance holding the majority of seats in the lower house of parliament.

The executive branch of the Indian government consists of the President, the Vice-President, and the Council of Ministers—the Cabinet being its executive committee—headed by the Prime Minister. Any minister holding a portfolio must be a member of one of the houses of the parliament...

- **Legislative Branch:** It comprises the upper house called the Rajya Sabha ("Council of States") and the lower called the Lok Sabha ("House of the People"). The Rajya Sabha is a permanent body that has 245 members. Most are elected indirectly by the state and territorial legislatures in numbers proportional to their state's share of the national population. All but two of the Lok Sabha's 545 members are directly elected by popular vote; they represent individual constituencies via five-year terms. The remaining two members are nominated by the president from among the Anglo-Indian community, in case the president decides that they are not adequately represented.
- **India's Judiciary:** India has a unitary three-tier judiciary, consisting of the Supreme Court, headed by the Chief Justice of India, 21 High Courts, and a large number of trial courts. The Supreme Court has original jurisdiction over cases involving fundamental rights and over disputes between states and the Centre; it has appellate jurisdiction over the High Courts. It is judicially independent and has the power both to declare the law and to strike down union or state laws which contravene the constitution of India. The Supreme Court is also the ultimate interpreter of the constitution. Sub divisions three. Indian States: India is a federation composed of 28 states and seven union territories. All states, as well as the union territories of Pondicherry and the National Capital Territory of Delhi, have elected legislatures and governments, the remaining five union territories are directly ruled by the Centre through appointed administrators. In 1956, under the States Reorganisation Act, states were reorganised on a linguistic basis. Since

then, their structure has remained largely unchanged. Each state or union territory is further divided into administrative districts. The districts in turn are further divided into tehsils and ultimately into villages.

Union territories are–Andaman and Nicobar Islands, Dadra and Nagar Haveli, Daman and Diu, Lakshadweep, National Capital Territory of Delhi. Pondicherry.

Science and Technology in India

Since Independence in 1947, India had developed a large infrastructure of Scientific and Technological Institutions around the country for Higher Education and Research. Some of the prominent ones are—IITs (Indian Institute of Technology), CSIR (Council of Science and Technology) laboratories, ICMR (Indian Council of Medical Research) laboratories, DST (Department of Science and Technology) Laboratories, DBT (Department of Biotechnology) laboratories, ICAR (Indian Council of Agricultural Research) laboratories etc. Besides these laboratories, a large number of Universities and other Indian Institutes are there where Science education and researches are conducted.

The HAL (Hindustan Aeronautics Limited) TEJAS is a light supersonic fighter developed by the Aeronautical Development Agency and manufactured by Hindustan Aeronautics in Bangalore.

India produces one of the largest numbers of PhD's in different subjects every year. Indian Institute of Science (IISC), Bhabha Atomic Research Centre (BARC), Defense Research and Development Organisation ((DRDO), Indian Satellite Research Organisation (ISRO) are some of the prominent organisations serving the Nation very satisfactorily.

China's nuclear capability, as well as its repeated threats to intervene in support of Pakistan in the 1965 war, convinced India to develop nuclear weapons of its own. India conducted its first nuclear weapons test in 1974 and carried out further underground testing in 1998. India maintains a "no first use" nuclear policy and is developing a nuclear triad capability as a part of its "minimum credible deterrence" doctrine. It is also developing a ballistic missile defense shield and, in collaboration with Russia, a fifth-generation fighter jet. Other major indigenous military development projects include *Vikrant*-class aircraft carriers and *Arihant*-class nuclear submarines.

India's Military

The President of India is the supreme commander of the nation's armed forces. With 1.6 million active troops, the Indian military is the world's third-largest. It comprises the Army, the Navy, the Air Force, and auxiliary forces such as the Paramilitary Forces, the Coast Guard, and the Strategic Forces Command. The official Indian defense budget for 2011 was US$ 36.03 billion, or 1.83 per cent of its GDP. As of 2012, India is the world's largest arms importer; in the period from 2006 to 2010, it accounted for 9 per cent of money spent on international arms purchases. Much of the military expenditure was focused on defense against Pakistan and countering growing Chinese influence in the Indian Ocean.

India's Economy

Indian agriculture dates from the period 7,000–6,000 BCE, employs most of the national workforce, and is the second in farm output worldwide. According to the International Monetary Fund (IMF), as of 2011, the Indian economy was worth US$1.843 trillion; it is the tenth largest economy by market exchange rates, and is, at US$ 4.469 trillion, the thirdlargest by purchasing power parity, or PPP. With its average annual GDP growth rate of 5.8 per cent over the past two decades, and reaching 10.4 per cent during 2010, India is one of the world's fastest-growing economies.

Now there are 467-million workers in Indian labor force. With this it has become the world's second-largest. The Indian service sector makes up 54 per cent of GDP; the agricultural sector contributes 28 per cent and the industrial sector 18 per cent. Major agricultural products include rice, wheat, oilseed, cotton, jute, tea, sugarcane, and potatoes. Major industries include textiles, telecommunications, chemicals, food processing, steel, transport equipment, cement, mining, petroleum, machinery, and software.

In 2006, the share of external trade in India's GDP stood at 24 per cent, a four times increase up from 6 per cent in 1985. In 2008, India's share of world trade was 1.68 per cent; India was the world's fifteenth-largest importer in 2009 and the eighteenth largest exporter. Major exports include petroleum products, textile goods, jewelry, software, engineering goods, chemicals, and leather goods. Major imports include crude oil, machinery, gems, fertiliser, and chemicals. Between 2001 and 2011, the contribution of petrochemical and engineering goods to total exports grew from 14 per cent to 42 per cent.

The economic growth rate of 7.5 per cent during the last few years attracted the attention of the World toward India. It has taken everybody to a surprise, especially the most advanced countries of the World. As a result, India has more than doubled its hourly wage rates during the last decade. Some 431 million Indians have left poverty line since 1985; India's middle classes are projected to a number around 580 million by 2030. The country is viewed as the second-most favorable outsourcing destination after the United States. India's consumer market, currently the worlds thirteenth-largest, is expected to become fifth-largest by 2030.

India's Telecommunication Industry is the world's fastest-growing industry now in 2012. It added 227 million subscribers during the period 2010–11. India's automotive industry, the world's second fastest growing, increased domestic sales by 26 per cent during 2009–10, and exports by 36 per cent during 2008–09. India's Power capacity is now 250 gigawatts, of which 8 per cent is of renewable type.

Despite impressive economic growth during the recent decades, India continues to face socio-economic challenges because of its vast populations. Driven by growth, India's nominal GDP per capita has steadily increased from US$ 329 in 1991, when economic liberalisation began, to US$1,265 in 2010, and is estimated to increase to US$ 2,110 by 2016. In a projection report published in 2011, India's GDP at purchasing power parity will overtake that of the United States by 2045. During the next four decades, Indian GDP is expected to grow at an annualised average rate of 8 per cent, making it potentially the world's fastest-growing economy until 2050. Among the key growth factors projected are—a young and rapidly growing workingage population; growth in the manufacturing sector due to rising education and engineering skill levels among the Indians; and sustained growth of the consumer market driven by a rapidly growing middle class and upper middle class. No success can be achieved easily. To achieve the above economic success, it is essential to continue to exploit its economic potential, and for that it must continue to focus on public sector reform, expansion of transport infrastructure, improvement in its Power production to provide energy security, agricultural expansion, an effective rural development programme, smoothening of labor laws, increasing educational facilities, and making better provisions of public health facility, control of population growth, increasing Child care programmes and installing an articulated nutritional programme.

Demographics

In the 2011 provisional Census, it has been reported that 1,210,193,422 residents are in India. India has thus continued to be the world's second-most populous country. Its population grew at 1.76 per cent per annum during 2001–2011, down from 2.13 per cent per annum in the previous decade (1991–2001). The human sex ratio, according to the 2011 census, is 940 females per 1,000 males. Medical advances made in the last 50 years as well as increased agricultural productivity brought about by the "Green Revolution" have caused India's population to grow rapidly. India continues to face several public health-related challenges. According to the World Health Organisation, 900,000 Indians die each year from drinking contaminated water or breathing polluted air. There are around 50 physicians per 100,000 Indians. The number of Indians living in urban areas has grown by 31.2 per cent between 1991 and 2001. Yet, in 2001, over 70 per cent lived in rural areas. According to the 2001 census, there are 27 million-plus cities in India, with Mumbai, Delhi, Kolkata, and Chennai being the largest. The literacy rate in 2011 was 74.04 per cent: 65.46 per cent among females and 82.14 per cent among males. Kerala is the most literate state; Bihar being the least.

In India, two major languages are spoken-Indo-Aryan (spoken by about 74 per cent of the population) and Dravidian (24 per cent). Hindi is the official language of the government. English is used extensively in business and administration and has the status of a "subsidiary official language"; it is mostly used in higher education ; there are many English-medium schools also. There is a growing tendency among the middle class to send their children to English medium schools.

Each state and union territory has one or more official languages, and the constitution recognises in particular 21 "scheduled languages". The Indian Constitution recognises 212 scheduled tribal groups which together constitute about 7.5 per cent of the country's population. The 2001 census reported that Hinduism, with over 800 million adherents (80.5 per cent of the population), was the largest religion in India; they are followed by Muslims (13.4 per cent), Christians (2.3 per cent), Sikhs (1.9 per cent), Buddhists (0.8 per cent), Jains (0.4 per cent), Jews, Zoroastrians, and Bahá'ís. India has the world's largest Hindu, Sikh, Jain, Zoroastrian, and Bahá'í populations, and has the third-largest Muslim population and the largest Muslim population for a non-Muslim majority country.

Culture

Indian cultural history spans more than 4,500 years. During the Vedic period (c. 1700–500 BCE), the foundations of Hindu philosophy, mythology, and literature were laid, and many beliefs and practices which still exist today, such as dhárma, kárma, yóga, and moksa, were established. India is notable for its religious diversity, with Hinduism, Sikhism, Islam, Christianity, and Jainism among the nation's major religions.

Hindi poet Tulsidas was composer of the *Ramcharitmanas*, one of the best-known vernacular versions of the *Ramayana*.

(B) Some of India's Art, Architecture and Literature

(a) Our Architectures! Some Masterpieces and Marvels

TAJMAHAL–AN ARCHITECTURAL BEAUTY-ONE OF THE SEVEN WONDERS OF THE WORLD.

Every Indian is proud to have Tajmahal at AGRA near NEW DELHI, our capital. Millions of people visit this place every year. Tajmahal assumes a romantic environment on a moon-lit night. So many people go to visit Taj Mahal on that day.

TAJMAHAL in AGRA, North India (above) attracted the attention of tourists from all over the World. It is one of the SEVEN WONDERS OF THE WORLD. It was built by Mughal Emperor, Shah-Jahan in memory of his beloved wife, MUMTAJ MAHAL.

Tajmahal's Origin and Inspiration

In 1631, Shah Jahan, emperor during the Mughal empire's period of greatest prosperity, was grief-stricken when his third wife, Mumtaz Mahal, died during the birth of their 14th child, Gauhara Begum. Construction of the Taj Mahal began in 1632. The court chronicles of Shah Jahan's grief illustrate the love story traditionally held as an inspiration for Taj Mahal. The principal mausoleum was completed in 1648 and the surrounding buildings and garden were finished five years later. Emperor Shah Jahan himself described the Taj in these words:

Shah Jahan, who commissioned the Taj Mahal-"Shah jahan on a globe" from the Smithsonian Institution Artistic depiction of Mumtaz Mahal.

Taj Mahal site plan.

1. The Moonlight Garden to the north of the Yamuna.
2. Terrace area: Tomb, Mosque and Jawab.
3. Charbagh (gardens).
4. Gateway, attendant accommodations, and other tombs.
5. Taj Ganji (bazaar)

In an inscription the following is written—

> Should guilty seek asylum here, Like one pardoned, he becomes free from sin. Should a sinner make his way to this mansion, All his past sins are to be washed away. The sight of this mansion creates sorrowing sighs; And the sun and the moon shed tears from their eyes. In this world this edifice has been made; To display thereby the creator's glory.

The Taj Mahal incorporates and expands on design traditions of Persian architecture and earlier Mughal architecture. Specific inspiration came from successful Timurid and Mughal buildings including; the Gur-e Amir (the tomb of Timur, progenitor of the Mughal dynasty, in Samarkand), Humayun's Tomb, Itmad-ud-Daulah's Tomb (sometimes called the *Baby Taj*), and Shah Jahan's own Jama Masjid in Delhi. While earlier Mughal buildings were primarily constructed of red sandstone, Shah Jahan promoted the use of white marble inlaid with semi-precious stones, and buildings under his patronage reached new levels of refinement.

Architecture

The tomb is the central focus of the entire complex of the Taj Mahal. This large, white marble structure stands on a square plinth and consists of a symmetrical building with an arch-shaped doorway topped by a large dome and finial. Like most Mughal tombs, the basic elements are Persian in origin.

The base structure is essentially a large, multi-chambered cube with chamfered corners, forming an unequal octagon that is approximately

55 metres (180 ft) on each of the four long sides. On each of these sides, a huge *pishtaq*, or vaulted archway, frames the iwan with two similarly shaped, arched balconies stacked on either side. This motif of stacked pishtaqs is replicated on the chamfered corner areas, making the design completely symmetrical on all sides of the building. Four minarets frame the tomb, one at each corner of the plinth facing the chamfered corners. The main chamber houses the false graves (sarcophagi) of Mumtaz Mahal and Shah Jahan; the actual graves are at the Lower level.

Taj Mahal Viewed from the East (above).

The marble dome that surmounts the tomb is the most spectacular feature. Its height of around 35 metres (115 ft) is about the same as the length of the base, and is accentuated as it sits on a cylindrical "drum" which is roughly seven metres (23 ft) high. Because of its shape, the dome is often called an onion dome or *amrud* (guava dome). The top is decorated with a lotus design, which also serves to accentuate its height. The shape of the dome is emphasised by four smaller domed *chattris* (kiosks) placed at its corners, which replicate the onion shape of the main dome. Their columned bases open through the roof of the tomb and provide light to the interior. Tall decorative spires (*guldastas*) extend from edges of base walls, and provide visual emphasis to the height of the dome. The lotus motif is repeated on both the chattris and guldastas. The dome and chattris are topped by a gilded finial, which mixes traditional Persian and Hindustani decorative elements.The main finial was originally made of gold but was replaced by a copy made of gilded bronze in the early 19th century. This feature provides a clear example of integration of traditional Persian and Hindu decorative elements. The finial is topped by a moon, a typical Islamic motif whose horns point heavenward. Because of its placement on the main spire, the horns of the moon and the finial point combine to create a trident shape, reminiscent of traditional Hindu symbols of Shiva. The minarets, which are each more than 40 metres (130 ft) tall, display the designer's penchant for symmetry. They were designed as working minarets—a traditional element of mosques, used by the muezzin to call the Islamic faithful to prayer. Each minaret is effectively divided into three equal parts by two working balconies that ring the tower. At the top of the tower is a final balcony surmounted by a chattri that mirrors the design of those on the tomb. The chattris all share the same decorative elements of a lotus design topped by a gilded finial. The minarets were constructed slightly outside of the plinth so that, in the event of collapse, (a typical occurrence with many tall constructions of the period) the material from the towers would tend to fall away from the tomb.

The Jagannath Temple in Puri, Odisha

It is a famous Hindu temple dedicated to Jagannath (Vishnu) and located in the coastal town of Puri in the state of Orissa, India. The name *Jagannath* (Lord of the Universe) is a combination of the Sanskrit words *Jagat* (Universe) and *Nath* (Lord of). The temple is an important pilgrimage destination for many Hindu traditions, particularly worshippers of Krishna and Vishnu, and part of the *Char Dham* pilgrimages that a Hindu is expected to make in one's lifetime. The temple was built in the 11th century atop its ruins by the progenitor of the Eastern Ganga dynasty, King Anantavarman Chodaganga

Puri–Jagannath Temple.

Deva. The temple is famous for its annual Rath Yatra, or chariot festival, in which the three main temple deities are hauled on huge and elaborately decorated temple cars. Since medieval times, it is also associated with intense religious fervour.

Puri Jagannath Temple is situated in Orissa almost on the sea shore. Its temple architecture is beautiful. Thousands visit the temple every year. Also they include another temple to visit, the famous KONARAK SURYA (SUN) Mandir. Puri's sea beach is also very famous and attractive.

Legendary account as found in the Skanda-Purana, Brahma Purana and other Puranas (ancient scriptures) and later Oriya works state that Lord Jagannath was originally worshipped as Lord Neela Madhav by a tribal chief named Viswavasu. Having heard about the deity, King Indradyumna sent a Brahmin priest, Vidyapati to locate the deity, who was worshipped secretly in a dense forest by Viswavasu. Vidyapati tried his best but could not locate the place. But at last he managed to marry Viswavasu's daughter Lalita. At repeated request of Vidyapti, Viswavasu took his son-in-law blind-folded to a cave where Lord Neela Madhav was worshipped.

Vidyapati was very intelligent. He dropped mustard seeds on the ground on his way to the cave. The seeds germinated after a few days, which enabled him to find out the cave later on.

On hearing from him, King Indradyumna proceeded immediately to Odra desha (Orissa) on a pilgrimage to see and worship the Deity. But the deity had disappeared by that time. The king was very disappointed. The Deity was hidden in sand. The king was determined not to return without having a darshan of the deity and observed fast unto death at Mount Neela, Then a celestial voice cried 'thou shalt see him'. Afterwards the king performed a horse sacrifice and built a magnificent temple for Vishnu. Sri Narasimha Murti brought by Narada was installed in the temple.

Ratha Jatra (a procession with the idols of Jagannath, Balaram and Subhadra) is celebrated every year with much enthusiasm. Thousand of people from all around the country participate in this event.

Ratha Jatra

As the story goes, during sleep, the king had a vision of Lord Jagannath. Also an astral voice directed him to receive the fragrant tree on the seashore and make idols out of it. Accordingly the king got the image of Lord Jagannath, Balabhadra, Subhadra and Chakra Sudarshan made out of the wood of the divine tree and installed them in the temple.

King Indradyumna put up for Jagannath the tallest monument of the world. It was 1,000 cubits high. He invited Lord Brahma, the cosmic creator, consecrate the temple and the images. Brahma came all the way from Heaven for that.

Seeing the temple he was immensely pleased with him. Brahma asked Indradyumna as to in what way can he (Brahma) fulfill the king's desire, since he was very much pleased with him for his having put the most beautiful Temple for Lord Vishnu. With folded hands, Indradyumna said, "My Lord if you are really pleased with me, kindly bless me with one thing, and it is that I should be issueless and that I should be the last member of my family." In case anybody left alive after him, he would only take pride as the owner of the temple and would not work for the society. There are other stories about the temple also. The temple is sacred to the Vaishnava traditions and saint Ramananda who was closely associated with the temple.

Konarak (also written as Konark) Sun Temple (shown below)

Architecture

Located on the shoreline, now a little over three km from the sea, the temple takes the form of the chariot of Surya (Arka), the Sun God, and is heavily decorated with stone carving. The entire complex was designed in the form of the God's huge chariot drawn by seven spirited horses on twelve pairs of exquisitely decorated wheels at its base. The huge wheels carved at the base of the temple are one of the major attractions. The spokes of the wheels serve as sundials and the shadows cast by these can give the precise time of the day. The pyramidical roof soars over 30 m (98 ft) in height.

Konark Sun Temple Chariot Wheel.

Front of the Sun Temple.

The entrance is guarded by two giant lions, which are each shown crushing a war elephant. Each elephant in turn lies on top of a human body. The temple symbolises the majestic stride of the Sun God. At the entrance of the temple is a Nata Mandir. This is where the temple dancers used to perform dances in homage to the Sun God. All around the temple, there are various floral and geometric patterns. The temple is now partly in ruins, and a collection of its sculptures is housed in the Sun Temple Museum, which is run by the Archaeological Survey of India.

The Nobel laureate Indian poet Rabindranath Tagore wrote of Konark: "***Here the language of stone surpasses the language of man.***"

Nata Mandir

The Sun Temple, built in the thirteenth century, was conceived as a gigantic chariot of the Sun God, with twelve pairs of exquisitely ornamented wheels pulled by seven pairs of horses. Majestic in conception, this temple is one of the most sublime monuments of India, famous as much for its imposing dimensions and faultless proportions as for the harmonious integration of architectural grandeur with plastic allegiance. Every inch of the temple is covered with sculpture of an unsurpassed beauty and grace, in tableaux and freestanding pieces ranging from the monumental to the miniature. The subject matter is fascinating. Thousands of images include deities, celestial and human musicians, dancers, lovers, and myriad scenes of courtly life, ranging from hunts and military battles to the pleasures of courtly relaxation. These are interspersed with birds, animals (close to two thousand charming and lively elephants march around the base of the main

temple alone), mythological creatures, and a wealth of intricate botanical and geometrical decorative designs. The famous jewel like quality of Orissan art is evident throughout, as is a very human perspective which makes the sculpture extremely accessible.

The temple is famous for its erotic sculptures (shown above), which can be found primarily on the second level of the porch structure. It will become immediately apparent upon viewing them that the frank nature of their content is combined with an overwhelming tenderness and lyrical movement.

The Sun temple belongs to the Kalinga school of Indian temples. The *Main Sanctum* which (229 ft. high) was constructed along with the *Audience Hall* (128 ft. high) having elaborate external projections. The *Main Sanctum* which enshrined the presiding deity has fallen off. The *Audience Hall* survives in its entirety, but only small portions of the Dancing Hall (Nata Mandir) and the Dining Hall (Bhoga-Mandap) have survived the vagaries of time. The Temple compound measures 857 ft (261 m) by 540 ft (160 m). The alignment of the Sun Temple is on the East-West direction. The Temple is located in natural surroundings, abounding with casuarina plantations and other types of trees such as mahogany, rosewood.

South Indian Temple Architecture

The Brihadeshwara temple, also known as Rajarajeswaram, India's largest temple and part of the UNESCO World Heritage Site "Great Living Chola Temples" (shown below).

Some architectural masterpieces of South Indian Temples are shown below.

Rameswaram Temple (Below)

Temple in Kerala

Many large *bannabs* (grand stone temples) still stand in South India. Ritual tends to be orthodox and elaborate especially in the large vedic

Sri Venkateshwara Temple of Tirupati.

brahminical temples, which follow the pan-Indian Sanskrit *agama* scriptural traditions. Apart from the main fixed stone deities, processional deities made of *panchaloha* (an alloy of gold, silver, copper, zinc and tin) are bathed, dressed, decorated with valuables and taken out in processions for festivals throughout the year. The richer the temple, the more elaborate the festivals. However, many ancient temples in small villages with great architectural and historical heritage value languish for lack of funds for maintenance.

Famous South Indian temples are Lord Sri Venkateshwara Temple, Tirumala Tirupati temple, Andhra; Mookambika temple, Kollur, Karnataka; Chennakesava temple, Belur (Karnataka); Sri Padmanabhaswamy Temple, Thiruvanathapuram Kerala; Sreevallabha Temple, Thiruvalla, Kerala; Sabarimala temple, Kerala; Guruvayur temple, Kerala; Kodungallor temple, Kerala; Kanyakumari temple, Tamil Nadu (TN); Madurai Meenakshi Amman Temple, Tamil Nadu; Srirangam Ranganathar temple and Thiruvanaikaval temple of Tiruchi, TN; Golden Temple of Sripuram, TN; Brihadeshwara temple (Rajarajeswaram), Thanjavur, TN; oldest temples such as Kailasanathar temple, Varatharajaperumal temple, Kamakshi temple and Ekambareshwarar temple of Kanchipuram, TN.

The Lotus Temple at New Delhi (Shown below)

It is open to all people regardless of religion, or any other distinction. The spirit of the House of Worship has been vested on the idea that it is a gathering place where people of all religions may worship God without

restrictions. The Bahá'í laws stipulated that only the holy scriptures of the Bahá'í Faith and other religions can be read or chanted inside in any language; while readings and prayers can be set to music by choirs, no musical instruments can be played inside. Furthermore, no sermons can be delivered, and there can be no ritualistic ceremonies practiced.

Architectural Wonder: Lotus Temple, New Delhi

Visitors at the Bahá'í House of Worship (below)—The Lotus temple

All Bahá'í Houses of Worship, including the Lotus Temple, share certain architectural elements, some of which are specified in Bahá'í scripture. A House of Worship is a nine-sided circular shape. While all current Bahá'í Houses of Worship have a dome, this is not regarded as an essential part of their architecture. Bahá'í scripture also states that no pictures, statues or images be displayed within the House of Worship. Inspired by the lotus flower, the design for the House of Worship in New Delhi is composed of 27 free-standing marble clad "petals" arranged in clusters of three to form nine sides. The nine doors of the Lotus Temple open onto a central hall slightly more than 40 meters tall that is capable of holding up to 2,500 people. The surface of the House of Worship is made of white marble from Penteli mountain in Greece, the very same from which many ancient monuments and other Bahá'í Houses of Worship are built. Along with its nine surrounding ponds and the gardens, the Lotus Temple property comprises 26 acres (105,000 m^2; 10.5 ha).

The site is in the village of Bahapur, in the National Capital Territory of Delhi. The architect was an Iranian, who now lives in Canada, named Fariborz Sahba. He was approached in 1976 to design it and later oversaw its construction. The major part of the funds needed to buy this land was donated by Ardishír Rustampúr of Hyderabad, who gave his entire life savings for this purpose in 1953. A portion of construction budget was saved and used to build a greenhouse to study indigenous plants and flowers that would be appropriate for use on the site.

Indian Culture

India is full of age-old cultures. Culturally significant monuments and shrines are scattered all around the Country. Many of those are architectural landmarks. These are a part of overall Indian culture. Tourists and Pilgrims flock there in thousands every year to enjoy these beauties and also to satisfy their divine belief, faith and convictions. India's age-old architectural beauty is world famous. In the pictures above, you will find some of these architectural masterpieces.

There are several masterpieces in different parts of India also—In the North there is Tajmahal in Agra, SWARNA MANDIR in Punjab, in the East there exists, PURI JAGANNATH TEMPLE and KONARK TEMPLE (Sun Temple), in South India there are many temples such as Lord Sri Venkateshwara Temple, Tirumala Tirupati temple, Andhra; Mookambika temple, Kollur, Karnataka; Chennakesava temple, Belur (Karnataka); Sri Padmanabhaswamy Temple, Thiruvanathapuram, Kerala; Sreevallabha Temple, Thiruvalla, Kerala; Sabarimala Temple, Kerala; Guruvayur temple, Kerala; Kodungallor temple, Kerala; and in the West India there exists the Buddhist Cave paintings and sculptures in AJANTA and ELLORA CAVES.

All these are very famous. These paintings and engravings are thousands of years old. They could still withstand the brunt of nature's fury over the years. They also symbolise the richness of our arts and culture, our sense of designs and architecture, craftsmanship and the aptitudes and expertise of our artisans and artists. We all should be feeling very proud of our cultural heritage and protect them very dearly. Although these are old structures but they still give us the feeling that India's artisans, painters and sculptors were the best in the World and were quite efficient in their own work so far as the then World was concerned. The same traditions continue, and should continue hereafter.

A Muslim Shrine in Hyderabad (known as Charminar) still stands as a testimony of the Muslim predominance during the time of the NIZAM of Hyderabad (See above).

Buddhist Culture in India

India is the birth place of Gautama Buddha, although he was a king, but later he took "Sanyas" and preached a new Religious Doctrine which was later spread as "Buddhism" in all South East Asian countries.

A Picture of Gautama Buddha in Meditation (Artist's concept, shown above).

Ajanta Padmapani Painting (Buddhist Culture)

Ajanta—Ellora Cave-Buddha Sculptures (Buddhist Culture).

It is a marvelous temple and is considered to be a sacred place of Worship by the Sikh Community in India and abroad. They are the followers of GURU NANAK.

Golden Temple, Amritswar—A Sikh Shrine.

Much of Indian architecture, including the Taj Mahal, and many other works of Mughal architecture, and South Indian architecture, blends ancient local traditions with imported styles. Vernacular architecture is also highly regional in it flavours. *Vastu shastra*, literally "science of construction" or "architecture" and ascribed to Mamuni Mayan, explores how the laws of nature affect human dwellings.

You will find in these architectures that geometry and directional alignments were the key tools. All these thoughts and ideas were applied in Hindu architecture in their construction of temples It has influenced the then poetry, dance, and sculpture.

(a) Our Family Structure–Indian Arts and Literature, Indian Society, Indian Cuisine, Indian Sports

Our Family structure is very important for the bondage we find among the members of our family.

Picture of a Sister and Brother (See above).

Below is a typical picture of an Indian Family showing the Father, Mother, Daughter and Son (A picture is shown this is normally the structure of our families.

Earlier, there were joint families with Grand parents, Uncle, Aunt, Cousin Brothers and Sisters, all living together. In the modern era, complexities of life increased and so family size became smaller. But still in some villages and towns we see joint family structures.

Wedding is a very special function in each family. In Indian Culture, through the wedding of a boy and a girl; besides them the two families also

Picture of an Indian Wedding is shown above.

come together to establish a long standing relationship. There is love, affection, faith and dependence on each other and one another.

We all know that Man had learnt to live in a family from early days; but what is meant by that Family has been described above.

An immediate family is composed of a father, a Mother, brothers and sisters. We also see our Grand father and Grand mother also in our family. Our Uncle and Aunts, Cousin Brothers and sisters also are part of an extended family. Very seldom we can see and meet our Great Grand Father (Father's father) and Great Grand mothers (Grand father's mother), There could be these people from our Mother's side as well. But we all should collect information about them. We should be feeling proud of our families. We bear the title and legacy of our family.

These days this extended family structures (Up to Grand father and Grand Mother Level) are very seldom seen, because of various complexities of life as mentioned above. But in some cases it still exists. How lucky those people are; they can enjoy the love and affection of their Grand Fathers and Grand Mothers. For educational purposes and also to get a proper job, people have to go out of the villages, towns, and even states; sometimes even outside their countries. Thus family size became shorter and shorter these days.

Man is a social animal. It had learnt to live in a collective manner from times immemorial. It had created its own society. It had developed many different cultural activities, religious festivals, games and plays. They differ

Above is the picture of an Indian Family engaged in a Religious Festival.

according to the regions they live in people from any one region cling to their style of living, faith, practices and culture.

If you travel from one corner to the other of our nation you will find diversities among the people. Their clothes, ornaments, life styles, their food habits and their religious faiths, beliefs, practices and convictions are different. But there is an Unity in Diversity. That is what Indian culture is. That is what has bonded us together in this great Nation, India.

Indian Literature

It has been detailed earlier that the earliest literary writings in India, composed between 1400 BCE and 1200 CE, were in the Sanskrit language. Prominent works of this Sanskrit literature include epics such as the Mahābhārata and the Ramayana, the dramas of Kālidāsa such as the *Abhijñānaúākuntalam* (*The Recognition of Úakuntalā*), and poetry such as the *Mahkvya*, which were developed between 600 BCE and 300 CE in South India.

From the 14th to the 18th centuries, India's literary traditions went through a period of drastic change because of the emergence of devotional poets such as Kabir, Tulsidas, and Guru Nanak. Their Bhajans and Religious songs and writings still touches the minds and hearts of many Indians.

20th-century Indian literature was influenced by the works of Bengali poet and novelist **Rabindranath Tagore**—the Nobel Laureate. Tagore's songs, poetry and dance drama introduced an altogether new phase in Bengali culture and made it richer than before. Still the Bengalees all over the world enjoy performing those dramas on stage, singing his songs as well as reciting his poetry. Tagore has become an institution by himself. In West Bengal many other stalwarts in the literary field; Sahitya Samrat Bankim Chandra Chattopadhyay, Sarat Chandra Chattopadhyay, Vidhrohi (Revolutionary) poet Kazi Nazrul Islam, Michael Madhusudan Datta (he created "Amritakswar Chanda" (a new style in Bengali poetry), "Chander Jadugar" Satyendra Nath Datta and many others.

The World had just celebrated the 150 birth Anniversary of Poet Rabindra Nath Tagore.

One of his famous poems (translated in English) is presented below:

Where the mind is without fear and the head is held high;
Where knowledge is free;
Where the world has not been broken up into fragments by narrow domestic walls;
Where words come out from the depth of truth;
Where tireless striving stretches its arms towards perfection;
Where the clear stream of reason has not lost its way into the dreary desert sand of dead habit;
Where the mind is led forward by Thee to ever-widening thought and action-Into that heaven of freedom, my father, let my country awake.

by Rabindranath Tagore

Performing Arts

Kuchipudi dance accompanied by Carnatic vocalisations is shown below:

Performing Arts had diversified in India along with many forms of Indian music which ranges over various traditions and regional styles. Classical music encompasses two genres and their various folk offshoots: the northern Hindustani and southern Carnatic schools. Regionalised popular forms include filmi and folk music; the syncretic tradition of the *bauls* is a well-known form of the latter. Indian dance also features diverse folk and classical forms. Among the better-known folk dances are the *bhangra* of the Punjab, the *bihu* of Assam, the *chhau* of West Bengal and Jharkhand, *sambalpuri* of Orissa, *ghoomar* of Rajasthan, and the *lavani* of Maharashtra. Eight dance forms, many with narrative forms and mythological elements, have been accorded classical dance status by India's National Academy of Music, Dance, and Drama. These are: *bharatanatyam* of the state of Tamil Nadu, *kathak* of Uttar Pradesh, *kathakali* and *mohiniyattam* of Kerala, *kuchipudi* of Andhra Pradesh, *manipuri* of Manipur, *odissi* of Orissa, and the *sattriya* of Assam.

Kathak Dance form of Lucknow.

Bharatanatyam dance form of Southern India.

Theatre in India melds music, dance, and improvised or written dialogue. Often based on Hindu mythology, but also borrowing from Kathak medieval romances or social and political events.

Manipuri Dance Form.

A Still from Rabindra Nritya Natya of Bengal.

Indian theatre includes the *bhavai* of Gujarat, the *jatra* of West Bengal, the *nautanki* and *ramlila* of North India, *tamasha* of Maharashtra, *burrakatha* of Andhra Pradesh, *terukkuttu* of Tamil Nadu, and the *yakshagana* of Karnataka.

The Indian film industry produces the world's mostwatched cinema. Established regional cinematic traditions exist in the Assamese, Bengali, Hindi, Kannada, Malayalam, Marathi, Oriya, Tamil, and Telugu languages. South Indian cinema attracts more than 75 per cent of national film revenue.

Indian Society

Traditional Indian society may be defined by strict social hierarchy. The Indian caste system embodies much of the social stratification and many of the social restrictions found in the Indian subcontinent. Social classes are defined by *jātis*, or "castes". Most Dalits ("Untouchables") and members of other lower-caste communities continue to live in segregation and often face persecution and discrimination, neglect and humiliation. Traditional Indian family values are highly respected, and patriarchal joint families have been the norm in India, though nuclear families are becoming common in urban areas. An overwhelming majority of Indians, with their consent, have their marriages arranged by their parents or other family members. Marriage is thought to be for life, and the divorce rate is extremely low in India. Child marriage is still a common practice, more so in rural India, with more than half of women in India is still marrying before the legal age of 18. It's a good sign that many young girls these days are refusing to marry at tender ages.

Many Indian festivals are religious in origin. The best known include Diwali, Ganesh Chaturthi, Thai Pongal, Navaratri, Holi, Durga Puja, Eid-ul-Fitr, Bakr-Id, Christmas, and Vaisakhi.

India has three National holidays which are observed in all states and union territories: Republic Day, Independence Day, and Gandhi Jayanti. Other sets of holidays, varying between nine and twelve, are officially observed in individual states.

Indian Dress

Traditional Indian dress varies in colour and style across regions and depends on various factors, including climate and faith. Popular styles of dress include draped garments such as the *sari* for women and the *dhoti* or *lungi* for men. Stitched clothes, such as the *shalwar kameez* for women and *kurta-pyjama* combinations or European-style trousers and shirts for men, are also popular. Delicate jewellery, modelled on real flowers, plants and various attractive designs used to be worn by the ladies in ancient India. This has been a part of a tradition dating back some 5,000 years; gemstones were also worn in India.

In the World, every country has its own culture, own religious faith, life styles, food habits and having their own belief and convictions. Even they speak different languages. So when we go to compare us with other nations and their people we find a great deal of differences and contradictions.

Indian Cuisine

Every country has their own cuisine according to their tastes and their own likings. Indian cuisine is known for its delicacies—use of herbs and spices of various kinds in individual preparations of both vegetarian and

Non-vegetarian dishes is a unique tradition available in different food preparations available n different parts of India. Indian tandoori preparations are of special importance giving you a specific kind of tastes.

The *tandoor* is a clay oven used in India for almost 5,000 years; it grills meats to an "uncommon succulence" and produces the puffy flatbread known as *naan*. The staple foods are wheat (predominantly in the north), rice (especially in the south and the east), and lentils. Many spices which have worldwide appeal are native to the Indian subcontinent, while chili pepper, native to the Americas and introduced by the Portuguese in India is now widely used by the Indians.

Indian Sport

In India, several traditional indigenous sports remain fairly popular, among them *kabaddi*, *kho kho*, *pehlwani*, and *gilli-danda*. Some of the earliest forms of Asian martial arts, originated in India. Chess, commonly held to have originated in India is regaining widespread popularity with the rise in the number of Indian Grandmasters. King Akbar (a celebrated Mughal King) used to play Chess on a giant marble court. Chess was also a very favourite indoor game for many Emperors and Kings. Rich and sophisticated people in India started playing this game later to pass their extra time.

Tennis in India

Lawn Tennis are becoming increasingly popular in India; this stems from the victorious India Davis Cup team and the recent successes of Indian tennis players in the Asian and International Tennis. Over the years, India has produced some outstanding tennis players, who have made the country feel proud both at the national and international stage. If players of the caliber of Ramanathan Krishnan and Vijay Amritraj excelled in the Grand Slams, the present crops of youngsters like Sania Mirza have earned plaudit for their achievements.

Going back to the history of tennis in India, in the 1960s, Ramanathan Krishnan rubbed shoulders with some of the established names in tennis, including Rod Laver, in the Wimbledon. Ramanathan was ranked third in the world. Krishnan's son Ramesh emulated his father, by reaching the quarterfinals of Wimbledon and US open.

During the 1970s, Vijay Amritraj dominated the sport of tennis in India. He reached the quarterfinals of Grand Slams on four occasions and his aggressive game got the better of some of the ace tennis players like Jimmy Connors, Ivan Lendl and John McEnroe. Indians can indeed win Grand Slam tournaments, was shown by Mahesh Bhupathi, when he achieved the feat in 1997 French Open. He teamed with the promising player Leander Paes to win a bagful of Grand Slam doubles title. In the present time, tennis star

Sania Mirza, with her amasing performance, has breathed in fresh air to the game in India. Some prominent Indian players are named below:

- Ramanathan Krishnan
- Ramesh Krishnan
- Leander Paes
- Vijay Amritraj
- Mahesh Bhupathi
- Sania Mirza

India's Joydeep Mukherjee earned reputation for his play in earlier days. The Tennis brothers, Vijay Amritraj and Anand Amritraj also earned reputations in World Tennis.

Other Games

India has a comparatively strong presence in shooting sports, and has won several medals, including Gold medals at the Olympics, the World Shooting Championships, and the Commonwealth Games. Other sports in which Indians have succeeded internationally include badminton, boxing, and wrestling. Football is popular in the North-East, West Bengal, Goa, Tamil Nadu, and Kerala. But India is yet to excel in Football.

Field Hockey

India's official national sport is field hockey; it is administered by Hockey India. The Indian national hockey team won the 1975 Hockey World Cup and have, as of 2012, taken eight gold, one silver, and two bronze Olympic medals, making it the sport's most successful team.

Cricket in India

Cricket is by far the most popular sport; the Indian national cricket team won the 1983 and 2011 World Cups, the 2007 ICC World Twenty–20, and shared the 2002 ICC Champions Trophy with Sri Lanka. Cricket in India is administered by the Board of Control for Cricket in India, or BCCI; the Ranji Trophy, the Duleep Trophy, the Deodhar Trophy, the Irani Trophy, and the NKP Salve Challenger Trophy are domestic competitions. The BCCI conducts a Twenty–20 competition known as the Indian Premier League. India has hosted or co-hosted several international sporting events: the 1951 and 1982 Asian Games; the 1987, 1996, and 2011 Cricket World Cups; the 2003 Afro-Asian Games; the 2006 ICC Champions Trophy; the 2010 Hockey World Cup; and the 2010 Commonwealth Games. Major international sporting events held annually in India include the Chennai Open, Mumbai Marathon, Delhi Half Marathon, and the Indian Masters. The first Indian Grand Prix featured in late 2011. Sachin Tendulkar earned International acclaim as the best batsman making largest number of runs in World cricket, surpassing even the legendary Don Bradman.

Biodiversity in India

India lies within the Indomalayan ecozone and contains three biodiversity hotspots. India hosts 12.6 per cent of all avian, 6.2 per cent of all reptilian, 4.4 per cent of all amphibian, 11.7 per cent of all piscine, and 6.0 per cent of all flowering plant species. Habitat ranges from the tropical rainforest of the Andaman Islands, Western Ghats, and North-East India to the coniferous forest of the Himalaya. Between these extremes lie the moist deciduous sal forest of eastern India; the dry deciduous teak forest of central and southern India; and the babul-dominated thorn forest of the central Deccan and western Gangetic plain. Less than 12 per cent of India's landmass bears thick jungle. The medicinal plant neem, widely used in rural Indian herbal remedies, is a key Indian tree. The luxuriant pipal fig tree, shown on the seals of Mohenjo-daro, shaded Gautama Buddha as he sought enlightenment. Mammals entered India from Asia. There are now many threatened species n India. These include the Asiatic lion, the Royal Bengal tiger, and the Indian white-rumped vulture, nearly went extinct.

The ecologically devastating human encroachment of recent decades has critically endangered Indian wildlife. In response the system of national parks and protected areas, first established in 1935, was substantially expanded. In 1972, India enacted the Wildlife Protection Act and Project Tiger to safeguard crucial wilderness; the Forest Conservation Act was enacted in 1980 and amendments added in 1988. India hosts more than five hundred wildlife sanctuaries and thirteen biosphere reserves, four of which are part of the World Network of Biosphere Reserves; twenty-five wetlands are registered under the Ramsar Convention.

Our Flora and Fauna

In India, we have many exotic species of nature's Gift. Our flowers, our plants, our animals, our birds, our reptiles etc., are exotic and most beautiful in the World. Some of their pictures are shown below and also elsewhere in this book. Try to know more about them, learn more about their details from the Wikipedia in the Internet.

You should realise that Diversity is the Rule of Nature. Through this slogan Nature has progressed thus far. This is the reason why and how evolution could progress up until this date.

In India, we have many exotic species of nature's Gift. Our flowers, our plants, our animals, our birds, our reptiles etc., are exotic and most beautiful in the World. Some of their pictures are shown below and also elsewhere in this book.

Wonderful Orchids–Nature's Magnificent Creation.

Let's not wipe them out

Rice-growing field and Vegetation
Both Men and Women Work in the Field. An Indian Scenerio.

Wildlife of India

One of Nature's Wonderful Creations—Royal Bengal Tiger (Panthers). It has become an endangered species already. It is becoming the victim of our aggressive encroachment of jungles in a variety of ways. The number

of Tigers is sharply decreasing. Poaching of Tigers for their skin is one of the main reasons why their numbers are decreasing day by day. Various efforts are going on to save them. There is already a Save Tiger Project in India—the purpose is to make all arrangements to protect them by all means. Count them from time to time to determine their numbers in a scientific mann.

Love Them and Save Them
Join Save Tiger Programmer

See below a Picture of a beautiful PEACOCK-India's national Bird. Oh! What a Beauty! Nature's Wonder. Let us save them. These are our heritage.

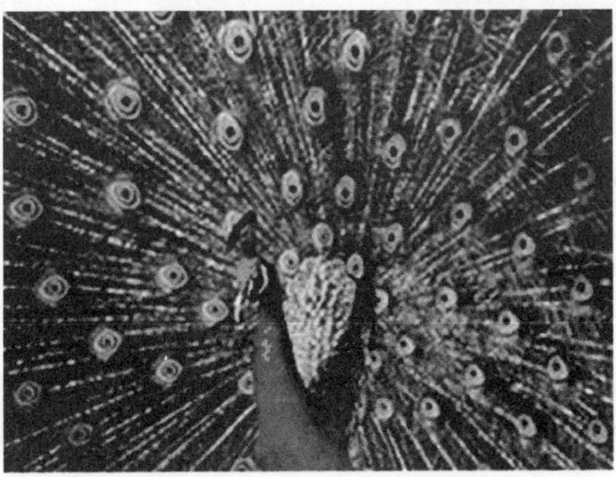

The Indian peacock (Pavo cristatus) is the national bird. It roosts in moist and dry-deciduous forests, cultivated areas, and village precincts. See two pictures above and below.

National Reptile of India–The COBRA. Dangerous, but Elegant.

Starting at GONGOTRI in high Himalayas and traveling across a distance of more than 2550 kilometers, across three states of India, such as Uttar Pradesh, Bihar and West Bengal, the river Ganges ultimately meets the Bay

Sunset in Holy River Ganges. India's Sacred River, India's Life-line.

of Bengal. The river Ganges is considered by the Hindus as a sacred river. Thousands of people throng together every year, in several holy places, such as Hrishikesh, Hardwar, Benaras, Goya, Kolkata, etc., situated on the banks of the river Ganges to take a dip as a part of their religious faith and conviction.

(C) India's Environmental Contrasts

(i) The Mighty Himalayas and its Ecology

Mount Everest–The Highest Peak in the World.

The Himalayan Mountains, usually called the Himalayas or Himalaya for short, is a mountain range situated at the north of the Indian subcontinent. The Himalayan mountain system is the world's highest, and home to the world's highest peaks, Mount Everest and K2. To comprehend the enormous scale of this mountain range, the Himalayan system includes over 100 mountains exceeding 7,200 m (23,600 ft).

The main Himalayan range runs west to east, from the Indus river valley to the Brahmaputra river valley, forming an arc 2,400 km (1,500 mi) long, which varies in width from 400 km (250 mi) in the western Kashmir-Xinjiang region to 150 km (93 mi) in the eastern Tibet-Arunachal Pradesh region.

Some of the world's major river systems arise in the Himalayas, and their combined drainage basin is home to some three billion people (almost half of Earth's population) in 18 countries. The Himalayas have profoundly shaped the cultures of South Asia; many Himalayan peaks are sacred in Hinduism, Buddhism and Sikhism.

Ecology

The flora and fauna of the Himalayas vary with climate, rainfall, altitude, and soils. The climate ranges from tropical at the base of the mountains to

Everest, the Highest Peak of the Himalayas-Kanchanjunga.

permanent ice and snow at the highest elevations. The amount of yearly rainfall increases from west to east along the front of the range. This diversity of climate, altitude, rainfall and soil conditions generates a variety of distinct plant and animal communities.

Kanchanjunga on the Border of China.

Kanchanjunga on the Border of Nepal.

Kanchanjunga from the East.

Lowland Forests

On the Indo-Gangetic plain at the base of the mountains, an alluvial plain drained by the Indus and Ganges-Brahmaputra river systems, vegetation varies from west to east with rainfall. The Northwestern thorn scrub forests occupy the plains of Pakistan and the Indian Punjab. Further east lie the Upper Gangetic plains moist deciduous forests of Uttarakhand and Uttar Pradesh and Lower Gangetic plains moist deciduous forests of Bihar and West Bengal. These are monsoon forests, with drought-deciduous trees that lose their leaves during the dry season. The moister Brahmaputra Valley semi-evergreen forests occupy the plains of Assam.

The Terai Belt

Above the alluvial plain lies the Terai strip, a seasonally marshy zone of sand and clay soils. The Terai has higher rainfall than the plains, and the downward-rushing rivers of the Himalaya slow down and spread out in the flatter Terai zone, depositing fertile silt during the monsoon season and receding in the dry season. The Terai has a high water table due to groundwater percolating down from the adjacent zone. The central part of the Terai belt is occupied by the Terai-Duar savanna and grasslands, a mosaic of grasslands, savannas, deciduous and evergreen forests that includes some of the world's tallest grasslands. The grasslands of the Terai belt are home to the Indian rhinoceros.

Origins and Growth

The Himalayas are among the youngest mountain ranges on the planet and consist mostly of uplifted sedimentary and metamorphic rock. According to the modern theory of plate tectonics, their formation is a result of a continental collision along the convergent boundary between the Indo-Australian Plate and the Eurasian Plate. This is referred to as a fold mountain. The Indo-Australian plate continues to be driven horizontally below the Tibetan plateau, which forces the plateau to move upwards. The Arakan Yoma highlands in Myanmar and the Andaman and Nicobar Islands in the Bay of Bengal were also formed as a result of this collision.

Himalayan Glaciers and River Systems

The Himalayan range encompasses about 15,000 glaciers, which store about 12,000 km of freshwater. The 70 km long Siachen Glacier at the India-Pakistan border is the second longest glacier in the world outside the polar region. Some of the other more famous glaciers include the Gangotri and Yamunotri (Uttarakhand), Nubra, Biafo and Baltoro (Karakoram region), Zemu (Sikkim) and Khumbu glaciers (Mount Everest region).

The higher regions of the Himalayas are snowbound throughout the year, in spite of their proximity to the tropics, and they form the sources for several large perennial rivers, most of which combine into two large river systems:

The western rivers combine into the *Indus Basin*, of which the Indus River is the largest. The Indus begins in Tibet at the confluence of Sengge and Gar rivers and flows southwest through India and then through Pakistan to the Arabian Sea. It is fed by the Jhelum, the Chenab, the Ravi, the Beas, and the Sutlej rivers, among others.

Most of the other Himalayan Rivers drain the *Ganges-Brahmaputra Basin*Its two main rivers are the Ganges and the Brahmaputra and the Yamuna, among other tributaries. The Brahmaputra originates as the Yarlung Tsangpo River in western Tibet, and flows east through Tibet and west through the plains of Assam. The Ganges and the Brahmaputra meet in Bangladesh, and drain into the Bay of Bengal through the world's largest river delta. The eastern-most Himalayan Rivers feed the Ayeyarwady River, which originates in eastern Tibet and flows south through Myanmar to drain into the Andaman Sea.

This image shows the termini of the glaciers in the Bhutan-Himalaya. Glacial lakes have been forming rapidly on the surface of the debris-covered glaciers in this region during the last few decades.

Snow-capped peaks and ridges of the eastern Himalaya Mountains create an irregular white-on-red patchwork between major rivers in south-western China.

Lakes

The Himalaya region is dotted with hundreds of lakes. Most lakes are found at altitudes of less than 5,000 m, with the size of the lakes diminishing

A high Himalayan Lake at an Altitude of Around 5,000 Metres Sikkim, India.

with altitude. Pangong Tso, which is spread across the border between India and China, and Yamdrok Tso, located in central Tibet, are amongst the largest with surface areas of 700 km², and 638 km², respectively. Other notable lakes include Gurudogmar lake in North Sikkim, Tsongmo lake, near the Indo-China border in Sikkim, and Tilicho lake in Nepal in the Annapurna massif.

The mountain lakes are known to geographers as *tarns* if they are caused by glacial activity. Tarns are found mostly in the upper reaches of the Himalaya, above 5,500 metres.

Impact on Climate

The Himalayas have a profound effect on the climate of the Indian subcontinent and the Tibetan plateau. They prevent frigid, dry Arctic winds blowing south into the subcontinent, which keeps South Asia much warmer than corresponding temperate regions in the other continents. It also forms a barrier for the monsoon winds, keeping them from traveling northwards, and causing heavy rainfall in the Terai region. The Himalayas are also believed to play an important part in the formation of Central Asian deserts, such as the Taklamakan and Gobi.

The mountain ranges also prevent western winter disturbances in Iran from traveling further, resulting in snow in Kashmir and rainfall for parts of Punjab and northern India. Despite being a barrier to the cold, northerly winter winds, the Brahmaputra valley receives part of the frigid winds, thus lowering the temperature in the North East India and Bangladesh.

The Himalayas, which are often called "The Roof of the World", contain the greatest area of glaciers and permafrost outside of the poles. Ten of Asia's largest rivers flow from here and more than a billion people's livelihoods depend on them. To complicate matters, temperatures are rising more rapidly here than the global average. In Nepal, the temperature has risen 0.6°C over the last decade, whereas the global warming has been around 0.7°C over the last hundred years.

Mountain Passes

The Himalayan Range at Yumesongdong in Sikkim, in the Yumthang River Valley.

The rugged terrain makes few routes through the mountains possible. Some of these routes include:

- Banihal is an important pass connecting the hill areas of Jammu to the Kashmir Valley.
- Zoji La lies between the vale of Kashmir and the Kargil district, and is the only Western entrance to the highlands of Ladakh.
- Rohtang Pass in Himachal Pradesh, India.
- Mohan Pass is the principal pass in the Siwalik Hills, the southern most and geologically youngest foothills running parallel to the main Himalayas in Sikkim.
- Kora La at 4,594 metres (15,072 ft) elevation on the Nepal-Tibet border at the upper end of Mustang. The Kali Gandaki Gorge (a graben), transects the main Himalaya and Transhimalayan ranges. Kora La is the lowest pass through both ranges between K2 and Everest, but some 300 metres (980 ft) higher than Nathula and Jelepla passes further east between Sikkim and Tibet.

- Arniko Rajmarg/Friendship Highway route from Kathmandu, Nepal crossing into Tibet at Kodari/Zhangmu, to Nyalam, Lalung-La pass (5,050 m/16,570'), Tingri, Xêgar, Lakpa La pass (5,250 m/17,225'), to Lhatse on the Yarlung Tsangpo/Brahmaputra River about 460 road kilometers west of Lhasa.
- Gangtok in Sikkim to Lhasa in Tibet, via the Nathula Pass and Jelepla Passes (offshoots of the ancient Silk Road).

Impact on People and their Culture

Mountain sheds like these are used by the rural populace as shelter for cattle in summer months as they take them for grasing in higher altitudes.

Some of the world's major rivers, the Ganges, Indus, Brahmaputra, Yangtze, Mekong, Salween, Red River (Asia), Xunjiang, Chao Phraya, Irrawaddy River, Amu Darya, Syr Darya, Tarim River and Yellow River, arise in the Himalayas, and their combined drainage basin is home to some three billion people (almost half of Earth's population) in Afghanistan, Bangladesh, Bhutan, People's Republic of China, India (almost half of the population of India live within 500 km of the Himalayan range), Nepal, Burma, Cambodia, Tajikistan, Uzbekistan, Turkmenistan, Kazakhstan, Kyrgyzstan, Thailand, Laos, Vietnam, Malaysia and Pakistan.

The Himalayas, due to their large size and expanse, have been a natural barrier to the movement of people for tens of thousands of years. In particular, this has prevented intermingling of people from the Indian subcontinent with people from China and Mongolia, causing significantly different languages and customs between these regions. The Himalayas have also hindered trade routes and prevented military expeditions across its expanse. For instance, Genghis Khan could not expand his empire south of the Himalayas into the subcontinent.

Panoramic View

Some noted mountaineers who were on the top of various mountain summits in Himalayas.

- Tensing Norgay (1914–1986) Nepalese Sherpa mountaineer. First man on Everest's summit along with Edmund Hillary.
- Maurice Herzog (b. 1919) First person to summit an Eight-thousander, Annapurna, in 1950. Lost all toes and most fingers due to frostbite. Peak not climbed again until 1970.

2004 photo mosaic the Himalayas with Makalu and Mount Everest from the International Space Station, Expedition 8.

- Sir Edmund Hillary (1919–2008) New Zealand mountaineer and explorer, the first man on Everest's summit along with Tensing Norgay.
- Tom Bourdillon (1924–1956) member of British Everest expeditions 1951, 1952, and 1953, reached 300 feet (90 m) from summit of Everest three days before Edmund Hillary and Tensing Norgay finally conquered it.
- Hermann Buhl (1924–1957) First ascent of Nanga Parbat in 1953 (feat accomplished solo and without oxygen). First ascent of Broad Peak. Died in fall on Chogolisa, body never found.
- Willi Unsoeld (1926–1979) United States. First ascent of Everest from West Face and first major traverse of a Himalayan peak, with Tom Hornbein 1963. Daughter Nanda Devi Unsoeld killed during Nanda Devi expedition 1976. Died during avalanche on Mount Rainier, 1979.
- Chris Bonington (b. 1934) First ascent of Annapurna (South Face), 4 ascents of Everest.
- Nawang Gombu (b. 1936) Indian mountaineer. First person to climb Everest twice: 1963 and 1965.
- Reinhold Messner (b. 1944) Italian mountaineer. First man to climb all fourteen mountains over 8000 metres (collectively known as the eight-thousanders).
- Jerzy Kukuczka (1948–1989) Polish mountaineer. Ascended all fourteen eight-thousanders faster than anybody else, establishing ten new routes
- Erhard Loretan Swiss climber. Ascended all 14,8000 ers, most establishing new routes and/or in alpine style.

- Nazir Sabir Pakistani mountaineer. First ascent of *two* eight thousanders (Broad Peak and Gasherbrum II) in a single attempt.
- Swami Sundaranand (b. 1926 India) Climbed 25 mountains with little or no equipment from 1950–1990 to experience open eyed Samâdhi using the ancient techniques of the Himalayan yogis. Noted also for his extensive photography of the Indian Himalayas.
- Casey Mackins An English mountaineer who climbed Mt Everest by a new route without oxygen from Tibet in 1984 and then again from Nepal in 1990 during his famous Sea to Summit expedition where he became the first person to climb Everest starting from sea level.
- José Antonio Delgado Sucre (1965–2006) was the first Venezuelan mountaineer to reach the summit of five eight-thousanders. He was one of the most experienced climbers in Latin America.
- Ed Viesturs (b. June 22, 1959) is the first American, and 12th person overall, to summit all fourteen eight-thousanders, and the sixth climber to do it without bottled oxygen.
- Pemba Dorjie (born c. 1977) a Sherpa who currently holds the world record for the quickest climb to the summit of Mount Everest from camp. On May 21, 2004 Dorjie set that record, with a total time of 8 hours and 10 minutes.
- Apa Sherpa (born c. 1960) on May 11, 2011, successfully summited Mount Everest for the 21st time, breaking his own record for most successful ascents.
- Krzysztof Wielicki (born 1950) Polish mountaineer, the fifth man to climb all fourteen eight-thousanders. Three of them (Mount Everest, Kangchenjunga and Lhotse) he ascended as the first man ever to do it in winter.

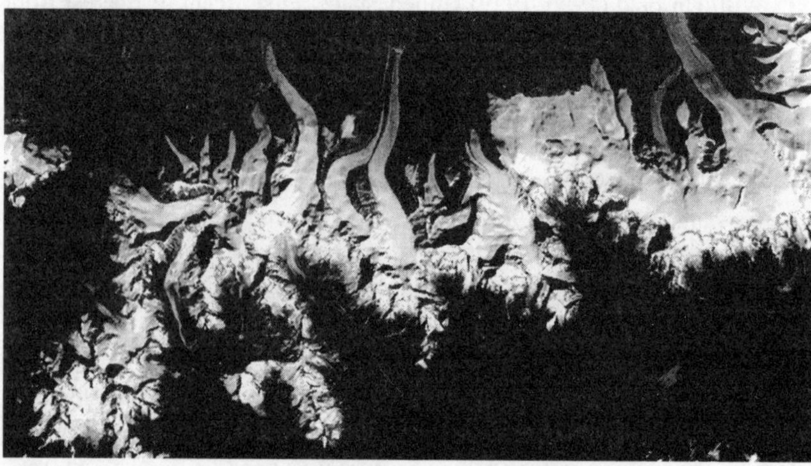

Himalayan Glaciers (see above).

Thar Desert-an Ecological Wonder

(a) Location and Description of the Thar Desert of Rajasthan

In India, the Thar Desert extends from the Sutlej River, surrounded by the Aravalli Range on the east, on the south by the salt marsh known as the Great Rann of Kutch and on the west by the Indus River. Its boundary to the large thorny steppe to the north is ill-defined, about 3/5th of the total geographical area of the State.

In Pakistan, the desert covers eastern Sindh and the southeastern portion of Punjab, Pakistan.

(b) Desert Soil

The soils of the Arid Zone are generally sandy to sandy-loam in texture. The consistency and depth vary according to the topographical features. Some of these soils contain a high percentage of soluble salts in the lower horizons, turning water in the wells poisonous.

(c) Origin of the Desert

The origin of the Thar Desert is a controversial subject. Some consider it to be 4000 to 10,000 years old, whereas others state that aridity started in this region much earlier.

Director General of Archaeological Survey of India asserted by "Radiocarbon dating that the Mature Harappan settlement at Kalibangan had to be abandoned around 2000-1900 BCE. The hydrological evidence indicated that this abandonment took place on account of the drying up of the Ghaggar-Hakra.

(d) Thar in Ancient Literature

The Indian epics describe this region as *Lavanasagara* (Salt-ocean). Ramayana mentions about *Lavanasagara* (Salt-ocean) when Rama goes to attack Lanka with the army of vanaras. Rama uses his *agneyashtra-amogha* to dry up the sea named *drumakulya* situated on north of *Lavanasagara.* A fresh water source named Pushkar surrounded by *Marukantara* was created. According to Jain cosmology, Jambûdvîpa is at the centre of Madhyaloka, or the middle part of the universe, where the humans reside. Jambûdvîpaprajñapti or the treatise on the island of Roseapple tree contains a description of Jambûdvîpa and life biographies of Rsabha and King Bharata. Jambûdvîpa continent is surrounded by ocean *Lavanoda* (Salt-ocean).

(e) Course of Sarasvati River through Thar Desert

The Sarasvati River is one of the chief Rigvedic rivers mentioned in ancient Hindu texts. The Nadistuti hymn in the Rigveda (10.75) mentions the Sarasvati between the Yamuna in the east and the Sutlej in the west, and later Vedic texts like Tandya and Jaiminiya Brahmanas as well as the Mahabharata mention that the Sarasvati dried up in a desert.

Mahabharata mentions about Kamyaka Forest situated on the western boundary of the Kuru Kingdom (Kuru Proper + Kurujangala), on the banks of the Saraswati River. It lay to the west of the Kurukshetra plain. It contained within it a lake called the Kamyaka Lake (2, 51). Kamyaka forest is mentioned as being situated at the head of the Thar Desert near the lake Trinavindu (3,256). The Pandavas on their way to exile in the woods left Pramanakoti on the banks of the Ganges and went towards Kurukshetra, traveling in a western direction, crossing the rivers Yamuna and Drishadvati. They finally reached the banks of the Saraswati River. The human habitations on the banks of rivers Saraswati and Drishadvati had shifted to the east and south directions prior to Mahabharata period. The present day Bikaner and Jodhpur areas were known as Kurujangala and Madrajangala provinces.

The Desert National Park, Jaisalmer has a collection of fossils of animals and plants of 180 million years old. Some fossils of Dinosaurs of 6 million years old have also been found in the area.

2. Biodiversity in the Desert

Indian Gazelle or *Chinkara*.

1. Wildlife

Stretches of sand in the desert are interspersed by hillocks and sandy and gravel plains. Due to the diversified habitat and ecosystem, the vegetation, human culture and animal life in this arid region is very rich in contrast to the other deserts of the world. About 23 species of lizard and 25 species of snakes are found here and several of them are endemic to the region.

Some wildlife species, which are fast vanishing in other parts of India, are found in the desert in large numbers such as the Blackbuck (*Antilope cervicapra*), the Indian Gazelle (*Gazella bennettii*) and the Indian Wild Ass (*Equus hemionus khur*) in the Rann of Kutch. They have evolved excellent survival strategies, their size is smaller than other similar animals living in different conditions, and they are mainly nocturnal. There are certain other factors responsible for the survival of these animals in the desert. Due to the lack of water in this region, transformation of the grasslands into cropland has been very slow.

Peacock on Khejri Tree Above.

The region is a haven for 141 species of migratory and resident birds of the desert. One can see eagles, harriers, falcons, buzzards, kestrel and vultures. Short-toed Eagles (*Circaetus gallicus*), Tawny Eagles (*Aquila rapax*), Spotted Eagles (*Aquila clanga*), Laggar Falcons (*Falco jugger*) and kestrels. There are also a number of reptiles.

The Indian Peafowl is a resident breeder in the Indian subcontinent particularly Thar region. The peacock is designated as the national bird of India and the provincial bird of the Punjab (Pakistan)It can be seen sitting on Khejri or Pipal trees in villages or Deblina.

Natural Vegetation in the Desert

The natural vegetation of this dry area is classed as Northern Desert Thorn Forest occurring in small clumps scattered more or less openly Density

Prosopis Cineraria* or *Khejri (Local name).

and size of patches increase from west to east following the increase in rainfall Natural vegetation of Thar Desert is composed of following tree, shrub and herb species.

(a) Tree Species

Many different species of trees and shrubs are present in the desert. **Some pictures are shown below**

***Albizia Lebbeck* (Siris Tree)**

***Tecomella Undulata* (Rohida Tree)**

Acacia Senegal (Gum-arabic Tree)

Acacia Nilotica (Babul Tree)

Shrubs

Calotropis Procera (Aak Shrub)

(b) Herbs and Grasses

Lycium Barbarum

***Tribulus Terrestris* (Gokharu herb)**

Grass

Saccharum Spontaneum
(Kans grass)

Sorghum Halepense
(Barru grass)

(c) Wild Life Sanctuary in the Desert Region

There are eleven national parks in the Thar desert area, the largest of which are the Nara Desert Wildlife Sanctuary and the Rann of Kutch.

Blackbuck Male and Female.

Others include: The Desert National Park, Jaisalmer (3162 km^2) is an excellent example of the ecosystem of the Thar Desert, and its diverse fauna. The endangered Great Indian Bustard (*Chirotis nigricaps*), Blackbuck, chinkara, fox, Bengal fox, wolf, and caracal can be seen here Seashells and massive fossilised tree trunks in this park record the geological history of the desert; Tal Chhapar Sanctuary a very small sanctuary in Churu District, 210 km from Jaipur, in the Shekhawati region. This sanctuary is home to a large population of Blackbuck while fox and caracal can also be spotted along with typical avifauna such as partridge and sand grouse; Jalore Wildlife Sanctuary (130 km from Jodhpur) is another small sanctuary that is privately owned where a sizeable population of rare and endangered wildlife is present including the Asian-Steppe Wildcat (Ornata), Leopard, Zird, Desert Fox and herds of Indian Gazelle.

(d) Attempt for Greening of the Desert Environment

Greening Desert with Plantations of Jojoba at Fatehpur, Shekhawati.

The soil of the Thar Desert remains dry for much of the year and is prone to wind erosion. High velocity winds blow soil from the desert, depositing some on neighbouring fertile lands, and causing shifting sand dunes within the desert, which bury fences and block roads and railway tracks. Permanent solution to this problem of shifting sand dunes can be provided by fixation of the shifting sand dunes with suitable plant species and planting windbreaks and shelterbelts. They also provide protection from hot or cold and desiccating winds and the invasion of sand.

(e) Indira Gandhi Canal

There are few local tree species suitable for planting in the desert region and these are slow growing. The introduction of exotic tree species in the desert for plantation has become necessary. Many species of Eucalyptus,

Indira Gandhi Canal is flowing in Thar desert near Sattasar village, Bikaner district, Rajasthan.

Acacia, Cassia and other genera from Israel, Australia, USA, Russia, Southern Rhodesia, Chile, Peru and Sudan have been tried in Thar Desert. *Acacia tortilis* has proved to be the most promising species for desert a forestation and the jojoba is another promising species of economic value found suitable for planting in these areas.

The Rajasthan Canal (Indira Gandhi Canal) system is the major irrigation scheme of the Thar Desert and is conceived to reclaim it and also to check spreading of the desert to fertile areas.

Due to severe weather conditions, there are few highways in the Thar Desert shown here is a road in Tharparkar District of Sindh, Pakistan.

(a) Agriculture

The Thar is one of most heavily-populated desert areas in the world and the main occupations of people living here are agriculture and animal husbandry. Agriculture is not a dependable proposition in this area—after the rainy season, at least 33 per cent of crops fail. Animal husbandry, trees and grasses, intercropped with vegetables or fruit trees, is the most viable model for arid, drought-prone regions. The region faces frequent droughts. Overgrasing due to high animal populations, wind and water erosion, mining and other industries result in serious land degradation.

Bajra is the Main Kharif Crop in Thar.

The agricultural production is mainly from the Kharif crops. The Kharif crops are the crops that are grown in the summer season and are seeded in the months of June and July. These crops are harvested in the months of September and October and include bajra, pulses, jowar (*Sorghum vulgare*), maize (*zea mays*), sesame and groundnuts. In past few decades the development of canals, tube wells etchas changed crop pattern. Now the desert districts in Rajasthan have started producing Rabi crops like wheat, mustard, cumin seed etccash crops also.

Thar region of Rajasthan is the main opium producer and consumer area. There are mainly two crop seasons. The water for irrigation comes from wells and tanks. The Indira Gandhi Canal irrigates northwestern Rajasthan.

Mustard Fields in a Village of Shri Ganganagar District (Rajasthan, India).

The Government of India has started a centrally sponsored scheme under the title of Desert Development Programme based on watershed management with the objective to check spreading of desert and improve the living condition of people in desert.

(b) Livestock

In the last 15–20 years, the Rajasthan desert has seen many changes, including a manifold increase of both the human and animal population.

Camel Ride in the Thar Desert near Jaisalmer, Rajasthan, India.

Animal husbandry has become popular due to the difficult farming conditions. At present, there are ten times more animals per person in Rajasthan than the national average, and overgrasing is also a factor affecting climatic and drought conditions.

Cows in Thar Desert.

A large number of farmers in Thar Desert depend on animal husbandry for their livelihood. Cow, buffalo, sheep, goats, camel, and ox consist of major cattle population. Barmer district has the highest cattle population out of which sheep and goats are in majority. Some of the best breeds of bullocks such as Kankrej (Sanchori) and Nagauri are from desert region.

Thar region of Rajasthan is the biggest wool-producing area in India. Chokla, Marwari, Jaisalmeri, Magra, Malpuri, Sonadi, Nali and Pungal breeds of sheep are found in the region. Of the total wool production in India, 40-50 per cent comes from Rajasthan. The sheep-wool from Rajasthan is considered best for carpet making industry in the world. The wool of Chokla breed of sheep is considered of superior quality. The breeding centers have been developed for Karakul and Merino sheep at Suratgarh, Jaitsar and Bikaner. Some important mills for making Woolen thread established in desert area are—Jodhpur Woolen Mill, Jodhpur; Rajasthan Woolen Mill, Bikaner and India Woolen Mill, Bikaner. Bikaner is the biggest *mandi* of wool in Asia. The live stock depends for grasing on common lands in villages. During famine years in the desert the nomadic rebari people move with large herds of sheep and camel to the forested areas of south Rajasthan or nearby states like Madhya Pradesh for grasing the cattle.

The importance of animal husbandry can be understood from the organisation of large number of cattle fairs in the region. Cattle fairs are normally named after the folk-deities. Some of major cattle fairs held are Ramdevji cattle fair at Manasar in Nagaur district, Tejaji cattle fair at Parbatsar in Nagaur district, Baldeo cattle fair at Merta city in Nagaur district, Mallinath cattle fair at Tilwara in Barmer district. Live stock is very important to the Thar Desert people.

(c) Agro-forestry

Prosopis cineraria (locally called Khejari) are a very useful and also commercially very profitable tree in the Desert. Khejari is frost-resistant, drought resistant and can withstand wild temperature extremes, ranging from 104-114°F in the summer to less than 50°F in the winter. It requires minimum rainfall. Khejari is the preferred plant species for livestock grasing in the area, and it provides shelter also to the grasing animals, people, birds with its shade.

Lopping of Khejri tree for fodder and fuel in Harsawa Village.

Prosopis cineraria (Khejri is the local name) are much valued as a fodder tree. The trees are heavily lopped particularly during winter months when no other green fodder is available in the dry tracts. The forage yield per tree varies a great deal. On an average, the yield of green forage from a full grown tree is expected to be about 60 kg with complete lopping having only the central leading shoot, 30 kg when the lower two third crown is lopped and 20 kg when the lower one third crown is lopped. The leaves are of high nutritive value. Feeding of the leaves during winter when no other green fodder is generally available in rain-fed areas is thus profitable. The pods have a sweetish pulp and are also used as fodder for livestock. Prosopis *cineraria* is readily eaten by camels, cattle, sheep and goats, constituting a major feed requirement of desert livestock. Locally it is called *Loong. Pods* are locally called *sangar* or *sangri. The* dried pods locally called *Kho-Kha* are eaten. Dried pods also form rich animal feed, which is liked by all livestock. Green pods also form rich animal feed, which is liked by drying the young boiled pods. They are also used as famine food and known even to prehistoric man. Prosopis *cineraria* wood is reported to contain high calorific value and provide high quality fuel wood. The lopped branches are good as fencing material. Its roots also encourage *nitrogen* fixation, which produces higher crop yields.

It should be understood that Forestry has an important part to play in the amelioration of the conditions in semi-arid and arid lands. If properly planned forestry can make an important contribution to the general welfare of the people living in desert areas. The living standard of the people in the desert is low. They can not afford other fuels like gas, kerosene etc. Fire wood is their main fuel; of the total consumption of wood about 75 per cent is firewood. The forest cover in desert is low. Rajasthan has a forest area of 31150 km. which is about nine per cent of the geographical area. The forest area is mainly in southern districts of Rajasthan like Udaipur and Chittorgarh. The minimum forest area is in Churu district only 80 km. Thus the forest is insufficient to fulfill the needs of firewood and grasing in desert districts. This diverts the much needed cattledung from the field to the hearth. This in turn results into the decrease in agricultural production. Agro-forestry model is best suited to the people of desert. Some Institutes have done good work in Agro-forestry.

The scientists of the Central Arid Zone Research Institute (CAZRI), have successfully developed improved varieties of traditional and non-traditional crops/fruits, such as Ber trees (like plums) that produce much larger fruits than before (lemon-size) and can thrive with minimal rainfall. These trees have become a profitable option for farmers.

Arid Forest Research Institute at Jodhpur is another national level institute in the region. It is one of the institutes of the Indian Council of

Forestry Research and Education (ICFRE) working under the Ministry of Environment and Forests, Govt. of India. The Objective of the Institute is to carry out scientific research in forestry in order to provide technologies to increase the vegetative cover and to conserve the biodiversity in the hot arid and semi arid region of Rajasthan, Gujarat and Dadar and Nagar Haveli union territory.

The most important tree species in terms of providing a livelihood in Thar Desert communities is *Prosopis cineraria* which provide wood for house-building, posts scantlings, doors and windows, and for well construction water pipes, upright posts of Persian wheels, agricultural implements and shafts, spokes, fellows and yoke of carts. It can also be used for small turning work and tool-handles. Container manufacturing is another important wood-based industry, which depends heavily on desert-grown trees.

Tecomella Undulata **Tree in the Village of Harsawa.**

Tecomella undulata seen above, locally known as Rohida, is found in Thar Desert regions of northwest and western India. It is another important medium sized tree of great use in Agro-forestry. It produces quality timber and is the main source of timber amongst the indigenous tree species of desert regions. The trade name of the tree species is Desert teak or Marwar teak. Its wood is strong, tough and durable. It takes a fine finish. Heartwood contains quinoid. The wood is excellent for firewood and charcoal. Cattle and goats eat leaves of the tree. Camels, goats and sheep consume flowers and pods.

Tecomella undulata plays an important role in the ecology of the Desert. It acts as a soil-binding tree by spreading a network of lateral roots on the top surface of the soil. It also acts as a windbreak and helps in stabilising shifting sand dunes. It is considered as the home of birds and provides shelter for other desert wildlife. Shade of tree crown is shelter for the cattle, goats and sheep during summer days. Tecomella *undulata* has medicinal properties as well. The bark obtained from the stem is used as a remedy for syphilis. It is also used in curing urinary disorders, enlargement of spleen, gonorrhea, leucoderma and liver diseases. Seeds are used against abscess.

4. Ecotourism

Desert safaris on camels have become increasingly popular around Jaisalmer. Domestic and international tourists frequent the desert seeking adventure on camels for anything from a day to several days. This ecotourism industry ranges from cheaper backpacker treks to plush Arabian night style campsites replete with banquets and cultural performances. During the treks tourists are able to view the fragile and beautiful ecosystem of the Thar desert. This form of tourism provides income to many operators and camel owners in Jaisalmer as well as employment for many camel trekers in the desert villages nearby.

(a) Industry

Rajasthan is pre-eminent in quarrying and mining in India. The Taj Mahal was built with white marble mined from Makrana in Nagaur district. The state is the second largest source of cement in India. It has rich salt deposits at Sambhar. Jodhpur sandstone is mostly used in monuments, important buildings, residential buildings, and such. This stone is termed "chittar patthar". Jodhpur has also got mines of red stone locally known as *ghatu patthar* used in construction. Sand stone is found in Jodhpur and Naguar districts. Jalore is biggest centre of granite processing units.

Lignite coal deposits are there at places Giral, Kapuradi, Jalipa, Bhadka in Barmer district; Plana, Gudha, Bithnok, Barsinghpur, Mandla Charan, Raneri Hadla in Bikaner district and Kasnau, Merta, Lunsar, etc., in Nagaur district. Lignite based Thermal power plant has been established at Giral in Barmer district. Jindal group is working on 1080 Megawatt power project in private sector at village Bhadaresh in Barmer district. "Neweli Lignite Barsinghpur Project" is under progress to establish two thermal power units of capacity 125 megawatts each at Barsinghpur in Bikaner district. Reliance Energy is working on establishing power generation through underground gasification technique in Barmer district with an outlay of about 3000 crore rupees.

There is large storage of good quality petroleum in Jaisalmer and Barmer districts. The main places with deposits of petroleum are Baghewal, Kalrewal, and Tawariwal in Jaisalmer district and Gudha Malani area in Barmer district.

Barmer district has started petroleum production on commercial scale. Barmer district is in the news due to its large oil basin. The British exploration company Cairn Energy is going to start the production soon in the year 2009 on large scale. Mangala, Bhagyam and Aishwariya are the major oil fields in the district. This is India's biggest oil discovery in 22 years. This promises to transform the local economy, which has long suffered from the harshness of the desert.

The Government of India initiated departmental exploration for oil in 1955-56 in the Jaisalmer area; Oil India Limited discovered natural gas in 1988 in the Jaisalmer basin. Also known for their fine leather messenger bags made from wild camels native to the area.

The Thar Desert seems an ideal place for generation of electricity from wind power. According to an estimate Rajasthan state has got a potential of 5500 Megawatt of wind power generation. As such it is in the priority of the State govt. Rajasthan State Power Corporation has established its first wind power based power plant at Amarsagar in Jaisalmer district. Some leading companies in the field are working on establishing wind mills in Barmer, Jaisalmer and Bikaner districts. Solar energy also has a great potential in this region as most of the days during a year are cloud free. Solar energy based plant has been established at Bhaleri in Churu district to convert hard water into drinking water.

(b) Salt Water Lakes

There are a number of salt water lakes in Thar Desert. These are Sambhar, Pachpadra, Tal Chhapar, Falaudi and Lunkaransar where Sodium chloride salt is produced from salt water. The Didwana Lake produces Sodium Sulphate salt. Ancient Archaeological evidences of habitations have been recovered from Sambhar and Didwana lakes which shows their antiquity and historical importance.

(c) People

Huts in the Thar Desert.

Young Muslim Woman in the Desert.

The Great Derawar Fort located within Bahawalpur, Pakistan.

A Girl from the Gadia Lohars Nomadic Tribe of Marwar, Cooking her Food.

The Thar Desert is mainly inhabited by Hindus, Muslims, and Sikhs. The portion in Pakistan is inhabited by primarily by Sindhis and Kolhis. A colourful culture rich in tradition prevails in the desert. The people have a great passion for folk music and folk poetry.

About 40 per cent of the total population of Rajasthan state lives in the Thar Desert.

The main occupation of the people in desert is agriculture and animal husbandry. In past years there has been a tremendous increase in human population as well as animal population. This has led to improper control of grasing and extensive cultivation resulting into the deterioration of vegetation resources. The increase of human and livestock population in the desert has led to deterioration in the ecosystem resulting in degradation of soil fertility. The living standard of the people in the desert is low. The Thar Desert is the most densely populated desert in the world, with a population density of 83 people per km^2 vs. seven in other deserts.

Jodhpur, the largest city in the region, lies in the scrub forest zone. Bikaner and Jaisalmer are located in the desert proper.

A large irrigation and power project has reclaimed areas of the northern and western desert for agriculture. The small population is mostly pastoral, and hide and wool industries are prominent.

In Pakistan part of Thar also has a rich multifaceted culture, heritage, traditions, folk tales, dances and music due to its inhabitants who belong to different religions, sects and castes.

(d) Water and Housing in the Desert

Water scarcity plays an important role in shaping life in all parts of Thar. Natural (tobas) or man-made (johads), both types of small, intermittent

Johads are Common Water Sources.

ponds, are often the only source of water for animals and humans in the true desert areas. The lack of a constant water supply causes much of the local population to live as nomads. Most human settlements are found near the two seasonal streams of the Karon-Jhar hills. Potable groundwater is also rare in the Thar Desert. Supplies are often sour due to dissolved minerals, and are only available deep underground. Wells that successfully bear sweet water attract nearby settlement, but are difficult to dig, possibly claiming the lives of the well-diggers.

Tanks for Drinking Water.

According to 1980 housing census in Pakistan, there were 241,326 housing units of one or two very small rooms. The degree of crowding was six persons per housing unit and three persons per room. For most of the housing units (approximately 76 per cent), the main construction material of outer walls is unbaked bricks whereas wood is used in 10 per cent and baked bricks or stones with mud bonding in eight per cent housing units. A large number of families still live in jhugis or huts which are housing units formed with straws and thin wood-sticks. The wind storm proves these jhugis unsustainable all the times. But the poverty leaves no other option to these jhugiwalas (people living in Jhugis).

The river Luni is the only natural water source that drains inside a lake in the desert. It originates in the Pushkar valley of the Aravalli Range, near Ajmer and ends in the marshy lands of Rann of Kutch in Gujarat, after travelling a distance of 530 km. The Luni flows through part of Ajmer, Barmer, Jalor, Jodhpur, Nagaur, Pali, and Sirohi districts and Mithavirana Vav Radhanpur region of Banaskantha, North Gujarat. Its major tributaries are the Sukri, Mithri, Bandi, Khari, Jawai, Guhiya and Sagi from the left, and the Jojari river from the right.

The Ghaggar is another intermittent river in India, flowing during the monsoon rains. It originates in the Shivalik Hills of Himachal Pradesh and flows through Punjab and Haryana to Rajasthan; just southwest of Sirsa, Haryana and by the side of *talwara jheel* in Rajasthan, this seasonal river feeds two irrigation canals that extend into Rajasthan. It terminates in Hanumangarh district. The Rajasthan Canal system is the major irrigation scheme of the Thar Desert and is conceived to reclaim it and also to check spreading of the desert to fertile areas. It is world's largest irrigation which is being extended in an attempt to make the desert arable. It runs south-southwest in Punjab and Haryana but mainly in Rajasthan for a total of 650 kilometers and ends near Jaisalmer, in Rajasthan. After the construction of the Indira Gandhi Canal, irrigation facilities were available over an area of 6770 km^2 in Jaisalmer district and 37 km^2 in Barmer district. Irrigation had already been provided in an area of 3670 km^2 in Jaisalmer district. The canal has transformed the barren deserts of this district into rich and lush fields. Crops of mustard, cotton, and wheat now flourish in this semi-arid western region replacing the sand there previously.

Besides providing water for agriculture, the canal will supply drinking water to hundreds of people in far-flung areas. As the second stage of work on the canal progresses rapidly, there is hope that it will enhance the living standards of the people of the state.

(e) Desert for Recreation

Thar Desert provides the recreational value in terms of desert festivals organised every year. Rajasthan desert festivals are celebrated with great

Desert Tribes Near Jaisalmer, India.

zest and zeal. This festival is held once a year during winters. Dressed in brilliantly hued costumes, the people of the desert dance and sing haunting ballads of valor, romance and tragedy. The fair has snake charmers, puppeteers, acrobats and folk performers. Camels, of course, play a stellar role in this festival, where the rich and colorful folk culture of Rajasthan can be seen.

Camels are an integral part of the desert life and the camel events during the Desert Festival confirm this fact. Special efforts go into dressing the animal for entering the spectacular competition of the best-dressed camel. Other interesting competitions on the fringes are the moustache and turban tying competitions, which not only demonstrate a glorious tradition but also inspire its preservation. Both the turban and the moustache have been centuries old symbols of honor in Rajasthan.

Evenings are meant for the main shows of music and dance. Continuing till late into the night, the number of spectators swells up each night and the grand finale, on the full moon night, takes place by silvery sand dunes.

(III) Andaman and Nicobar Islands

A place of Natural Beauty—A must for the Tourists to visit.

It is a place where the Modern and primitive people are there side by side. Among the places to go are Havelock Island, Mount Harriot, Cellular Jail, Barren Island, etc., Andaman and Nicobar Islands are a group of islands in the Bay of Bengal and a Union Territory of India.

Vegetation in the Island

The territory of Andaman and Nicobar Islands is 150 km (93 mi) north of Aceh in Indonesia and separated from Thailand and Burma by the Andaman

Sea. It comprises two island groups, the Andaman Islands and the Nicobar Islands, separated by the 10°N parallel, with the Andamans to the north of this latitude, and the Nicobars to the south. The Andaman Sea lies to the east and the Bay of Bengal to the west.

Tourist Lodge.

The territory's capital is the Andamanese town of Port Blair. The territory's population as per the most recent (2011) Census of India was 379,944. The total land area of the territory is approximately 6,496 km^2 (2,508 sq mi).

First Inhabitants

The Andaman and Nicobar islands have been inhabited for several thousand years, at the very least. The earliest archaeological evidence yet documented goes back some 2,200 years; however, the indications from genetic, cultural and isolation studies the Middle Paleolithic. In the Andaman Islands, the various Andamanese people maintained their separated existence through the vast majority of this time, diversifying into distinct linguistic, cultural and territorial groups. By the 1850s when they first came into sustained contact by outside groups, the indigenous people of the Andamans were:

- the Great Andamanese, who collectively represented at least 10 distinct sub-groups and languages;
- the Jarawa;
- the Jangil (or *Rutland Jarawa*);
- the Onge;
- the Sentinelese (most isolated of all the groups).

In total, these people numbered somewhere around 7,000 at the time of these first encounters. As the numbers of settlers from the mainland increased (at first mostly prisoners and involuntary indentured labourers, later purposely recruited farmers), these indigenous people lost territory and numbers in the face of punitive expeditions by British troops, land encroachment and the effects of various epidemic diseases. The Jangil and most of the Great Andamanese groups soon became extinct; presently there remain only approximately 400–450 indigenous Andamanese, the Jarawa and Sentinelese in particular maintaining a steadfast independence and refusing most attempts at contact.

The indigenous people of the Nicobars (unrelated to the Andamanese) have a similarly isolated and lengthy association with the islands. There are two main groups:

- the Nicobarese, or *Nicobari*, living throughout many of the islands;
- the Shompen, restricted to the hinterland of Great Nicobar.

Pre-colonial Era

[Rajendra Chola (1014 to 1042 CE)], one of the Tamil Chola dynasty kings, occupied Andaman and Nicobar Islands to use it as a strategic naval base to launch a naval expedition against Sriwijaya Empire (a Hindu-Malay

empire based on the island of Sumatra, Indonesia). The cholas called the 'Nicobar' island as 'Nakkavaram' which is inscribed on the Tanjore inscription of 1050 CE. Nakkavaram in Tamil means "naked man" or "land of the naked" which should have been evolved to the modern name "Nicobar" Marco Polo (12-13th Century CE) also referred this island as 'Necuverann'.

The Aerial View of Andaman and Nicobar Islands

The name of the island has always been 'Andaman' and might represent Handuman, the Malay form of Hanuman.

The islands provided a temporary maritime base for ships of the Marathas in the 17th century. The legendary admiral Kanhoji Angre established naval supremacy with a base in the islands and is credited with attaching those islands to India.

Danish Occupation of the Nicobar Islands

The history of organised European colonisation on the islands began when the Danish settlers of the Danish East India Company arrived on Nicobar Islands on 12 December 1755. On January 1, 1756, the Nicobar Islands were made a Danish colony and renamed 'New Denmark'. In December 1756, the Nicobar Islands was renamed 'Frederiksøerne' (Frederiks Islands). During 1754–1756 they were administrated under the name of Frederiksøerne from Tranquebar (in continental Danish India); missionaries from the Moravian Church Brethren's settlement in Tranquebar attempted a settlement on Nancowry and died in great numbers from disease; the islands were repeatedly abandoned due to outbreaks of malaria between 14 April 1759–19. August 1768, from 1787–1807/05, 1814–1831, 1830–1834 and finally from 1848 gradually for good.

From 1 June, 1778 to 1784, they were occupied by Austria, and renamed 'Theresia Islands', attempting to establish a colony on the islands on the mistaken assumption that Denmark had abandoned its claims to the islands. Danish involvement ended formally on 16 October, 1868 when the Danish rights to the Nicobar Islands were sold to Britain which made them part of British India by 1869 when the British took possession.

British Colonial Period

After an initial attempt to set up a colony in the islands by the British, it was abandoned after only a few years (1789–1796). A second attempt from 1858 proved to be more permanent. The primary purpose was to set up a penal colony for dissenters and independence fighters from the Indian subcontinent.

The British used the islands as an isolated prison for members of the Indian independence movement. The mode of imprisonment was campaign 1941-1942.

Indian Control

The islands were only nominally put under the authority of the Arzi Hukumate Azad Hind of Netaji Subhash Chandra Bose, and the Islands were practically under Japanese control, who committed tremendous atrocities there.

Netaji visited the islands during the war, and renamed them as "Shaheed-dweep" (Martyr Island) and "Swaraj-dweep" (Self-rule Island). General Loganathan, of the Indian National Army, INA (set up by Netaji Subhas Chandra Bose) was made the Governor of the Andaman and Nicobar Islands. On 22 February, 1944 he along with four INA officers—Major Mansoor Ali Alvi, Sub. Lt. Md. Iqbal, Lt. Suba Singh and stenographer Srinivasan—arrived at Lambaline Airport in Port Blair. On 21 March, 1944 the Headquarters of the Civil Administration was established near the Gurudwara at Aberdeen Bazaar. On 2 October, 1944, Col. Loganathan handed over the charge to Maj. Alvi and left Port Blair, never to return. The islands were reoccupied by British and Indian troops of the 116th Indian Infantry Brigade on 7 October, 1945, to whom the remaining Japanese garrison surrendered.

At the independence of both India (1947) and Burma (1948), the departing British announced their intention to resettle all Anglo-Indians and Anglo-

Burmese on the islands to form their own nation, although this never materialised. It became part of the Indian union in 1956. It was declared a union territory on 1956.

Recent History

On 26 December, 2004 the coasts of the Andaman and Nicobar Islands were devastated by a 10 m (33 ft) high TSUNAMI following the 2004 Indian Ocean earthquake. At least 5,930 people were believed to have been killed on the Nicobar and Andaman Islands during the disaster. The worst affected Nicobar islands were Katchal and Indira Point, the latter the southern most point of India, which was submerged by the ocean.

While newer settlers of the islands suffered the greatest casualties from the tsunami, most of the aboriginal people survived because oral traditions passed down from generations ago warned them to evacuate from large waves that follow large earthquakes.

Geography

There are 572 islands in the territory having an area of 8,249 km^2 (3,185 sq mi). Of these, only 38 are permanently inhabited. The islands extends from 6° to 14° North latitudes and from 92° to 94° East longitudes. The Andamans are separated from the Nicobar group by a channel (the Ten Degree Channel) some 150 km (93 mi) wide. The highest point is located in North Andaman Island (Saddle Peak at 732 m (2,402 ft). The Andaman group has 325 islands which cover an area of 6,408 km^2 (2,474 sq mi) while the Nicobar group has only 24 islands with an area of 1,841 km^2 (711 sq mi).

The northernmost point of the Andaman and Nicobars group is 901 km (560 mi) away from the mouth of the Hooghly River and 190 km (120 mi) from Burma. The southernmost island, Great Nicobar's southernmost point, called *Indira Point*, lies only 150 km (93 mi) from Sumatra in Indonesia. The capital of the union territory, Port Blair, is located 1,255 km (780 mi) from Kolkata, 1,200 km (750 mi) from Visakhapatnam and 1,190 km (740 mi) from Chennai.

Andaman and Nicobar Islands are blessed with a unique tropical rainforest canopy, made of a mixed flora with elements from Indian, Myanmarese, Malaysian and endemic floral strains. So far, about 2,200 varieties of plants have been recorded, out of which 200 are endemic and 1,300 do not occur in mainland India.

The South Andaman forests have a profuse growth of epiphytic vegetation, mostly ferns and orchids. The Middle Andamans harbours mostly moist deciduous forests. North Andamans is characterised by the wet evergreen type, with plenty of woody climbers. The North Nicobar Islands (including Car Nicobar and Battimalv) are marked by the complete absence of evergreen forests, while such forests form the dominant vegetation in the central and southern islands of the Nicobar group. Grasslands occur only in the Nicobars, and while deciduous forests are common in the Andamans, they are almost absent in the Nicobars. The present forest coverage is claimed to be 86.2 per cent of the total land area.

This a typical forest coverage is made up of twelve types, namely:

1. Giant evergreen forest.
2. Andamans tropical evergreen forest.
3. Southern hilltop tropical evergreen forest.
4. Cane brakes.
5. Wet bamboo brakes.
6. Andamans semi-evergreen forest.
7. Andamans moist deciduous forest.
8. Andamans secondary moist deciduous forest.
9. Littoral forest.
10. Mangrove forest.
11. Brackish water mixed forest.
12. Submontane hill valley swamp forest.

Timber

Andaman Forest abounds in a plethora of timber species numbering 200 or more, out of which about 30 varieties are considered to be commercial. Major commercial timber species are Gurjan (*Dipterocarpus* spp.) and Padauk (*Pterocarpus dalbergioides*). The following ornamental woods are noted for their pronounced grain formation:

1. Marble Wood (*Diospyros marmorata*)
2. Padauk (*Pterocarpus dalbergioides*)
3. Silver Grey (a special formation of wood in white chuglam)
4. Chooi (*Sageraea elliptical*)
5. Kokko (*Albizzia lebbeck*)

Padauk being sturdier than teak is widely used for furniture making.

There are burr wood and buttress formations in Andaman Padauk. The largest piece of buttress known from Andaman was a dining table of 13 × 7 ft (4.0 × 2.1 m). The largest piece of burr was again a dining table to seat eight persons at a time.

The holy Rudraksha (*Elaeocarps sphaericus*) and aromatic Dhoop/Resin trees also are found here.

Fauna

These islands because some like turbo, trochus and nautilus etc., are used as novelties supporting many cottage industries producing a wide range of decorative items and ornaments. Shells such as giant clam, green mussel and oyster support edible shell fishery, a few like scallop, clam, and cockle are burnt in kilns to produce edible lime.

Demographics

The major languages spoken in the Andamans in numerical order are Bengali (32.6 per cent), Hindi (25.95 per cent), Tamil including Sri Lankan Tamils (17.84 per cent), Nicobarese and Telugu (18.93 per cent). Other languages include Malayalam and English. More than 2,000 people belonging to the Karen tribe live in the Mayabunder tehsil of North Andaman district, almost all of whom are Christians. Despite their tribal origins, the Karen of Andamans has OBC status in the Andamans. The majority of Andamans are Hindus, with significant Christian, Muslim and Sikh minorities.

Foreigners wishing to visit the Andaman and Nicobar Islands require a Restricted Area Permit; permits are now available on arrival at Port Blair's Veer Savarkar Airport.

Administration

In 1874, the British had placed the Andaman and Nicobar Islands in one administrative territory headed by a Chief Commissioner as its judicial administrator. On 1 August 1974, the Nicobar Islands were hived off into another revenue district with district headquarters at Car Nicobar under a Deputy Commissioner. In 1982, the post of Lieutenant Governor was created who replaced the Chief Commissioner as the head of administration. Subsequently a "Pradesh council" with representatives of the people was constituted to advise the Lieutenant Governor.

Administrative Divisions

Andaman and Nicobar Islands are divided into three districts. Each of the districts is again sub-divided into Sub-Divisions and taluks.

North and Middle Andaman District Headquarters: Mayabunder

- Diglipur Sub-Division
    - Diglipur Taluk
- Mayabunder Sub-Division
    - Mayabunder Taluk
    - Rangat taluk

South Andaman District Headquarters: Port Blair

- Port Blair Sub-Division
  - Port Blair Taluk
  - Ferrargunj Taluk
- Little Andaman Sub-Division
  - Little Andaman Taluka (Hut Bay)

Nicobar District Headquarters: Car Nicobar

- Car Nicobar Sub-Division
  - Car Nicobar Taluk
- Nancowrie Sub-Division
  - Nancowrie Taluk
  - Kamorta Taluk
  - Teressa Taluk
  - Katchal Taluk
- Great Nicobar Sub-Division
  - Great Nicobar Taluk (Campbell Bay)
  - Little Nicobar Taluk

Economy

Little Andaman Island seen by Spot satellite.

Ross Island a Couple of days before the Tsunami of December 2004.

Agriculture

A total of 48,675 hectares (120,280 acres) of land is used for agriculture purposes. Paddy, the main food crop, is mostly cultivated in Andaman group of islands, whereas coconut and arecanut are the cash crops of Nicobar group of islands. Field crops, namely pulses, oilseeds and vegetables are grown, followed by paddy during Rabi season. Different kinds of fruits such as mango, sapota, orange, banana, papaya, pineapple and root crops are grown on hilly land owned by farmers. Spices such as pepper, clove, nutmeg, and cinnamon are grown under a multi-tier cropping system. Rubber, red oil, palm and cashew are grown on a limited scale in these islands.

Industry

There are 1,374 registered small-scale, village and handicrafts units. Two units are export-oriented in the line of fish processing activity. Apart from this, there is shell and wood based handicraft units. There are also four medium sized industrial units. SSI units are engaged in the production of polythene bags, PVC conduit pipes and fittings, paints and varnished, fibre glass and mini flour mills, soft drinks and beverages etc. Small scale and handicraft units are also engaged in shell crafts, bakery products, rice milling, furniture making, etc. The Andaman and Nicobar Islands Integrated Development Corporation has spread its wings in the field of tourism, fisheries, industries and industrial financing and functions as authorised agents for Alliance Air/Jet Airways.

Tribals Exploited by Tourists

In 2012, the country was shocked by the news of tourists and locals exploiting the tribals in Andaman for food. The videos captured in contravention of Supreme Court of India orders of 2002 show Jarawa girls dancing topless. It should be mentioned that the traditional costume of Jarawa women are straw skirts without tops. In that video, nobody tried for forced removal of clothes.

A Picture of Tribals (*Source:* Wikipedia).

(VI) Kashmir-A Heaven on Earth

Visiting Kashmir is always a Tourist's Delight, Breathtaking natural beauty, Panoramic views of the valley, A wonderful view of the Mount Everest, A Sikara Ride in Dal lake, etc., are some of the enjoyable trips that the Tourists can enjoy. Other details are given below.

Panoramic View of Dal Lake, Srinagar City and Kashmir Valley.

Jammu and Kashmir is the northernmost state in India. In the seventeenth century the Mughal emperor Jahangir set his eyes on the valley of Kashmir. He said that if paradise is anywhere on the earth, it is here, while living in a houseboat on Dal Lake. "Gar firdaus, ruhe zamin ast, hamin asto, hamin asto, hamin ast." If there is ever a heaven on earth, its here, it's here, its here. In Jammu and Kashmir the most important tourist places are Kashmir, Srinagar, the Mughal Gardens, Gulmarg, Pahalgam, Jammu, and Ladakh. Some areas require a special permit for non-Indians to visit.

Regions

- Jammu—most will only stop here to change from train to bus en route to Kashmir, Jammu is the winter capital of state, it is famous for its temples.
- Kashmir Valley—some say it is Heaven on Earth, friendly people, beautiful gardens, vast lakes and pristine streams and stunning landscapes, it is all that but please see "Stay safe" below.
- Ladakh—truly amasing landscapes high up in the Himalayas, popular for trekking and with those on a search for the most serene place in the world.

Cities

- Jammu—the winter capital.
- Srinagar—the summer capital of the state, set around famous Dal Lake, with its floating houseboats.

- Gulmarg—decent skiing and the World's highest gondola.
- Katra—in the foothills of the Trikuta Mountains and home of the holy Mata Vaishno Devi shrine.
- Leh—the jumping off point for treks and adventures around Ladakh.
- Pahalgam—a calm and serene place offering multiple trekking routes. Starting point of Amarnath Yatra.
- Patnitop—a small hill station in Jammu.
- Udhampur.
- Zab Baihk.

Overview

Before militancy intensified in 1989, tourism formed an important part of the Kashmiri economy. The tourism economy in the Kashmir valley was worst hit. However, the holy shrines of Jammu and the Buddhist monasteries of Ladakh continue to remain popular pilgrimage and tourism destinations. Every year, thousands of Hindu pilgrims visit holy shrines of Vaishno Devi and Amarnath which has had significant impact on the state's economy.[1] The Vaishno Devi yatra alone contributes Rs. 475 crore to the local economy annually

Tourism in the Kashmir valley has rebounded in recent years and in 2009, the state became one of the top tourist destinations of India. Gulmarg, one of the most popular ski resort destinations in India, is also home to the world's highest green golf course. However with the decrease in violence in the state has boosted the states economy specifically tourism. It was reported that 7.36 lakh tourists visited Kashmir in 2010 including 23,000 foreigners. In 2011, the number of tourist arrivals in Kashmir touched the mark of 10 lakh.

Language

The state's official language is Urdu. However, the main languages spoken are Kashmiri in the Kashmir Valley, Ladakhi in Ladakh and Dogri in Jammu. Most people can speak Hindi as a second language.

As elsewhere in India, English is fairly widely spoken among the educated classes and those involved in the tourist industry.

Entry

By Plane

Flights operate to Jammu, Srinagar and Leh. Try Indian Airlines, Jet Airways, Kingfisher, Indigo Airlines and Spice Jet.

By Train

The last stop on the railway line north is Udhampur, where you can catch onward buses and hire SUVs/MUVs (Tata Sumo/Toyota Innova/ Mahindra Scorpio). However it is better to get down in Jammu and catch a taxi from there as these are more readily available.

The Kashmir Railway is a railway line being built in India to connect the state of Jammu and Kashmir with the rest of the country. The Project officially coded USBRL (Udhampur Srinagar Baramulla Railway Link) starts from the city of Udhampur, 55 kilometres (34 mi) north of Jammu, and travels for 290 kilometres (180 mi) to the city of Baramulla on the northwestern edge of the Kashmir Valley. The route crosses major earthquake zones, and is subjected to extreme temperatures of cold and heat, as well as inhospitable terrain, making it an extremely challenging engineering project.

By Bus

There are two ways to get in by land—via Jammu and up to Srinagar or via Manali in Himachal Pradesh and up to Leh.

Transportation Within

- Buses are operated by J&K SRTC to most points around the state. They offer package tour to Gulmarg, Shonmarg, Yusmarg, Ular lake, City tour, etc. There is Tourist information center, where one get the tickets plus info.
- 4wd jeeps are quicker, a little more expensive and reach more locations, Private hire jeeps are also available.

Notable visitor attractions.

Gulmarg

Gulmarg is well known for its amasing natural beauty and it is counted as one of the unique tourist destinations in the world. Gulmarg is surrounded by dense forest. This place is famous for its golf hikes and beautiful highland golf course. The natural beauty accompanied with clean fresh air and a beautiful environment highlights Gulmarg as a major tourist destination.

Sonamarg

The way to reach Sonamarg or the Meadow of the gold is from the Sindh valley. This valley also shows more amasing facet in Kashmir. Sonamarg is located at an altitude of around 2730 meters from the sea level; it has Snow Mountains as its backdrop against the sky.

Raghunath Temple

Raghunath Temple is dedicated to the Hindu Lord Shri Rama. All the inner walls of this temple are covered with gold, on three sides. Galleries of this temples are covered with 'Saligrams'. The other surrounding temples are related to other gods from the Ramayana. This temple is located in the centre or we can say in the heart of Jammu.

Bahu Fort

Bahu fort was modified and improved by Dogra Rulers of jammu but first built it was built by the Raja Bahulochan. This fort is located at a distance of around five km. from the main city and perhaps is the oldest edifice in the Jammu. This fort is facing the Tawi River. There is a temple of goddess kali in the fort.

Mubarak Mandi Palace

Mubarak Palace was built with the touch of three different styles, Rajasthani, Mughal and Gothic. Most famous part of this Palace is the Sheesh Mahal segment. There is a Dogra Art Museum, which is a treasure house of miniature paintings from various hill schools.

Peer Baba

This is of the holy places for Muslim saints. Here, people from all the religions comes in large number to pray, on Thursday.

Chadar Trek

Zanskar is located at a very high altitude in Jammu and Kashmir. It is one of the best trekking destinations around the world. In Winter, Zanskar river freezes up, and get converted into an amasing adventures trek called *Chadar-The Frozen River Trek.*

Khillonmarg is another beautiful senic beauty and a favourate tourist destination the famour liddar valley is prominent feature.

The traditional name for the Zanskar Trek is Chadar Trek as the river becomes a snow sheet during winters due to heavy snowfall. It boasts of some of the lowest temperatures making it a challenging trek for the adventurers. The most isolated and inaccessible for nearly eight months in a year due to heavy snowfall resulting in closure of all the access passes; Zanskar has the distinction of being the least interfered with microcosms of Ladakh, and thus one of the last few surviving cultural satellites of Tibet. This geographical isolation together with the esoteric nature of Buddhism practiced here has enabled its ten thousand inhabitants to preserve and perpetuate their cultural identity.

In Kashmir Valley

- Vernag Spring and Mughal Garden—A fresh water spring and a Mughal garden next to it, spring is chief source of Jhelum River.

Skiing is popular in Gulmarg, showing cable car in a snow clad mountain.

- Srinagar-Capital of Jammu and Kashmir, a popular hill station.
    - Dal lake-famous lake in Srinagar, with house boats called shikharas.
    - Manasbal Lake.
    - Shalimar Gardens—Mughal Garden.
    - Nishant Gardens—Mughal Garden.
    - Chashme Shahi—Mughal Garden.
    - Badamwari Garden.
    - Pari Mahal—old monument of Pari Mahal, one can have full view of Dal Lake.
    - Shankaracharya Temple—Ancient Temple of Lord Shiva.
    - Hari Parbat—Ancient Temple of Goddess Sharika Bhagwati and an old fort on this hill.
    - Kheer Bhawani Temple.
- Gulmarg—Popular hill station and skiing destination.
- Pahalgam—Hill station.
- Betaab Valley—A lush green valley 15 km from Pahalgam where the movie Betaab was shot.
- Sonmarg—Hill station.
- Yusmarg—Hill station.
- Aru—scenic valley.
- Amarnath temple—Pilgrimage site for Hindu devotees of Shiva.
- Eco-tourism places: Gurez, Dudhpathri, Bangus valley.

In Jammu

Patnitop: A view towards the mountains:

- Vaishno Devi—Famous shrine.
- Patnitop—Hill station.
- Bhaderwah—Hill station.
- Poonch.
- Sanasar.
- Eco-tourism places: Mantalai and Shivkhori.
- Punj old fort.
- Shahdra Sharif shrine.
- Bhimgarh Fort.
- Ramnagar Fort in Udhampur District.
- MANSAR LAKE-Mansar lake, with its length more than a mile and width half-a-mile, is a very attractive lake in the midst of lusting greeneries surrounded by forest-covered hills. It is considered as a very holy site known from mythological periods sharing the sanctity and legacy of Mansa Sarovar. It is a very popular base of tourists.

A temple for a snake god, Sheshnag, is located on the banks of lake. It is believed that it is auspicious for newly wed couples to seek blessings of Sheshnag by performing three parikarma around the lake. Holy dip in the Mansar Lake is assumed to be purifying the sins.

A temple of Durga and two other ancient temples Narasimha and Parvathi Shiva (Umapati Mahadev) are located in the close proximity of the Mansar Lake. Mansar Lake is an ideal spot for boating, amidst the lusting greeneries of Jammu. There is a wildlife sanctuary nearby.

Jammu

1. Head north-east on Jammu Flyover 600 m.
2. Sharp right to stay on Jammu Flyover Pass by Dogra Chowk (on the left in 1.0 km) 1.2 km.
3. Continue onto NH 44 Go through 1 round about 3.6 km.
4. At the roundabout, take the 1st exit to stay on NH 44 Pass by District Collector Secreteriat (on the left in 30.0 km) 31.2 km 5 Turn left onto Mansar Udhampur Road 21.4 km Mansar Lake KULDEEP RAJPUT.

In Ladakh

Tso Moriri in Ladakh

2

The Outer/Distant Environment Around India

(A) Our Planetary System–Our Universe and Our Galaxies

We need to know more about our outer Environment, the Planetary System, The Galaxies and of course about our *Earth*. Interestingly, Our Earth is the only Planet known so far where Life Exists. It took millions of years to have the proper kind of Environmental conditions to be available on our planet Earth to enable the life forms to thrive and survive. The uniqueness of mother Earth's relative position in our Galaxy possibly helped it to create proper kind of atmospheric and environmental conditions to have proper type of water with distinctive ionic balance to support life. It is also amasing that soil was enriched with all different nutrients such that our vegetables can grow in plenty and provide us with our foods. Our atmospheric air was provided with right kind of gases (oxygen, nitrogen, moisture etc.) that can help sustaining the various life forms.

In the following picture is shown the planetary system in relation to one another.

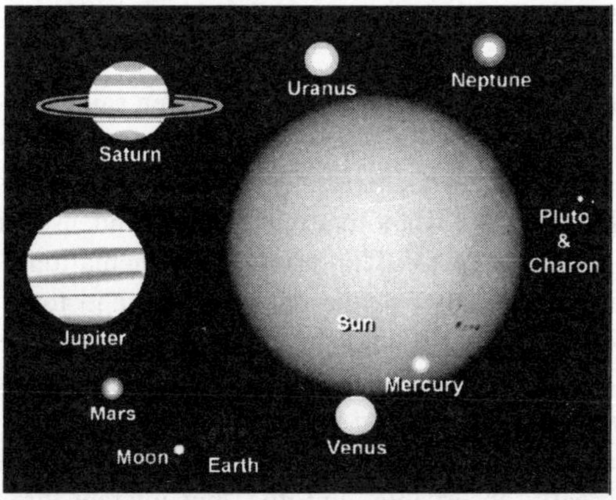

Our Planetary System.

It is only on earth the right kind of environmental conditions exist that could sustain the life processes, such as water, air and food. The seasonal variations of weather brings in the right kind of heat and cold and rainfall allowing to grow different types of foods round the year.

(B) Evolution of the Planet Earth

Before we start learning about Earth's Environment, we must know something about our Universe, Our Galaxies, Our Planets, The Atmosphere, how did the evolution of Earth happen, earth's surrounding Environment, the early living organisms and the evolution of first living Cell and of course of the Human beings. The original "Big Bang Theory" sought to explain the sudden appearance of everything from nothing, New Concept emerged regarding the Big Bang was that the entire universe was compacted into a tiny little ball, which exploded at some point of time into all space, time, matter and energy in an instant manner. The Big Bang theory is the prevailing cosmological model that explains the early development of the Universe. According to the Big Bang theory, the Universe was once in an extremely hot and dense state which expanded rapidly. This rapid expansion caused the young Universe to cool and then resulted in its present continuously expanding state.

(C) Our Universe and the Galaxies

Early in our Universe, Galaxy was formed. It took millions of years to undergo many different transformations, reactions and interactions, explosions, etc., for the Galaxy to take the shape it had. But those reactions and interactions still continue.

The study of Galaxy formation through the evolutionary process tells us that a heterogeneous universe was formed from a homogeneous beginning. Galaxy formation is hypothesised to occur, in the aftermath of the Big Bang. You may note that Clustering and merging is how galaxies gained in mass, shape and structures.

How did the first galaxies form? As have been said above, after the Big Bang, the Universe was homogeneous. There was almost no structure in the universe, and therefore no Galaxies. It is suggested that as the Universe cooled gradually, clumps of dark matter began to condense, and within them gas began to condense also. The primordial fluctuations gravitationally attracted gas and dark matter to the denser areas, and thus the seeds later became Galaxies. At the early stage the universe was composed of hydrogen, helium and dark matter. Soon after the first proto-galaxies formed, the hydrogen and helium gas within them began to condense and made the first stars. The majority of mass in our Galaxies is made up of Dark Matter, a substance which is not directly observable, and does not interact through any means except gravity.

According to the California Institute of Technology report, six stars formed the galaxies about 13.2 billion light years (light travel distance) away and was created when the universe was only 500 million years old. The discovery of a galaxy more than 13 billion years old was reported in 2011 which existed only 480 million years after the Big Bang.

Properties of Galaxies

Some observed features of Galaxy structure are described below:

Hubble Tuning Fork Galaxy structure. Spiral and the Galactic disks are quite thin, dense, and rotate very fast. The Milky Way disk is 100 times longer than it is thick. Some galaxies divide into blue-star forming Galaxies that are more like spiral types, and red-non-star forming galaxies that are more like elliptical galaxies. Many galaxies in the universe are gravitationally bound to other galaxies, that is to say they will never escape the pull of the other galaxy.

(D) Relative Placements of Our Planet Earth, Moon and the Planet Mars

Some scientists believe that our Earth was created from Mars on the right is our Earth; on the left is MARS as shown in the picture above. Some reports suggest that Mars may have atmospheric conditions which might

support Life. But it is not conclusive yet. The atmosphere on Mars consists of 95 per cent Carbon dioxide, three per cent Nitrogen and 1.6 per cent Argon and also contains traces of oxygen and water. The atmosphere here is quite dusty. It contains dust particles of the size about 1.5 μm in diameter which give the Martian sky a brownish or orange color when seen from the surface. It is thus evident that the mars atmosphere is not ready yet to support life.

The relative placements of Sun, Earth and Moon along with the orbits that the Earth and Moon rotates are shown in the above picture. In our planetary system, the relative placements of Sun, Moon and Earth at a given point of time determines the climatic changes on Earth. The Day and Night cycle and the season changes are also guided by that. Our Galaxy is full of Myth and Mystery, new surprises and excitements. There had been many Satellite expeditions by USA, USSR (now Russia), UK, France, Now India and China, even sending Men and animals in the space with newer and newer objectives each time such as:

1. To place satellites in a particular orbit to send information about weather conditions, transmit messages from one part of the world to another part, to facilitate telephone connections, to take picture of various part of the world in different seasons, to map the earth's surfaces, to follow the movements of fish from one place to another, to take picture of enemy locations etc.
2. Manned satellites were sent for various purposes, such as to know the effects of withstanding such artificial atmosphere on human body, how long one can stay in the space without damage to the body systems such that they can remain functional, to carry out various experiments to find answers to myriads of questions, to investigate whether there is any planet in the Universe that will support the life systems etc. Scientist's queries and questions have resulted in many information, which only raised more questions keeping the door open for more research seeking new information in order to increase our knowledge.

(E) Our Planet Earth where Life could Sustain Only

The Planet Earth is a unique one so far as its environment is concerned. It is the only planet known thus far where LIFE exists. It took millions of years for this planet to be created. Over the years, the optimum type of Environmental conditions evolved so that life can sustain. These are water to drink, air to breathe and food to eat. Man had done substantial improvements over the years utilising his brainpower, hard work and honest pursuit leading into new Discoveries and inventions. Life has improved a lot. However, for more comfort and easy life-styles man had increased its needs and side by side was driven by his own greeds, being driven to get more and much more. Thus, he has now been immersed into his own creation—an increasing order of life-threatening pollution problems. So much so that even the weather has started changing such that the very existence of our life is facing a great danger of extinction some day. But never mind, nothing is going to happen suddenly and all on a sudden. But we should be cautious and careful enough to ensure that we do not do anything that might hasten the process of our extinction.

Extinction of Species during Evolution

It may be remembered that several billion years passed by before the evolution of life forms on the surface of our planet. About four billion years ago, our ecosphere has been developing into different forms of life. All these forms are an integral part of mother nature. Quite a large number of different plant and animal species make up our Ecosystem stable. The elimination of even one species affects the whole and disturbs its balance—it has a knock-on effect on estimated 18 to 30 other species.

With the increase in population our demands have been constantly increasing and it constantly reduced the Biodiversity of our Ecosystem. At this moment, we are going through an extinction spasm, caused mainly by habitat degradation, environmental pollution, the introduction of non-native species and huge exploitation by man. In particular, human activity has destroyed areas that are species-rich, like the Tropical Rain Forests and Coral Reefs. If we continue with the present business-as-usual approach, half of the species of this planet could be extinct within next 50 years.

Since the year 1600, 83 known mammal species and 113 bird species have become extinct. In 2003 the *World Conservation Union's* Red List claimed that more than 12,000 species (out of 40,000 assessed) faced some extinction risk, including one bird in eight, 13 per cent of the world's flowering plants, and a quarter of all mammals. We must realise that every species which came into being today is a unique product of an unpredictable chain of events through history. Each event is linked with the one before. If events had taken even a slightly different turn hundreds of millions of years ago, there would be no Humans today.

(F) The Uniqueness of Life-forms

Cell–the Smallest Unit of Life

All Biology students know that a single cell is the smallest unit of life. Competition for resources modifies the cells until they are perfectly adapted to the new environment. Cells that give it greater access to the resources will gain an edge and its numbers will increase. In the real world, the environment constantly changes. Cooperation with one's own or other species may be a solution to survival. In nature, symbiosis has shown remarkable success, so could many species survive for a long time.

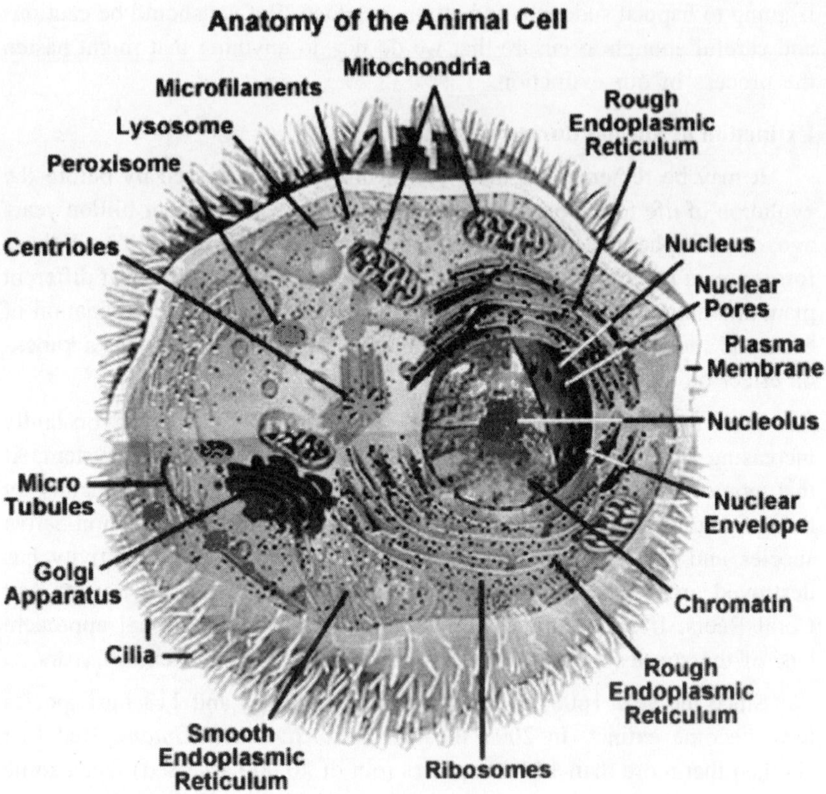

Animal Cell Structure (in figure above)

The complexity of animal and Plant cell structure is shown above and below. You will learn more about the cell structure and their functions in any Text Book of Biology. So I am not going to elaborate it here.

If the above two types of Cell structures are examined in detail, it will be seen that there exists some fundamental differences between the two types of cells. The animal cells have cilia and plasma membrane, but the plant cells have cell wall and cell membrane structures. Plant cell has chloroplast, amyloplast; the animal cell has centriole, lysosome, peroxisome, centrioles, and microtubules. Some common organelles are—Nucleus, Nucleolus, Mitochondria, Golgi apparatus (Golgi bodies), both smooth and rough Endoplasmic Reticulum etc.

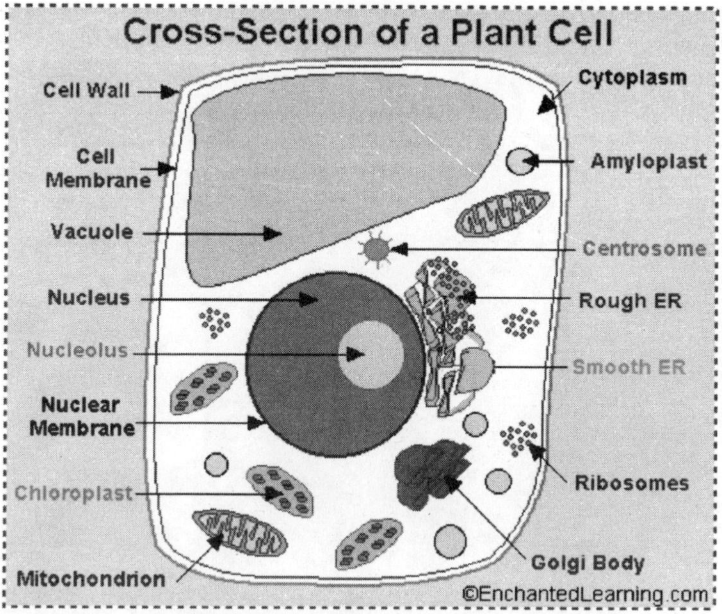

(G) Appearance of the First Single Cell: The Virus World

It is always very fascinating to know as to how the First single cell appeared on earth. What are its ancestors? How did the transformations take place? Many believe that from the ancient Virus World cells originated. There was a distinct flow of Genes (segments on DNA structure-the hereditary molecule) emerging from those that existed from the very beginning. Those genes retained its identity. It has been suggested that all viruses evolve from other viruses. It seems that the mobile elements from viruses integrated into the host genomes, but propagated in the selfish mode. Once such elements lost their ability to reproduce autonomously, they emigrated from the virus world to the cellular world. Most often, having no function, they perished upon immigration. According to this concept the bulk of our genome seems to be derived from the ancient Virus World. Life may have remained in the virus stage for many millions of years before a suitable assemblage of elementary units was brought together in the first cell. More information about the viral genomes will reveal many information regarding virus evolution and the origin of different types of cells.

A Prokaryotic and Eukaryotic cells—From single cell appeared multi-cell organisms. Life in variety of forms; Data indicate that from prokaryotes (bacteria) resulted eukaryotes (animal and plant cell)–The following pictures show various pro-and euro-karyotic species.

Biodiversity in Various Plant Forms are Shown Above

The above picture represents that life appeared on Earth in a continuous manner, in a chain of events, in the changing circumstances of environmental progression, only through the process of adaptation, to the future environmental conditions. Experiments with microbes grown in a test tube do not prove that the evolution of intelligent beings was inevitable, what they reveal is the power of natural selection to find adaptive solutions to change. All life, in order to survive, needs to be able to sense any dangers and opportunities to its health and existence. To communicate with fellow beings, in order to exchange information, i.e., learn and to participate in group activities, i.e., family sharing. Group activities assume rules of behaviour, e.g., colonial insects like ants, bees, animal and bird migrations and flock behavior and so on. Human communities include tribes, armies, sport teams and orchestras. Communication is also necessary for procreation to succeed and in bringing up the young, generations after generations.

In addition, humans have invented ways to technologically extend our senses using microscopes to view the most tiny worlds and telescopes to gain information about the most distant worlds. Today Instruments exist to record all types of radioactivity (alpha, beta and gamma) and electromagnetic radiation as well, from radio waves to X-rays. Human evolution has included the convergence of many sensing facilities, and this convergence has enabled humanity to see the connectivity of many diverse features.

(H) Human Adaptation and Evolution

Genetic variation in a population is what gives it the flexibility to adapt to its changing environment. It has been indicated that "while past events do shape the outcome of adaptation and evolution, but in the long run they do not constrain it. If a particular set of adaptation is well-suited. Our senses of perception are continuously receiving information. In fact, our brain receives much more information than we are aware of. We are in fact overloaded with information. Our consciousness has therefore evolved to be highly selective. We select by experience—experience of what has been useful before, of what makes "sense". Some people who cannot stop hearing everything suffer from a malady called "superior canal dehiscence". They hear their heartbeat, the hum of distant cars, the ticking of the clock, the scratching of insects etc. It is all for data overload. In our dreams, in visions or hypnosis, some of our unconsciously recorded sense receptions emerge. But psychotic or paranormal people do not experience that.

Human Evolution

Early Human

The evolution of Human beings on this planet perhaps is the greatest of all the creations. But it took millions of years during the evolutionary transformation process started forming a VIRUS, with Proteins (composed

of amino acids composed of Carbon, Oxygen, Hydrogen and Nitrogen) and Nucleic Acids (such as DNA and RNA, composed of Nucleotides made up of Carbon, Oxygen, Hydrogen, Nitrogen, Phosphorus). We will know more about it when we study the subject of Biology, Biochemistry, Genetics and Biotechnology. The term "human" in the context of human evolution refers to the genus *Homo*, but studies of human evolution usually include others as well. Early humans may have originated from chimpanzees about five to seven illion years ago. One view among scientists concerning the origin of modern humans is the hypothesis known as "Out of Africa". Recent African origin hypothesis argues that *Homo sapiens* arose in Africa. Then they migrated out of the continent around 50,000 to 100,000 years ago. Then they replaced the then populations of *Homo erectus* in Asia and Neanderthals in Europe. Molecular evidence suggests that between eight and four million years ago, first the gorillas, and then the chimpanzees split off from the line leading to the humans. Human DNA is approximately 98.4 per cent identical to that of chimpanzees. Current research has established that humans are genetically highly homogenous. Distinctive genetic characteristics have arisen from the result of small groups of people moving into new environmental conditions. These adapted traits are a very small component of the *Homo sapiens* genome. It includes various characteristics such as skin color and nose form, in addition to internal characteristics such as the ability to breathe more efficiently at high altitudes.

Dawn of Civilisation–the Beginning of Inventions and Discoveries

Discovery of fire and tools showed the dawn of our civilisation.

Fire is One of the Greatest Human Inventions

Models of human evolution: Today, all humans belong to one population of *Homo sapiens,* undivided by species barrier. Anthropologists have been divided as to whether current human population evolved only in East Africa. There are differing theories on whether there was a single exodus or several. There is African model as well as out-of-African model of first human population. World populations is a mixture of different types of people originating from different parts of the World, through the process of both intra-culture and inter culture mixing.

PART-II
INDIAN MYSTIC ENVIRONMENT

3

The Exotic Environment and Our Natural Resources

(I) The Exotic Environment and Our Natural Resources—Environment the Provider of Our Needs

In earlier Chapters, we have learnt about our distant and immediate/near Environment where we live in, Our Country, its environmental contrasts. Our ancient glory, Our people, Our family, Customs, food habits etc.

In this Chapter, we will learn about the basic needs of human life, Our Natural Resources and how it is getting polluted due to man-made activities. We will focus our attention on what needs to be done about the protection of those basic ingredients that we need to survive, and how many of those are getting extinct. Therefore, we have to learn to insure protection of all those items that we need to survive.

Among the major and basic needs of our survival are the following:

(A) Foods that we get from our immediate and near environment

We will discuss here on others the following aspects in some details.

- (a) Macro nutrients and Micro nutrients.
- (b) Preservation of Food,
- (c) Availability of Foods,
- (d) Different types of food–Indian and International,
- (e) Food habits,
- (f) Food Preservation.

(B) Water–the Basic unit of life,

- (a) Why we need Water?
- (b) Water pollution sources,
- (c) Water Purification,

(C) Air

- (a) Air Pollution,
- (b) Green House Effect and Global Warming,
- (c) Practices to follow to keep air clean.

(D) Shelter–a basic necessity of all animals.

(E) Clothing–Nature of clothings change with cultures, climates, professions and countries

(F) Cultural Activities–Every country has its own culture that changes even within the country itself around their mother tongue; its expressions through observance of various local activities, cultural functions (songs and dance, theaters, festivals etc.

(G) Health and Hygiene—Observance of proper health and hygiene is important for survival in a pollution free environment.

(H) Transport and Communication—Good Transport and communication systems are essential for any country to progress and develop.

(A) Food, water, and air are the three basic needs of human beings for our growth and development.

Our Environment provides them all. Some details are described below:

(a) Food

We need food to grow and develop. Food provides the building blocks, the proteins, and also provides other necessary nutrients, such as carbohydrates, fats and oils, minerals, vitamins and also some water which are needed for our growth, to build muscles and to help maintaining our internal organs functional. Any imbalance in the process of food and nutrient supply may cause disorders or diseases. Food is the essential need of a child. It must be wholesome with respect to its nutrient content. It should be kept in our mind that there are variations in the type of food that should be supplied to very young, just after birth during the early stage of development, compared to the growing and adult children. In each stage, the child needs different varieties of food supply.

(b) Which are our Foods? Foods should have the following Nutrients

We must know which are our foods, why we need our food and what they contain.

In general, our foods contain the following nutrients.

- Proteins,
- Carbohydrates,
- Fats,

- Vitamins and
- Minerals
- Water is also essential.

Nutrients

What are called Nutrients?

Nutrients are those which support our life systems. It helps our metabolic processes, replenishes our body proteins, fats, blood constituents, helps in cell division, and reconstitutes those elements that gets destroyed or damaged. Above nutrients help each individual cell to divide to make a balance between the cellular destruction and body-building processes.

You must know that during the entire growth period, during our childhood and boyhood in particular, we grow continuously. Our cells divide faster, from one cell to two and from two to four and so on. So we need lot of nutrients' supply, which actually comes from our food and drink. If there is a shortage of supply of any particular type of nutrient, our growth hampers.

Micro Nutrients and Macronutrients

Nutrients can be divided into—Micronutrients and Macronutrients according to the very size of their chemical structures, small or large.

As has been said above, some of the foods contain Macronutrients, such as Proteins, Carbohydrates, Fats and Oils, Nucleic acids etc.

Proteins

What are the Proteins?

Proteins are large chemical compounds which are composed of smaller units called amino acids. Proteins can be broken into amino acids by a process known as Hydrolysis. Some of the smaller units of proteins are named as serine, threonine, tyrosine, tryptophan, glutamine, cystine, glycine, valine, threonine etc.

Protein hydrolysis can be done by heating a sample of the protein in hydrochloric acid to 100–110°C for 24 hours or longer. Proteins will be broken into amino acids. Each amino acid is composed of an amino (NH_2) in one side; the other side contains carboxylic groups (COOH). In order to form a protein molecule, NH_2 group of one amino acid has to bind with the COOH group of another amino acid to form a—CONH-bond known as Peptide bond. In the process, one molecule of water (H_2O) is released. This is how a large molecule of Protein is formed through a chain reaction by joining various amino acids one after the other, such as serine-arginine-histidine-valine-leucine and so on. This is how larger molecules of peptides are formed. This is how polypeptides and oligopeptides are formed. A naturally-occurring protein is an oligopeptide. The imprints of each protein are there in the DNA code.

Protein Structure

One of the most distinguishing features of polypeptides is their ability to fold into a globular form. The extent to which proteins fold into a defined structure varies widely. Some proteins fold into a highly rigid structure with small fluctuations and are therefore considered to be having a single structure. Other proteins undergo large rearrangements from one conformation to another. This conformational change is often associated with a signaling event. Thus, the structure of a protein serves as a medium through which to regulate either the function of a protein or the activity of an enzyme (which is also a protein having catalytic function). Not all proteins require a folding process in order to function, as some function in an unfolded state.

Like other biological macromolecules such as polysaccharides and nucleic acids, proteins are an essential part of organisms and participate in virtually every process within the cells.

Some proteins act as hormones in the body; our blood has many proteins such as albumin, hemoglobin, immunoglobulins (which act as antibody in our immune functions to protect us against infections), etc.

Proteins which function as enzymes are called Functional proteins that catalyse (helping or facilitating a reaction to cause) various biochemical reactions and are vital to our metabolic process.

Proteins also have structural or mechanical functions As for examples, we may look at actin and myosin in muscle and the proteins in the cytoskeleton structure, which form a system of scaffolding that maintains cell shape. Many other proteins are important in cell signaling, immune responses, cell adhesion and the cell cycle.

Proteins are also necessary in animals' diets, since animals cannot synthesise all the amino acids they need and must obtain those essential amino acids from various foods. Through the process of digestion, animals break down ingested proteins into free amino acids which are then used in our metabolism in order to synthesise the desired proteins.

Early nutritional scientists believed that protein was the most important nutrient for maintaining the structure of the body, because it was generally believed that "flesh makes flesh." The central role of proteins as enzymes in living organisms was not known initially until it was observed that the enzyme urease was in fact a protein. The first protein to be sequenced was insulin, by Frederick Sanger, who won the Nobel Prize for this achievement in 1958.

Carbohydrates

A carbohydrate is an organic compound. It consists only of carbon, hydrogen, and oxygen, with a hydrogen: oxygen ratio of 2:1 (as in water). Carbohydrates can be viewed as hydrates of carbon, hence their name. The term is most common in biochemistry, where it is a synonym of saccharide. The carbohydrates (saccharides) are divided into four chemical groupings: monosaccharides, disaccharides, oligosaccharides, and polysaccharides. In general, the monosaccharides and disaccharides, which are smaller (lower molecular weight) carbohydrates, are commonly referred to as sugars. The blood sugar is the monosaccharide glucose, table sugar is the disaccharide sucrose, and milk sugar is the disaccharide lactose.

Carbohydrates perform numerous roles in living organisms. Polysaccharides (contain a number of monosaccharides, such as glucose, fructose, lactose etc.) serve for the storage of energy (e.g., starch and glycogen), and as structural components (e.g., cellulose in plants). The 5-carbon monosaccharide ribose (a 5-carbon sugar molecule) is an important component of ATP (Bioenergy molecule), and the backbone of the genetic molecule known as RNA (ribonucleic acid). The related deoxyribose is a component of DNA (deoxyribonucleic acid). Saccharides and their derivatives include many other important biomolecules that play major roles in the immune functions, fertilisation, preventing pathogenesis, blood clotting, growth and our development.

The term carbohydrate often means any food that is particularly rich in the complex carbohydrate starch (such as cereals, bread, noodles, and pasta) or simple carbohydrates, such as sugar (found in candy, jams, Jelley, sweets, and desserts).

Nucleic Acid

Nucleic acids are major biological molecules that are very essential for our life. There are two types of Nucleic acid molecules—DNA (deoxyribonucleic acid) and RNA (ribonucleic acid). DNA molecule is also known as the "Hereditary Molecule" as it carries the genetic information from the parents and passes on to the offspring. Like father like son, and like mother like daughter Dogma is carried out through the imprints on this molecule.

Together with proteins, nucleic acids make up the most important macromolecules in our body; each is found in abundance in all living things. As has been said above, the nucleic acids are important molecules that encode, transmit and express genetic information. Experimental studies of nucleic acids constitute a major part of modern biological and medical research, and form a foundation for genome and forensic science, as well as the biotechnology and pharmaceutical industries. You will learn more about it when you study Biochemistry, Genetics, Biotechnology etc.

Nucleic acids are known to be found in all life forms, including animal, plant, bacteria, and viruses. All living cells and organelles contain both DNA and RNA, while viruses contain either DNA or RNA, but usually not both. There is DNA virus and also there exists RNA virus.

The basic component of biological nucleic acids is the nucleotide, each of which contains a pentose sugar (ribose or deoxyribose), a phosphate group, and a nucleobase. Now with the sophisticated technology, nucleic acids can be prepared within the laboratory. A DNA Double Helix structure is shown below:

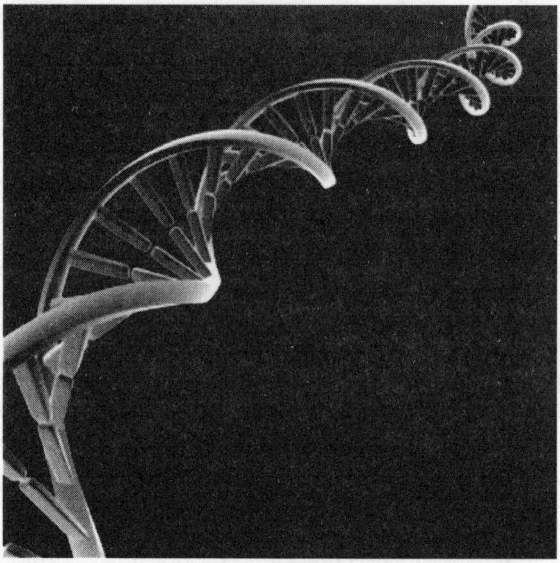

Molecular Composition and Size of Nucleic Acids

Nucleic acids can vary in size, but are generally very large molecules. Indeed, DNA molecules are probably the largest individual molecules known. Well-studied biological nucleic acid molecules range in size from 21 nucleotides (small interfering RNA) to large chromosomes (human chromosome 1 is a single molecule that contains 247 million base pairs).

In most cases, naturally occurring DNA molecules are double-stranded and RNA molecules are single-stranded. Nucleic acids are linear polymers (chains) of nucleotides. Each nucleotide consists of three components: a purine or pyrimidine nucleobase (sometimes termed *nitrogenous base* or simply *base*), a pentose sugar, and a phosphate group. Nucleic acid types differ in the structure of the sugar in their nucleotides—DNA contains 2'-deoxyribose while RNA contains ribose sugar. Also, the nucleobases found in the two nucleic acid types are different: adenine, cytosine, and guanine are found in both RNA and DNA, connected.

Transfer RNA (t-RNA) molecules, that bind with amino acids and transfer them to ribosomal structure for peptide or protein formation, contain a particularly large number of modified nucleosides.

Thus from the above you can well realise that Macronutrients (larger molecules) are formed by linking smaller molecules together through a chain reaction. The smaller units of Proteins are known as Amino acids. Carbohydrates are formed by chaining sugar molecules with one another.

Fats and Oils

Fats and oils are also macromolecules consisting of glycerides (made of joining a Glycerine molecule with Fatty acids (the compound formed is known as glycerides). Since a Glycerine molecule may bind three molecules of fatty acids, it is called Triglyceride). Fats are those molecules that remain solid at room temperature, such as animal Fats, Ghee, Butter, etc., while oils are those that remain in the liquid form at room temperature.

The following triglyceride vegetable oils account for almost all worldwide production, by volume. All are used as both cooking oils or to make biodiesel. The total world consumption of major vegetable oils in 2007/08 is shown below in the chart. There are many vegetable oils in or midst. The palm oil is the most widely produced vegetable oil. It is used also in the production of Biofuel. About half of worldwide edible oil comes from Soybean. Olive oil and Cocoanut oil. These are used for cooking and also for soap making; olive oil is also used in making cosmetics.

Oil source	*World consumption (million tons)*	*Notes*
Palm	41.31	The most widely produced tropical oil, also used to make biofuel
Soybean	41.28	Accounts for about half of worldwide edible oil production
Rapeseed	18.24	One of the most widely used cooking oils, canola is a (trademarked) variety (cultivar) of rapeseed.
Sunflower seed	9.91	A common cooking oil, also used to make biodiesel
Peanut	4.82	Mild-flavored cooking oil
Cottonseed	4.99	A major food oil, often used in industrial food processing
Palm kernel	4.85	From the seed of the African palm tree
Coconut	3.48	Used in soaps and cooking
Olive	2.84	Used in cooking, cosmetics, soaps and as a fuel for traditional oil lamps

Note that the above figures include industrial and animal feed use. The majority of European rapeseed oil production is used to produce biodiesel, or used directly as fuel in diesel cars.

You may learn more about these molecules In Chemistry, especially biochemistry. A fatty acid is a carboxylic acid with a long unbranched aliphatic tail (chain), which is either saturated or unsaturated. Fatty acids that have double bonds are known as unsaturated fatty acids. Fatty acids without double bonds are known as saturated. Most of the naturally occurring fatty acids have a chain of an even number of carbon atoms, from four to 28. Fatty acids are important sources of fuel or Bioenergy. Many cell types can use either glucose or fatty acids for the purpose of making ATP. The brain cannot use fatty acids as a source of fuel; it relies on glucose or ketone bodies.

Types of Fatty Acids

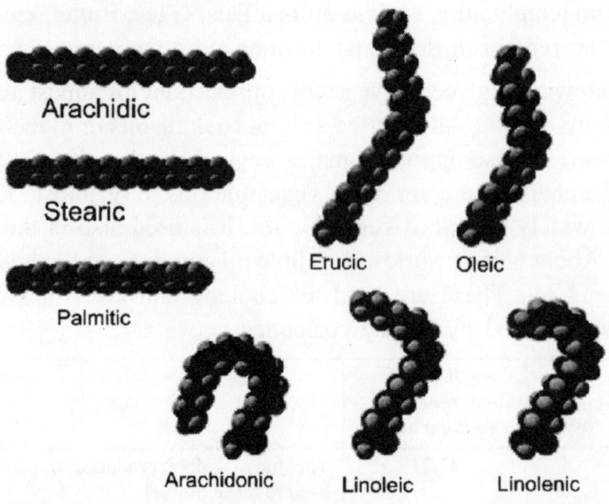

Three Dimensional Representations of Several Fatty Acids.

Length of Free Fatty Acid Chains

- Fatty acid chains differ by length, often categorised as short, or long.
- Short-chain fatty acids (SCFA) are fatty acids with aliphatic tail (Straight chain molecules) of fewer than six carbons (i.e., butyric acid).
- Long-chain fatty acids (LCFA) are fatty acids with aliphatic tails longer than 12 carbons.
- Very long chain fatty acid (VLCFA) is fatty acids with aliphatic tails longer than 22 carbons.

Unsaturated Fatty Acids

Unsaturated fatty acids have one or more double bonds between carbon atoms. Examples of some unsaturated fatty acids are Linoleic acid, Linolenic acid, Arachidonic acid, Oleic acid.

In fact, the Macronutrients are converted into Micronutrients by the metabolic process within our body. These Micronutrients are—amino acids (from proteins), sugars (from carbohydrates), fatty acids (from fats and oils), vitamins, minerals etc. Our body absorbs the micronutrients for our use. These nutrients go to the blood stream and from there reaches every single cell to help them to do their specific jobs.

Food Preservation and its Importance

It is important to realise that unless food items are preserved properly, the food value may be lost, If foods are not preserved properly, it may get spoiled. Food gets spoiled because of bacterial or fungal contamination. Unless properly preserved, it may be infested with germs which are harmful to our body. Foods may be putrefied or get dried if improperly kept. So the knowledge of food preservation is very important.

Do not keep your food open. Always keep it covered. For long time preservation, keep it in the Refrigerator. Cooked food, such as Fish, Meat, Milk, Egg, Bread, Vegetables, Jam, Jelly, etc., would remain in good condition in the cold. For long time preservation, especially food grains like rice, wheat, dal, lentils, etc., food items are usually stored in go–downs using pesticides or insecticides to prevent insect or rodent infestations in order to protect them from getting spoiled. Food items should be washed and cleaned properly before using them since those chemicals are very harmful for human health. For various fruits and vegetables especially like potatoes, onions, tomatoes, etc., and also for fruit preservation cold storage facility is essentially required. In case of many food items, unfortunately non-permitted coloring matters are added to make it attractive. One should be very careful about their use. Usually sweets and powdered spices are colored with chemicals to make them look brighter and more appealing. Non-permitted colors are very often found in various food items. Beware of them, it may be very harmful.

In order to make more profits, some businessmen adulterate foods by mixing small stones in rice and dahl, glass powder or sand to sugar, toxic pesticides to atta (wheat flour), mineral oil to edible oils, etc., in order to increase its weights. Be always careful to buy such things. When buying, one should ensure whether it is packaged and it has ISI/BIS/AGMARK / ISO standard mark or not. Such food items are reasonably safe. If there is any suspicion, one should be in touch with the "Consumer's Safety Department' seeking help and guidance.

Food adulteration /contamination were a major problem in our country. The Government has enacted a Food adulteration ACT and there are food inspectors whose job is to collect samples from the market and analyse them from time to time. Although we have come a long way, but problems exist. We all should be very watchful/careful about it. Willful contamination/ adulteration of food is a crime. Although it is rarely seen these days in big cities, it has not been eliminated completely from villages. Law enforcement department can be contacted to seek help. There are consumer rights protection group in the state. They may be contacted also for prevention of adulteration of foods.

Food Habits

India is a vast country. Many different type of people live here. They have different types of food habits also. North and South Indian food-habits are entirely different. Food habits in Eastern India are also different from the West Indians. A large number of our people are Vegetarians. Some are Non-vegetarians.

Availability of different types of Cuisine: National and International–A matter of Tourists' Interests.

Foods are very special to a person. Each person has different tastes and likings so far as foods are concerned. In India you can taste different types of Indian foods as well as foods prepared according to the recipe of other nations of the World. These foods are available in any part of India; foods from different countries are available in the restaurants in different parts of India. These are—Chinese food Thai foods, Korean, Japanese, Middle Eastern, Italian, Continental, American and Mexican foods. It is so amasing that each type of food is cooked with their special Recipe, which smells and tastes different.

Indian Foods

North Indian Mutton preparations (Mutton kasha, Tanduri, Korma, Kabab, Kofta, Curry) and Chicken preparations (Tanduri Chicken, Chicken Kabob, Chicken Curry, Chicken Korma, Chicken Karhai), Fish preparations (Fish Curry, Fishes prepared with mustard or Cocoanut, Fish fry, etc., are very popular among the non-vegetarians. Among other dishes are—Biriyani, Pulao, Fried Rice, Romali Roti, Luchi, Paretha, Tanduri Roti, Chapatti, Basmati Rice and various other rice preparations, various Dal and vegetable preparations are also available in every part of our country; Our South Indian foods like Yellow Rice, Dosa, Idli, Bada, Sambar and Rasam are also very popular in different parts of India. Some of the Indian dishes are also very popular in other countries as well. East Indian Fish curry, different types of Vegetable preparations, Rassogulla, Sweet Dahi, Flavored Gur,

Sandesh and West Indian Pomphret preparations, Bombay Chat, Pohe, Goanese foods are also of special interests to many people in India.

Foreign Foods

Some of these are described below:

Many different foreign foods are available in India and in other countries of the World these days. Italian food such as Pizza, Pasta; different types of American and European food as are found in Various types of Sandwitches with Vegetable salads, sliced and cooked Ham, Chicken (also in spicy forms), Cheese, etc., and also Hot Dogs; French Fries, Fried Chicken, various types of steaks are very popular.

Mexican foods are becoming also very popular these days just like the Chinese foods for a long time in the Western world. Chinese and Thai Foods and their soup preparations are a special treat. Soups of different kinds (Vegetable, Chicken, Pork, Egg; MOMO, Spring Roll, Fried Rice-with Chicken, Pork, Shrimp, Egg, etc., Chilli Fish and Various Chicken preparations (chicken with Chinese vegetables, bamboo shoots; Egg Fuyong etc. These dishes are available with normal, medium and hot sauces. Besides, you may get also Pakistani, Bangladeshi, Afgani, Middle Eastern, and Greek restaurants in various parts of the World. This is the reason why we get a large number of Foreign Tourists every year, since they do not find it very difficult to get their kind of Foods in different parts of India, especially in Big Six star, Five star and Four star hotels with all modern amenities. When Indians visit other countries they also find their choices of foods in other countries as well. These days Western food chains of McDonalds, Kentucky Fried Chicken, Pizza Huts, Giovanies Pizza, etc., are all available in different parts of India.

(B) Water

Water is another most essential item a child need. In fact, every human being, animals and plants need water. One may survive a few days without food, but none can survive long without water. Everyday we need to drink several glasses of water to replenish the water loss and also to help maintaining our metabolic process within the body. These days water has become so polluted that people are scared to drink water from outside their homes. Bottled water is available in most of the places. Most people opt for drinking bottled water when they are outside their own homes.

Why do we need Water?

- Water keeps our body cool
- Water helps softening our food.
- It helps in breaking down our food (metabolism).
- It helps to replenish the loss due to perspiration and passing out of urine.

- It helps in our fluid balance.
- Water has a major role for the thermal regulation of our body also.

Water Purification

It is essential that we gather some knowledge as to how water can be purified. Unfortunately most of our natural sources of water are polluted to day! Therefore, water should be boiled, cooled, gravity-filtered or filtered through other types of filters available in the market and then used for drinking. Boiling is the best method!

For water purification, different types of filter candles, charcoal filters, aqua-guard, resin containing filters, UV-filters, Reverse Osmosis process filters are available in city markets.

In villages, water can be purified by keeping four earthen pitchers one above the other. It is called 'Permutit Process'. The top pitcher may contain gravels, the second one may contain sand, the third one may contain charcoal powder and the fourth one may serve as the reservoir of purified and filtered water.

(C) Air

We must learn what air is and why we need it. Air is composed of Oxygen and Nitrogen in a major way. Among other substances are—Carbon dioxide, Carbon monoxide, Methane, Sulphur dioxide, Dusts, volatile hydrocarbons, Chlorine, etc., which pollute our Air environment. These substances go to air as a result of various man-made activities, such as Industrial emissions, car exhausts, agricultural activities, Coal, wood or Fossil-fuel burning etc. Many of these gases, such as CO_2, Methane, Chlorinated hydrocarbons, CFCs (Chlorofluorocarbons) H_2S etc., are responsible for causing Green House EffectThis is a process wherein the Infra red rays are bounced back to the surface raising the surface temperature of Earth. CFCs and other chlorinated hydrocarbons can destroy the Ozone layer in the upper atmosphere. Ozone layer normally covers and thus protects the Earth's surface from the harmful UV rays. Ozone hole is made by the CFCs and other gases mentioned above allowing UV to directly fall upon Earth's surface. Already Ozone hole has been noted in the North Pole areas. UV ray is dangerous. It can cause cancer, cataract in our eyes, skin disorders etc. It can also increase the surface temperatures. Thus, both the Green house gases including UV are responsible for the Global Change phenomena, changing the atmospheric weather conditions, abnormal summer and winter, too much rain and snow, severe floods, hurricanes, tornadoes, volcanic eruptions, earthquakes, tsunamis etc.

Every person breathes air to take oxygen from the air. We cannot see or taste air. Air has no shape, smell or colors either. But we can only feel air. If we go to any oxygen-free environment and stay there for some time, we will feel breathing difficulties and may eventually die. High above the mountains, we will feel suffocated for want of enough of oxygen. So the mountaineers and deep-sea divers carry oxygen-cylinders at their backpacks as a source of oxygen. Air keeps us cool in summer months. Air is filled in footballs, cycle tire tubes, car tires etc, so that it can run smoothly. Air can also help us in producing electricity. When air moves speedily, the wind rotates the fans of the wind-mills that are connected with big turbines, which rotates to produce electricity. Oxygen is vital for our "cellular function". Shortage of oxygen kills the cell, so also the tissues. As a result, the individual may die.

Practices to follow to keep air clean:

We need to follow certain practices to keep our AIR clean. These are described as follows:

- The vehicle owners should use eco-friendly fuel like CNG (Compressed Natural Gas). In Western nations people have started using GASOHOL. Electric cars are also Eco-friendly.
- Bursting of crackers should be avoided.
- Burning of coal, wood and fossil fuel should be minimised.
- Factories should only be allowed to function far away from the residential areas, so that they cannot pollute our immediate neighbourhood.
    - The industries should plant at least five saplings in place of each tree they cut for the space for construction of industries. Similar principles should be followed by housing complexes, town planners etc.
- Polluting industries should develop a GREEN belt around it so that it can prevent/minimise both dusts and smoke to go outside the green belt area. Similar principles.

(D) Shelters

Children's mind is always curious. They ask questions seeking answers for it. A child should know what the status of their houses was. Houses or shelters in the primitive stage were not as nice as it is today. Early men used to live in caves. Caves served as their shelters. They needed privacy and so some covered their living places with large leaves, logs and bamboos, and sometimes put mud or clay around the bamboo structures to save them from the attack of animals and from the heat of the sun, rain water and cold.

Large animals like Lion and Tiger also lived in cages. So men were in danger always. Some started living under the shade of large trees. Some others started making tree-houses also.

In many cases, large number of people used to live in a single cave grouping together. It created space problems, anger, jealousy, greed etc. They used to fight with each other for food and other materials. Later men built a better place as their own shelter that could protect them from their enemies and also save them from the rage of nature—heat, rain, cold weather and storm. Thus the concept of housing was appreciated in course of time...

Gradually, men learnt to build their huts with straws, bamboos, wooden logs, large leaves and mud. This set the beginning of modern living by man and woman. This gave birth also to the concept of family-living. Gradually, houses were built to make them roomy with enough ventilation so that air can pass through and sunlight can enter into the house. Proper sanitation arrangement became a part of every shelter or a house when it was constructed.

Building one's own shelter is a biological instinct, also seen among the lower animals. You must have seen birds making their own nests on trees and in air vents of buildings. Such tendency is normally seen among many other small and large animals such as the ants, snakes, tortoise, mice, birds and many other animals. Ants live in small holes. Snakes are found in deep forests and jungles and in burrows. Mice live in large holes or burrows. Fish is found in water. Crocodiles live in both water and land. Penguins make their nests on grounds with pebbles. We see a lot of Penguins in Australia, Antarctic regions Cuckoo cannot make their nests. They lay their eggs in row's nest by fooling them to get their own babies born there. Honeybees make their hives on the branches of trees or in the corner's of a building. Hives contain honey. Spiders make web, which catches insects which they eat.

Usually large domestic animals cannot make their own shelters. They depend on us for building their shelters for them. We make stable for horses, shed for cows, aquarium for small ornamental fishes, cage for birds etc. So you see that animals need our love, affection and care for their survival. Sharing and caring is a normal instinct that a biological being inherits. Besides humans, it is seen among all animals.

(E) Clothing

Early men used to move around with very little cover of their body. They used to cover only their private parts. As they become more civilised, they started covering their whole body. It was necessary to protect the body from heat and cold, dusts, insect bites, accidental injury etc. Early men used to make dresses made of barks of trees, big leaves, straws etc. As men learnt making of cloths, clothing of different type came into being. These are—Shirts, pants, frocks, dhoti, hosiery item, underpants etc. Later, clothes made of nylon, rayon, polyesters, silk, wool became available. We wear different types of dresses suitable for various weather conditions. In summer, we use light dresses like loose, comfortable, cotton clothes. These are known as casual dress like Shorts, T-shirts, Saree, Dhoti-Kurta, Kurta-Pyjama, Salwar-Kameez etc.

In winter, we need warm garments. Warm garments are made of wool and/or polyester. These garments are—Sweaters, Jackets, Shawl, Coats and pants, Scarves, Caps etc. In the rainy season, people need umbrella, hat, rain-coat, gumboots etc. All these are called Seasonal dresses. Styles and colors of dresses change from one region of the country to another. It may vary from one country to another also. People in Kashmir dressentioned in their traditional characteristic style, which is different from both North and South Indians. The Tibetan Lamas, the Nagas in Nagaland, People from Manipur, Punjab, Tamil Nadu, West Bengal etc., all these people dress in their traditional style. People in Saudi Arabia dresses in their characteristic style than the people of UZBEKISTAN. All those are called regional dresses.

Apart from the above-mentioned traditional dresses, there are Special dresses, which are worn during some special events or occasions, such as Marriage, Graduation (Convocation) Ceremony, Religious festivals etc. Dresses used during the marriages are called bridal dress. Dancers use a particular type of dress according to various regional types of very distinctive costumes. Such as Manipuri (Manipur), Bharat Natyam (South India), Kuchipudi (Orissa), Bengali Dance (Rabindrik), Santhali Dance (Santhal Parganas), Kathak (North India), Bhangra (Punjab) dances. The swimmers use another type of costumes, called swimming costumes.

People in their Traditional Dresses in Different Parts of India

Sikh Family from Punjab, India at a Wedding.

Woman Wearing a Churidar and Kameez.

Indian Men Wearing Mundu.

Girls Wearing Gagra Choli.

People of South India.

Women of Top and Pants.

People in different occupations use particular type of dresses known as uniforms. In this category are—Doctors, Lawyers, Nurses, Policemen, Military and Air-force personnel, Drivers, Postman, School students etc. In the Church, fathers wear a specific type of dress. Dress gives people an identity as to what kind of profession they are engaged in.

(f) Functions and Festivals

You have seen many functions in your school and festivals in your locality. From early days every community organises social and cultural functions, community festivals etc. Many people attend these functions and festivals. This gives them a feeling of togetherness and help them living in a community as friends.

Different festivals are organised in different parts of our vast country. They are:

- GURU POORNIMA and BAISAKHI in Punjab.
- PONGAL in South India.
- BIHU UTSAB in Assam.
- PAUSH MELA in Santiniketan, West Bengal.
- DURGA PUJA, DASSEHRA and RATHA JATRA in West Bengal, and other parts of India.
- GANESHA FESTIVAL in Maharastra.
- HOLI (festival of colors), and DIWALI festivals (or festival of lights and crackers) all over India.
- ID-UL-FITR and MUHARAM all over India.
- BUDDHA Jayanti, MAHABIR Jayanti are also celebrated in different parts of India.
- CHRISTMAS is celebrated every year on 25 December, the birth day of Jesus Christ all over India.

Merry-Making

People celebrate these festivals with great enthusiasm. They wear new dresses, offer presents, distribute sweets and exchange greetings to each other. They decorate their houses with lights and flowers, organise Langars (Mass feast) or community dinners and visit religious places to offer prayers to GOD. People also organise different cultural functions and MELA which are attended by many.

Some major National festivals, such as the Republic Day on 26th January, Independence Day on 15th August and Gandhi Jayanti on October 2 are celebrated with dignity and great enthusiasm all over the country.

(G) Health and Hygiene

Health is wealth. If you have a good health, you will have a healthy mind. You will be able to think better and work efficiently. You should take care of your health with proper care and attention.

For proper health care, you have to maintain adequate hygiene. For maintaining proper hygienic practices, the following are suggested:

- Rise every day in the early morning and go to bed at proper time.
- Make a habit of going to the toilet in the morning. Wash your hands with soap after you come back from the toilet.
- Brush your teeth regularly in the morning and also after every major meal you take. It will save your tooth from cavity and make it strong. With clean tooth, your smile would look beautiful.
- Keep your tongues clean using a tongue cleaner.
- Take your bath regularly and clean your body with soap.
- Shampoo your hair once in a while and comb it regularly.
- Keep your clothes clean. Wash them with soap or detergents to remove dusts, dirts, colors etc.
- Keep your nails clean and cut it at periodic intervals so that dusts and dirts cannot accumulate. Dusts and dirts carry germs. Germs cause disease.
- Take special care of your sense organs like eyes, ear and nose etc. Wash your eyes with cold water couple of times everyday in the morning. When you read, keep your book about a foot away. Be sure that enough light is there.
- Keep your ear drum clean with ear buds. Do not use sharp objects like pin or pencil
- Keep your nose clean also
- Always keep your house and your surroundings clean.
- Do not throw away waste papers, peels of fruits and vegetables, wrapping papers of chocolates, and chewing gums, kitchen garbage, etc., anywhere in or outside your house. It should be kept in waste paper box, dustbins, and garbage cans or in places meant for it.

For proper health care, we need to do several other things. These are given below:

- Play or do some exercise everyday in the early morning in open and fresh air.
- Have some breakfast and drink milk everyday.

Good Habits

Apart from the above, you need to practice some good habits as a good student:

- Study everyday and complete your home work.
- Dress yourself with school uniform. Be sure your School bag has everything you need.
- Be attentive to your teachers.
- Do not loiter with friends.
- Do not make the class dirty.
- During the school break, take your tiffin.
- Play with your friends.
- Do not quarrel and make noise.
- As soon as the school bell rings, go to your class.
- Be sure your school uniform is washed, cleaned and ironed regularly,
- Shine your shoes and keep your socks clean.
- At the end of the school, collect your books, note-books, tiffin box, water bottles, umbrella, etc., make sure you are not forgetting anything.

While coming back home, watch road signs carefully while crossing the roads; ride buses or trains with enough of caution.

After return from the school, change your school uniforms. Keep them in proper place. Wash your hands, feet and face with clean water. Get ready for playing and play for an hour with others. Come back home before it is dark. Take showers and change your dress. Take some light food and sit down for study.

Have dinner as per routine. With permission from your parents, you may see some children programme on TV or listen to music or read a story book according to your liking.

Healthy Living

Remember that maintaining proper hygiene, playing and exercising everyday, also having good food and Rest will make you healthy. You will feel happy. You will not suffer from frequent diseases. You will get enough energy to do lot of work and become a successful person later.

(H) Transport and Communication Facilities in India

Transport

We need different types of transport to go from one place to another. Bus, Tram, Taxi, Cycle, Motor Bike, etc., play on roads. Boat, Steamer and Ship sail on water. Aero plane flies in the air. All of them carry people and goods from one place to another.

Different Types of Transport

Transport facilities differ from one place to another. In big cities, we find many types of transport facilities. Villages have altogether a different picture. In big cities like Bombay, Kolkata, Madras and New Delhi, we have Bus, Taxi, A/C Cars, Lorry, Zeep, Scooters, Motor bikes, Cycles, Cycle-rickshaws, and Trains etc. In Kolkata and Delhi, there are underground METROS. Kolkata has TRAMS as well.

Just outside the cities, in suburbs, there are Cycle rickshaws, Tonga (horse-driven cart) Camel-cart, Bullock-cart, Three wheelers, Autos, Cycle, Bus, Train and Taxi.

Transportation in villages include–Cycle, cycle rickshaws, Bus, Trains, Vans or Trekkers, Three wheelers, Autos, Bullock carts, Tonga, Camel cart, Tractors etc. In some areas, where canals, rivers and oceans are there, Ferry boat, Speed Boat, Steamer and Ship are used by people as water transport.

There are three types of vehicles in India-Engine driven, Animal driven and manually driven. The first one needs petrol, Diesel or Coal. The second and third one needs physical and mechanical strength. Train is the fastest of all the vehicles. Electric trains are in use these days. Earlier, trains used coal instead.

Helicopters and aero-planes still run faster than road vehicles or water transports. Aero planes are the fastest. Supersonic planes run faster than sound. To day there are jumbo jets, which can carry 500-600 people at the same time.

In earlier days, when these vehicles were not there, people used to use sledges or wheel-less carts to carry things from one place to another. Rafts were used in water. With the invention of wheel, other forms of carts and carriers became available.

Communication

What is Communication?

As we are getting more and more modern, our Communication systems are getting better and better and more modern. Communication is the process of exchanging our thoughts and ideas, giving messages and transmitting news of importance between one person to another. There are several modes of communication. The traditional one is by sending letters through the post office. To day, in addition to normal post office services, there are courier services, which can send your letters faster than the post office. You can send letters also by FAX or by e-mail. These are faster modes of communication.

Our post offices provide various services-same day and overnight mail service, Money order service, Speed post, Telephone and Telegraph services. Besides that, there are door-to-door Courier service, Fax, and Cell phone service.

One can reach out to the farthest point on this planet within a few seconds over the cell phone or STD/ISD, direct dial facility or trunk calls. These have become possible because of several communication Satellites which have been placed in the earth's orbit by different countries, including India.

Computer, Television and Radio are the electronic media of mass communication. News and views, cultural and educational programmes, song, Dance and music programmes, games, movies, etc., can be watched, seen and heard through these media. You can see a cricket match or a football game being played at a far-off place, just sitting in your home. You can also listen to the lecture delivered by our Prime Minister on August 15 every year from Delhi Red Fort. You can see the Republic Day parade on 26th of January transmitted directly from Delhi. Obviously you may feel proud of the progress and development of our country.

Books, Newspapers and Magazines also carry lot of information. These are also a part of mass communication.

More communication means more contact, more message transfer, more business, more profits and so more progress and development of the country.

Do you know what is she doing? She is using her cell phone. Cell phones have reached already the remotest part of our country providing a quick and instant method of communication in the hands of millions of our country-men/women.

(II) Man and his Environment

Basic ingredients of our Environment and how they are getting influenced by human activities.

In this Chapter, we will discuss some of the major ingredients of Our Environment. We discussed in the previous chapter some other aspects of it, i.e., what we need for our life processes, some chemical details about them and why we need them. More of these substances will be discussed here, especially how the basic ingredients are getting polluted.

We must appreciate that Water, Air, Soil and Plants and Forests are all needed by us for our living and sustenance. They are all part of our immediate Environment. Let us know more about these basic needs of mankind and how they are getting influenced/ polluted and/or getting extinct. This will be discussed below.

Water

Water is a major life sustaining material: We cannot survive without water. Man can survive without food for some days, but it cannot survive without water for long.

As has been said above, Water can be equated with "life". Water is essential for the sustenance of all living organisms including all plants and animals. All plants, animals including human beings have 60–95 per cent water in their bodies. Part of this water is released from our body in the form of sweat, excreta, urine and vapour.

All species require a good amount of water daily. About 4 litres of water we need everyday. During the summer months we need more water because of the increasing order of water loss from our body. Much of this water is needed for our body growth, nutrition and transport of soluble nutrients to different cells in the body.

Plants carry out Photosynthesis (a process by which plants make their carbohydrate food) with the help of water (H_2O), carbon dioxide (CO_2) and sun's rays (as source of Energy). In plants also water helps in transportation of micronutrients from one part to another part of the plant. It serves as the medium of Transportation within the body. Water also serves as the medium to maintain our body temperature (Thermoregulation). So any form of life cannot be sustained without water.

Earth's Water Distribution

We all know that about 97 per cent of Earth's water supply is from the ocean. Ocean water is unfit for human consumption and other uses (irrigational purposes) due to its high salt content. Of the remaining three per cent, 2.3 per cent is buried in the polar ice caps. Thus it will appear that major amount of water is not suitable for our use. The remaining only 0.7 per cent remains as fresh water in rivers, lakes, streams, ponds and in the underground water for our use.

Therefore, one can well appreciate that usable or utilisable water is in short supply. Besides, the World population is steadily increasing. It is about seven Billion today. India itself has already crossed 1.25 Billion marks. Because of increasing order of industrialisation and agricultural activities together with population pressure, drinking water is already in short supply. With this comes another problem, since a large amount of available water gets polluted because of various human activities and is no longer suitable for drinking purposes. Many in the cities have to even purchase water for drinking water. Many more suffer in both villages and cities because of drinking/using polluted water. Enteric and gastrointestinal disorders, typhoid, cholera has been increasing day by day and are also taking many lives of our citizens.

Among the net amount of annual rainfall, about 70 per cent is lost by evaporation and transpiration by plants, while the remaining 30 per cent goes into our streams. Out of all the stream water about eight per cent is utilised for irrigation, two per cent for domestic use, four per cent in industries and 12 per cent for other utilities.

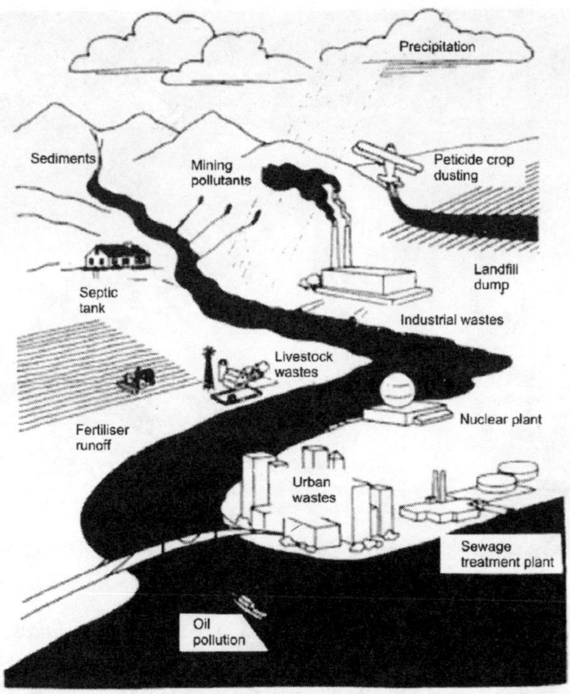

It must be appreciated that our usable water resources is finite and is likely to be exhausted within the next dew centuries or so. Moreover, it is getting polluted as we have discussed above and are becoming unfit for use.

The picture above shows how our water bodies may get polluted from a variety of sources, such as urban wastes, oil spillage, livestock wastes, fertiliser runoff and pesticide run-off from the agricultural lands, in addition a massive amount of untreated industrial wastes landfill dump, septic tank precipitation, etc., also contribute to it to a large extent.

Therefore, Water crisis is more serious a problem than food or population crisis since food production or population problems are irrelevant without water supply. Therefore we all have to save water in every possible manner we can and do not indulge in polluting water or even allow others to pollute it. We should not allow having water famine someday.

Sources

There are three main sources of water:

(i) Surface water (streams, rivers, lakes)

(ii) Ground water (underground or emerging as springs)

(iii) Rain water.

(i) Surface Water: Water from *streams, rivers, ponds, lakes, dams* and reservoirs is rarely potable; its direct use is likely to require treatment measures.

Lake water (seen above) provides us with one of the major sources of drinking water. They are usually rain water, protected and saved to supply drinking water.

Water coming down from the hills (as in the above picture) provides us stream water with minerals such as Magnesium, Calcium etc.

River Water (seen above): It gets polluted because it traverses a long distance carrying large amount of different types of pollutants on its way. It has to be treated to supply drinking water to people.

Dam Water (see above in the picture) is a major source of water for agricultural purposes and also for domestic purposes. Large excesses of water are maintained in reservoirs to protect them from getting wasted and used when needed.

Pond Water is a major source of water for domestic purposes.

Sea water can be used for almost everything except drinking and irrigation purposes as it contains all types of impurities and soluble salts.

On locations where no adequate sources of fresh water exist but where sea water is near, desalinisation is one possible but costly option to desalinate water for supply.

Our sea is the vast source of water (about 3/4th of the world surface is full of sea water, but it is not suitable for either drinking nor for irrigation; because of its high salinity (very high salt concentration). it is not used for either purposes. However modern science has developed methods for desalination of sea water to make it useful for drinking purposes. These methods are called Reverse Osmosis. Desalination plants are now available in some areas of our country. These plants are very costly, however.

Spring Water

Springs are the ideal source of groundwater. This comes out from an opening in the earth through pressure. Water from a spring is usually pure at the source and can be piped to storage and distribution points. The yield of water from a spring may vary widely with the seasons. It will be at its minimum at the end of the dry season and early in the rainy season.

It is reasonably pure and rich in minerals, but gets polluted when it travels down through human habitats.

Spring Water.

(ii) Groundwater: Groundwater is contained in aquifers. Aquifers are rocks or groups of rocks under the surface of the earth that are capable of transmitting, storing and yielding water. They may be formed by loose sediments (silt, sand, gravel); fractured rocks or otherwise porous rocks (fractured lavas, granites, metamorphic rocks, sandstones, etc.). The microbiological quality of groundwater is usually very good in view of the filtration undergone by water in its transit through rock pores.

Groundwater can be raised by infiltration galleries, tube wells, dug wells or boreholes. Infiltration galleries extract groundwater horizontally; for example through tunnels and/or ditches. The choice of method will depend on the depth of the water table (the level of water present above the rocks), yield, soil conditions and availability of expertise and equipment. Any new well or borehole must first be developed to full yield by an initial period of pumping at a fast rate. This pumps out finer soil particles, allowing water to pass more easily into the well. Yields can be raised by increasing the size of the well below the water table, for example in the case of a shallow well, by an infiltration gallery across the line of groundwater flow. If wells are sited too close together, yields will be reduced.

(iii) Rainwater: This is the purest form of natural water and relatively free from microorganisms. Reasonably pure rain water can be collected in areas with suitable shelter and individual household storage facilities in areas where there is adequate and reliable year-round rainfall.

Picture above shows how rain water can be preserved for various uses.

WATER IS A MAJOR RESOURCE- SAVE IT AND PROTECT IT

As has been said above, rain water, groundwater from springs and wells or water from municipal and private systems are usually of better quality than surface water from rivers, lakes or dams and should be used if available.

Water Cycle

This precious resource, Water, gets recycled from one form to another and gets back to its original form again. This is known as Water Cycle.

The Water Cycle means how surface water from the land rotates in various forms–from surface water it gets converted into water vapor and goes to the sky; there it gets transformed into cloud in the colder environment. As water vapor gets condensed it becomes heavy and comes down as rain water. On the high mountains, the water vapor is converted into ice, which in summer gets melted and comes down on the land as water again. The Sun's heat provides energy to evaporate water from the Earth's surface (ponds, rivers, oceans, lakes, etc.). Plants also lose water to the air (this is called transpiration of plants).

Some of the underground water is trapped between rocks or clay layers; this forms groundwater. But most of the water flows downhill as runoff (above ground or underground), eventually returning to the seas as slightly salty water.

We all know that ground water reaches the surface to fill our ponds and lakes, and we keep water stored in reservoirs and dams etc. These surface waters get vaporised due to Sun's heat and go up in the form of water vapor. The water vapor gets condensed into water droplets gradually and becomes heavy to come down on the surface of earth as rain or snow (where temperature is too low (below 0°C). Such water then traverses from the surface of the soil and goes underneath the ground to form ground water. Thus it completes the water cycle shown below in the picture.

The picture below shows how water gets circulated from one form into another.

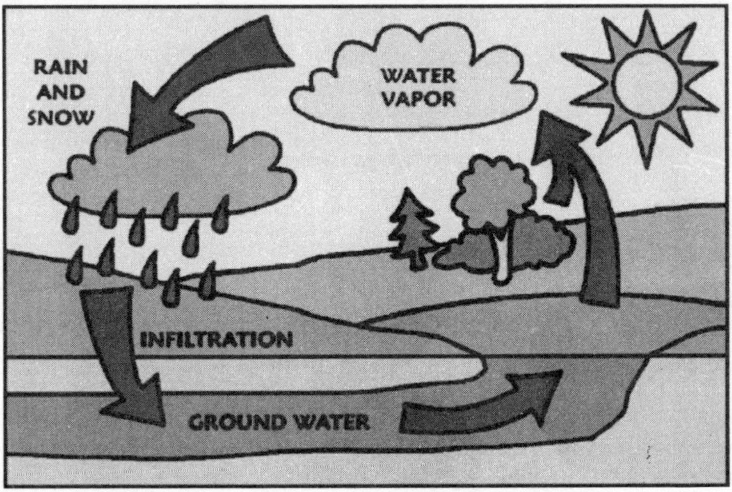

The pictures on the sides (above and below) show in two different manners our Water Cycle.

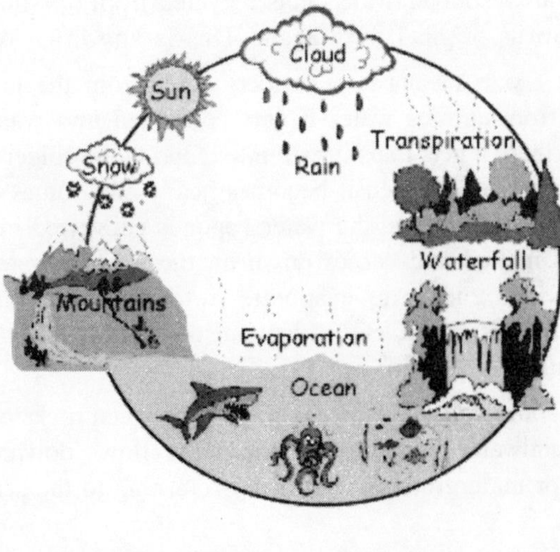

The water cycle (also known as the hydrologic cycle) is the pathways that water follows through its various states and forms, such as vapor, liquid, solid—as it moves through the ocean, atmosphere, groundwater, streams, mountains etc. (The picture above in the left depicts it).

MASS AWARENESS PROGRAMME

A List of some activities that both the students in schools, and also others in area such as Clubs/NGOs can organise from time to time for increasing awareness among them the general public.

The activities suggested below are neither exhaustive nor prescriptive. Teachers may design their own set of activities keeping in view the overall objectives of teaching and learning of Environment Education at this stage. They will have to make use of local flora and fauna and available resources and facilities and take cognizance of local environmental problems. Students should be encouraged initiate action on their own.

1. Collect samples of soil from various places and study similarities and differences between them based on their physical characteristics.
2. Visit nearby localities and study the relation between the types of vegetation and the nature of soil.
3. Collect samples of rainwater in the beginning and midday through a rain spell and compare the samples for impurities present.
4. Collect information from different sources for two weeks (newspapers, radio, and television) about temperature, humidity and rainfall and study the pattern of changes in respect of each parameter.
5. Collect information from different sources for two weeks (elders in the community, newspapers, radio and television, Internet and official records) about the water bodies like ponds, wells, and *jhohars* lost in the locality, village or region. Find out the reasons (like silting, disuse, filling for reclamation of land). Participate in discussions on the impact of these changes on availability of water, vegetation, habitat and social life.
6. Collect information about changes in land use, availability of water, forests, livestock and internal resources of the locality/village/region from different sources (elderly in the community, news papers, television, internet and official records) and have discussions on them.
7. List the crops grown in your area and prepare a record about the snowing season, duration of maturity, sources and periodicity of irrigation and yield of each crop.

8. Collect information about the prevalent methods of growing plants for forestry in the region.
9. Plant trees in the school compound (or any other area) and look after them (this may be done as a class or group activity), as a part of *Van Mahotsava* programme, wherever possible.
10. Visit nearby localities to observe how plantation prevents soil erosion.
11. Identify and collect relevant information about commercial, industrial and social activities at the local level that may have an impact on the environment. Disseminate information through hand-outs and school Bulletin Board.
12. Make a collection of clippings of news items, features, photographs, posters, cartoons, advertisements or any other format, about various issues of environment, including community hygiene, sanitation and pollution. Collate and disseminate information through charts, posters, collages, bulletin boards or through any other mode.
13. Participate in Co-scholastic activities like observance of World Environment Day and *Van mahotsava*, eco-clubs, study tours, debates, exhibitions and quiz competitions.

(b) Air

The atmosphere around us serves as the reservoir of air. The atmosphere covers up the earth as a blanket. It maintains humidity and temperature on the surface of Earth. It is also the source of various gases and is also the medium for dispersal of gaseous wastes. The vital Oxygen is a major gas in our atmosphere.

Earth's atmosphere can be divided into two parts-near atmosphere and far atmosphere.

As has been said above, the atmosphere of the Earth is a mixture of different gases, particulate matters and aerosols, collectively known as AIR which envelops the Earth. It reaches over 560 kilometers (348 miles) from the surface of the Earth. Life on Earth is supported by this atmosphere, solar energy, and our planet's magnetic fields.

The atmosphere absorbs the energy from the Sun, recycles water and other chemicals, and works with the electrical and magnetic forces to provide a moderate climate. The atmosphere also protects us from high-energy radiation and the frigid vacuum of space. The envelope of gas surrounding the Earth changes from the ground up. Four distinct layers have been identified using thermal characteristics (temperature changes), chemical composition, movement, and density. These are: (1) Troposphere, (2) Stratosphere, (3) Mesosphere, and (4) Ionosphere.

Earth's Upper Atmosphere

Troposphere

The troposphere starts at the Earth's surface and extends 8 to 14.5 kilometers high (five to nine miles). This part of the atmosphere is the

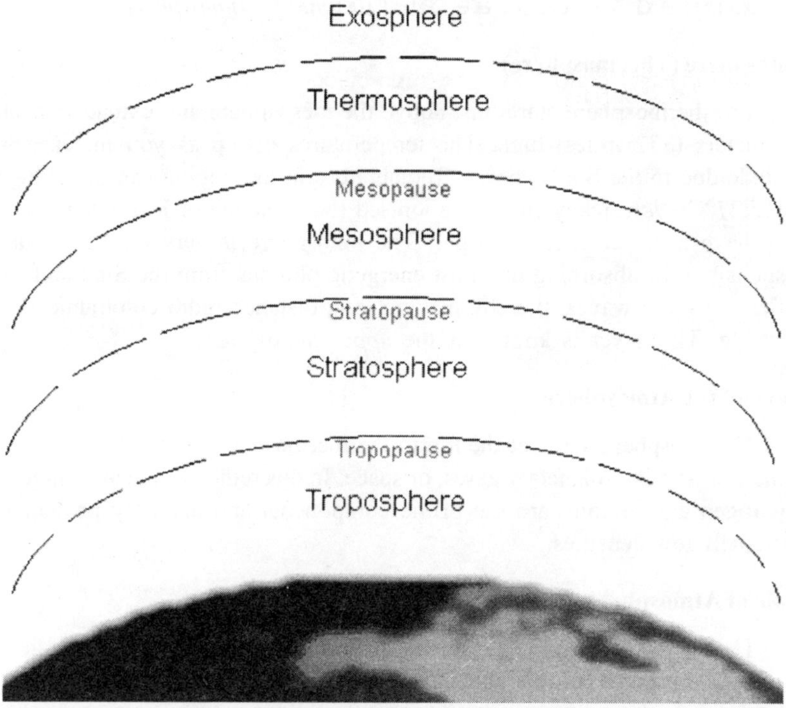

densest part. As you climb higher in this layer, the temperature drops from about 17 to 52°C. The tropopause separates the troposphere from the next layer. The tropopause and the troposphere are known as the *lower atmosphere.*

Stratosphere

The stratosphere is 50 kilometers (31 miles) high. Compared to the troposphere, this part of the atmosphere is dry and less dense. The stratosphere starts just above the troposphere and the temperature in this region increases gradually to–3°C. The thin ozone layer in the upper stratosphere has a high concentration of Ozone. It is a reactive form of oxygen. The Ozone layer is primarily responsible for absorbing the ultraviolet radiation (UV) from the Sun. Ninety-nine per cent of "air" is located in the troposphere and stratosphere. The stratopause separates the stratosphere from the next layer.

Mesosphere

The mesosphere starts just above the stratosphere and extends to 85 kilometers (53 miles) high. In this region, the temperatures again fall as low as 93°C. The mesopause separates the mesophere from the thermosphere. The regions of the stratosphere and the mesosphere, along with the stratopause and mesopause, are called the *middle atmosphere*.

Ionosphere (Thermosphere)

The thermosphere starts just above the mesosphere and extends to 600 kilometers (372 miles) high. The temperatures go up as you increase in altitude due to the Sun's energy. Temperature in this region can go as high as 1,727°C. *Here* many atoms are ionised (have gained or lost electrons so they have a net electrical charge). The ionosphere is very thin. It is also responsible for absorbing the most energetic photons from the Sun, and for reflecting radio waves, thereby making long-distance radio communication possible. This layer is known as the *upper atmosphere*.

Beyond the Atmosphere

The exosphere starts at the top to the thermosphere and continues until it merges with interplanetary gases, or space. In this region of the atmosphere, Hydrogen and Helium are the prime components and are only present at extremely low densities.

Role of Atmosphere

The earth's atmosphere is the environment for most of its biological activity and exerts a considerable influence on the ocean and lake environment. Weather in this region consists of the day-to-day fluctuations of environmental variables and includes the motion of wind and formation of weather systems such as hurricanes.

Climate is the normal or long-term average state of the atmospheric environment. The atmosphere protects us by filtering out deadly cosmic rays, powerful ultraviolet (UV) radiation from the Sun, and even meteorites on collision course with Earth. The ozone layer also protects the earth from the sun's harmful ultraviolet rays. Meteors strike the thermosphere and mesosphere and burn from the heat generated by air friction.

Composition of Our Atmosphere–A Source of Gases

There are a number of atmospheric gases, which make up our air. The main gases are nitrogen (N_2, 78 per cent) and oxygen (O_2, 21 per cent), which make up most of the volume of air. Remaining one per cent is filled with other gases.

Nitrogen

The molecules of nitrogen (N_2) are composed of two atoms of nitrogen (N) atoms. It is a colourless, odourless, and tasteless gas. Nitrogen is very essential for the nutrition of both plants and animals. Nitrogen is a constituent part of all proteins of our body. It is also a part of the genetic material (DNA) of all organisms.

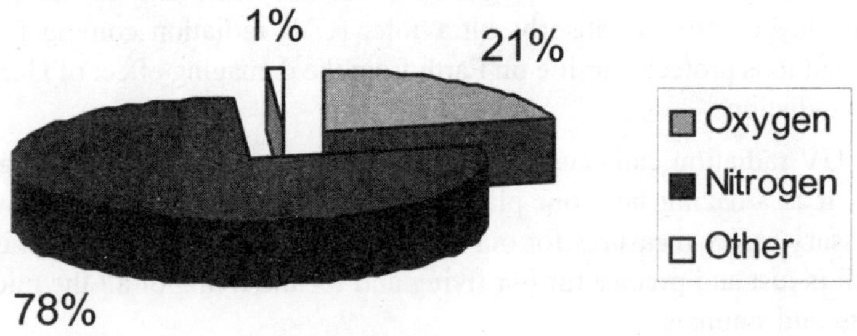

Several species of bacteria can absorb nitrogen from the air and convert it into ammonium salts, which plants can use. This process is called "Nitrogen fixation". It is the principal natural mechanism by which atmospheric nitrogen is added to the soil. Legumes, such as beans, can fix nitrogen from the atmosphere. This is accomplished by a type of bacteria called "Nitrogen-fixing bacteria" living in the nodules of the plant roots.

Nitrogen molecules can be broken by the energy generated by lightning strikes and volcanic action. Whenever lightning flashes in the atmosphere, some nitrogen combines with oxygen and forms the gas called nitric oxide (NO). This nitric oxide is converted to nitric acid (HNO_3) by combining with water. It is highly soluble in water and falls to the ground with rainwater, to be absorbed later by soils.

Oxygen

The gas oxygen (O_2) is composed of two atoms of oxygen. Like Nitrogen it is also colorless, odorless, and tasteless. Oxygen also comprises 86 per cent of the ocean water. Sixty per cent (60 per cent) of the human body is composed of O_2. Oxygen (O_2) is the third most abundant element found in the Sun. Oxygen is utilised primarily by all animals, including humans, but also to a small degree by plants, in a process termed as "Respiration" (wherein food products are metabolised to generate energy).

Oxygen is very reactive. It binds with most of the elements to form their oxides. A chemical reaction in which an oxide is formed is known as "Oxidation". The process of burning or combustion involves a very rapid oxidation.

Carbon in fossil fuels, for example, can be quickly oxidised to carbon monoxide (CO) and then to carbon dioxide (CO_2). A considerable amount of heat is generated in the process. Such a reaction is called an 'Exothermic Reaction'. Within the stratosphere, oxygen molecules combine with free oxygen atoms to form Ozone gas (O_3). As has been said earlier that this Ozone layer normally absorbs ultraviolet (UV) radiation coming from the Sun, and thus protects our life on Earth from the damaging effect of Ultraviolet (UV) radiation.

UV radiation can cause skin cancer, kurtosis and can also damage our eyes. It is amazing how our planet, Earth, was formed or created with all necessary safety measures for our survival in this Environmental conditions, which is just and precise for our living and for the living of all the microbes, plants and animals.

Trace Gases

Besides Nitrogen (N_2) and Oxygen (O_2), the remaining one per cent of the atmospheric gases is known as trace gases because they are present in very small concentrations. The most abundant of the trace gases is the noble gas Argon (approximately one per cent by volume). Noble gases, which also include neon, helium, krypton and xenon, are very inert and do not generally, engage in any chemical transformation within the atmosphere.

Hydrogen is also present in trace quantities in the atmosphere, but because it is so light, over time much of it has escaped Earth's gravitational pull to the space.

Despite their relative scarcity, the most important trace gases in the Earth's atmosphere are the '*Greenhouse gases'*, which include carbon dioxide, methane, nitrous oxide, water vapor and ozone. It is so called because they are involved in the Earth *natural greenhouse effect* which keeps the planet warmer than it would be without an atmosphere.

Apart from water vapor, the most abundant greenhouse gas (by volume) is carbon dioxide. Despite being present in only 370 parts per million by volume of air, carbon dioxide and the other greenhouse gases help to keep the Earth 33°C warmer than it would otherwise be without an atmosphere. Through emissions of more of greenhouse gases, as a result of several of Man's activities, a substantial increase in the concentrations of Greenhouse gases has been caused resulting in the "Greenhouse effect", which is responsible for more of warming of the Earth surface.

Other trace gases in the atmosphere arise from natural phenomena such as volcanic eruptions, lightning strikes and forest fires. Gases from these sources include nitric oxide (NO) and sulphur dioxide (SO_2). Sulphur dioxides are also released from various untreated industrial emissions.

Water Vapour

Moisture or water vapor is one of the most important components of the atmosphere. It not only provides the supply for clouds formation and rainfall, but it also plays a vital role in energy exchanges within the atmosphere, which affect the Earth's energy balance. When water is heated to 100°C it boils and evaporates into the air. Water at 100°C contains enough heat to break all the bonds, which link together the molecules in liquid water. However, even at temperatures below 100°C some evaporation from water surfaces takes place, with water molecules breaking free and escaping into the air. These free water molecules are collectively known as water vapor or moisture. There is always water vapor present in the atmosphere. Water vapor enters the atmosphere by evaporation from all surface bodies of water. These include puddles, ponds, streams, rivers, lakes and oceans. Water also enters the atmosphere by transpiration from the leaves of plants and trees.

When air containing water vapor cools in the atmosphere, the water vapor condenses to form tiny droplets of liquid water (or ice) in clouds. Eventually the water stored within clouds is returned to the Earth's surface in precipitation—rain, hail, sleet or snow. Water vapour in the atmosphere behaves like a greenhouse gas, trapping heat that is trying to escape from the Earth to space. The presence of water vapour in the atmosphere significantly strengthens the Earth's natural greenhouse effect.

Our Atmosphere

"Our atmosphere is nothing but a medium for dispersion of gaseous materials including wastes".

During the past about 200 years, mankind has begun to significantly alter the composition of the atmosphere by generating activities responsible for adding pollution to our environment. The more we are becoming modern, the more pollution we are adding to our environment. Massive Industrialisation and an aggressive agriculture are basically responsible for increasing the order of pollution in our environment. Because of Population, there had been a need for greater urbanisation of cities and towns adding large number of housing projects, roads, schools, colleges, hospitals, vehicles etc. All these activities added pollution to our atmosphere.

Although air is still made up mostly of oxygen and nitrogen, mankind, through its pollution, has increased the levels of many trace gases, and in some cases, released completely new gases to the atmosphere. In addition to natural sources of nitric oxide and sulphur dioxide there are now many man-made sources, including pollutant emissions from cars (CO, CO_2, the carcinogen, Benz-a-PYRENE etc.), agricultural activities (Fertilisers, Pesticides), Industrial activities (SO_2, N_2O and NO, hydrocarbons, acid vapour, dusts) and electricity generation through the burning of fossil fuels (dusts, smokes,

H_2S). Some of these gases present in an elevated concentration can be harmful to both humans and the environment as a whole.

Air pollution can result in poor air quality, both in cities and also in the countryside. Some air pollutants make people sick, causing breathing problems and increasing the likelihood of developing cancer. Others are harmful to plants, animals, and the ecosystems. Some air pollutants return to Earth in the form of acid rain, which corrodes statues and buildings, damages crops and forests, and makes lakes and streams unsuitable for fish and other plant and animal life.

Man made air pollution (gaseous pollutants are coming out untreated and are releasing in the open sky various toxic gaseous substances.

Man-made air pollution is also changing the Earth's atmosphere so that it lets in more harmful radiation from the Sun. Although we have now banned products which can harm the Earth's ozone layer, unfortunately such harmful gaseous emissions have not yet stopped completely. Ozone holes have been recognised over Antarctica and the Arctic. The chlorofluorocarbons (CFCs) formed from refrigerators damage the ozone layer. At the same time, various human activities are responsible for releasing more of greenhouse gases to the atmosphere, preventing heat from escaping back into space and leading to a rise in global average temperatures.

Global warming phenomena have far-reaching impact on the entire environment, for example it will raise the sea levels and change climates all over the world. Some places will become hotter and drier, others wetter. The incidence of severe storms and flooding is likely to increase. Global warming will also affect food supply and increase the spread of tropical disease.

(C) Soil Resources

Soil is a valuable resource for mankind. Soil is the medium for growth of plants. It is also a habitat for large number of soil organisms that help balancing our cology. Soil also serves as the facilitator for percolation and retention of water.

What is Soil?

Soil gets transformed into rock in its final state of its decay. After millions of years of weathering, it is converted into fine mineral particles. Water, wind, chemical actions, temperature variations, and earth's movement, etc., act on the rock cracking it and also dividing it into smaller pieces and particles which creates our soil.

Soil Structure

Soil is made up of four different distinct layers called *soil horizons*. These are:

(A) Horizon or Top soil: This layer is closest to the surface and contains large amounts of organic remains called humus. It is full of tiny living organism. The plant grows in this layer.

(B) Horizon or sub soil: This layer is low in organic matter but rich in minerals which have leached from a horizon due to water movement through the layer of soil. This is not suitable for plant growth.

(C) Horizon or water table: This layer contains broken up bits of bedrock in various stages of weathering submerged in water.

(D) Horizon or Bed rock: This is the lowest layer consisting of unweathered parent rock material.

Composition of Soil

Thus it is now clear that Soil is made up of—Weathered rock, Organic remains, Water, Air and a great variety of living organisms. Apparently, soil may look simple; however it is an extremely complex system. It is most often described by its physical, chemical and biological properties. Soil is composed of both organic and inorganic materials; inert and active; living and non-living substances. Soil contains many organisms: bacteria, nematodes, fungi, earthworms, and small animals.

Soil can be described in a simple manner that it consists of only four major components: air, water, organic matter, and mineral matter. In an ideal soil, air and water fill the pore space and compose about 50 per cent of the volume; organic matter accounts for about one to five per cent of the soil volume; and mineral matter accounts for the remaining 45 to 49 per cent.

Soil organic matter is present in the surface horizon of soils in much higher concentration than below. It comes in a variety of chemical forms from complex plant residues and humus to very simple organic compounds like sugars and amino acids.

Humus is synthesised or builds up from other intermediate organic components, particularly proteins and lignins. It is different from the other organic compounds in that it is fairly resistant to decomposition. Therefore, it persists in the soil for fairly long times. It is also much richer in nitrogen, phosphorus, and sulfur that the original plant residues. Therefore, it is an excellent plant nutrient source.

Soil Texture

Soil particles vary in size, shape and chemical composition. Some are so small that they can be seen only with a microscope. Three categories of soil particles have been established—sand, silt and clay. This is called texture of soil. The three groups are usually divided by their particle size.

Clay particles are the smallest one (less than 0.002 mm). Clay is smoother when dry and sticky when wet. Soils high in clay content are called heavy soils. Clay also can hold a lot of nutrients, but doesn't let air and water to pass through it well. You may need an electron microscope to see clay particles, since they are so small. *Silt particles* (between 0.002 mm and 0.06 mm) feel smooth and powdery. When wet it feels smooth but not sticky. A microscope must be used to see silt particles. *Sand particles* are the largest ones (between 0.06 mm and 2 mm). They can be seen by the naked eye. When you rub it, it feels rough. This is because it has sharp edges. Sand doesn't hold many nutrients. Particle size has a lot to do with a soil's drainage and nutrient holding capacity. To better understand how big these three soil particles are, you may think of them like this—If a particle of sand were of the size of a basketball, then silt would be the size of a baseball, and clay would be the size of a golf ball.

Soil Types

Soil types depend upon the rock from which the soil weathered the climate and the life within the soil.

(A) Basically soil is split into three types, Acid soil and alkaline soil, with neutral soil in between.

Soil acidity is measured from 0–14 pH (a measure of acidity and alkalinity) with 0 as acid and 14 as alkaline.

Acid Soil—This is mainly made up of decaying matter which releases chemicals into the soil and this is where the acid balance comes in question. Acid soils can go as high as 5.5 pH. The soil is usually quite dark and has obvious matter content. The more the matter rots, the less acid there is.

Alkaline Soil—Areas with high limestone content will normally have a more alkaline soil (pH more than 7.0).

(B) Soil can also be classified depending upon the size of particles present and water retaining capacity. This is given in table below:

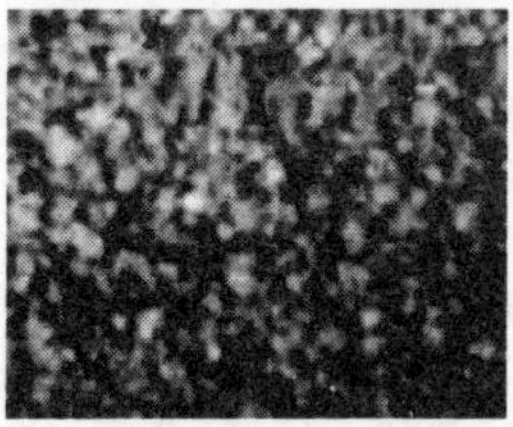

Sandy/Rocky soil

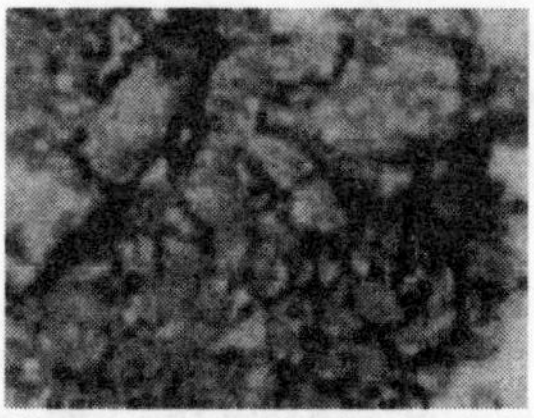

Clayey soil

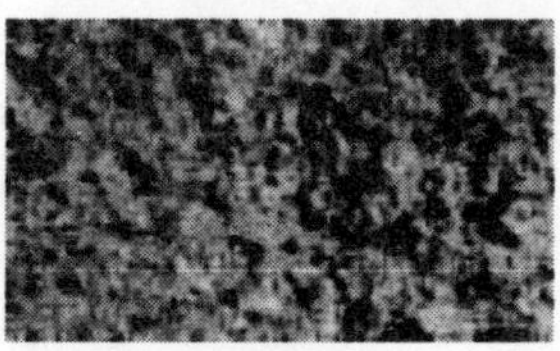

Loamy soil

Functions of Soil

1. Soil is a medium for growth of plants: Soil is important for plants because it holds its roots, stores nutrients, and provides support for the growth of plants. The mineral and organic matter of the soil are the solids and serve as the storehouse and exchange sites for plant nutrients and other chemicals; thus, they are important from both fertility and environmental point of view.

2. Habitat for organisms: Many organisms and creatures inhabit in the soil and use the air and water for living. Some of them are bacteria, fungi, insects, worms and burrowing animals like snakes, frogs, rodents, lizards etc.

3. Facilitator for percolation and retention of water: Soil acts as a sponge to take up and retain water. Movement of water into soil is called *infiltration,* whereas, downward movement of water within the soil is called *percolation, permeability or hydraulic conductivity.* Pore space in soil is the conduit that allows water to infiltrate and percolate. It also serves as the storage compartment for water. Infiltration rates can be near zero for very clayey and compacted soils or in excess of 10 inches per hour for sandy and well aggregated soils. Low infiltration rates lead to ponding on nearly level ground and runoff on sloping ground. Permeability also varies with soil texture. This is the mechanism by which water reaches the subsoil and rooting zone of plants. It also refers to the movement of water below the root zone. Water that percolates deep in the soil may reach a groundwater aquifer.

(D) Vegetation and Forests

Vegetation: From time immemorial, vegetation on the soil is a vast source of our food. Without that we would not have survived. Vegetation on the surface of the soil has been provided by the nature during the very early stages of development. It serves as the major source of our food, both for animals and humans. It serves as the place for living of many small animals. It provides us with all kinds of vegetable foods like Tomatoes, brinjal, Okra (ladies finger), beans, cucumber, and also potatoes, onions, ginger beneath the surface soil, and gourd, bitter gourd as creepers. Various other vegetables such as rice, wheat, lentils, various types of dahl (lentils), oil plants, fruit plants, flower plants, etc., and many more comprise our vegetation world.

Very early in Evolution, there exist indications that on the top of our soil, vegetation started spreading. Over the years grass, weeds, small plants, various types of vegetables appeared.

Forests: Our Forests are the habitat for larger plants and animals Forests serve as an agent for percolation and retention of water, for maintaining ground water level, for prevention of soil erosion. Forests maintain humidity of air Forests are a source of firewood, bamboo, timber, fruits, lac, and resins and is a vast resource of medicinal plants as well.

Forest means a place with dense growth of trees, together with other plants, covering a large area of land. Forests have natural vegetation, i.e., plants growing on their own. The trees which make up the main area of the forest create a special environment which, in turn, affects the kinds of animals and plants that can exist in the forest. The science concerned with the study, preservation, and management of forests is called *forestry.* A forest is an ecosystem—a community of plants and animals interacting with one another and with the physical environment.

Several types of forests are shown below:

Types of Forests

The *forests of the world* are often broadly classified by biomes, which are forest types corresponding to the climatic regions of the earth in which they occur. There are three major forest biomes: tropical, temperate, and coniferous. These are described below:

Tropical Forests

Tropical forests have the greatest diversity of species (lots of birds, small mammals, and insects); they are located near the equator. There is no winter there and these forests only have two seasons: rainy and dry. They have 12 hours of daylight, temperature is about the same all year around (68°F to 77°F), and average rainfall is more than 78 inches per year. One square kilometer may contain more than 100 species of trees. Here soil is not nutrient rich. Such type of forests Cover entire area of Indonesia, Amazon and Congo basins.

Temperate forests or deciduous forests: These types of forests have winter and other seasons; temperature varies from –22°F to 86°F, rainfall occurs throughout the year, averages 30 to 60 inches per year. The soil of this type of forests is nutrient rich; 3-4 tree species are seen per square kilometer (include such species as oak, hickory, beech, hemlock, maple, basswood, cottonwood, elm, and willow). This forest has both small and large mammals including squirrels, rabbits, skunks, birds, deer, mountain lion, bobcat, timber wolf, fox, and black bear. These are located in eastern North America, north eastern Asia, and western and central Europe.

Coniferous Forests

The largest type of biome (zone) occurs on land. They have short, moist summers and long, cold dry winters. Most of the precipitation is snow

(15 to 40 inches per year) and has mostly evergreen conifers trees that are tall and pointed with needle leaves (pine, fir and spruce trees). These forests are the habitats of both large and small mammals and birds Hawks, moose, bear, weasel, lynx, fox, wolf, deer, hares, chipmunks, shrews, and bats may live here. You may find such forests in Siberia, Alaska, Scandinavia and Canada.

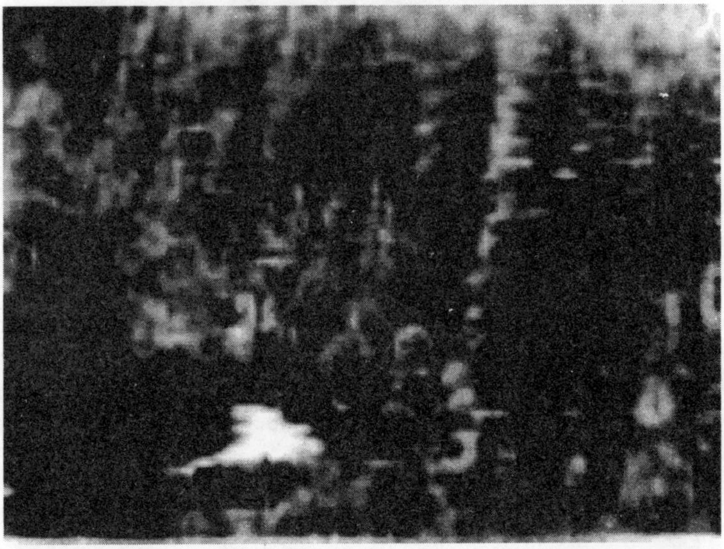

India has a diverse range of forests: from the rainforest of Kerala in the south to the alpine pastures of Ladakh in the north; from the deserts of Rajasthan in the west to the evergreen forests in the north-east. In India, forests can be broadly classified into many types; some of which are the Taiga type (consisting of pines, spruce, etc.), the mixed temperate forests with both coniferous and deciduous trees, the temperate forests, the sub tropical forests, the tropical forests, and the equatorial rainforests.

Some other types of forests present in India include: Thorny forest–trees which have thorns and long roots and can survive without water for a long time. This type of forest is present in Rajasthan and some parts of Madhya Pradesh and Uttar Pradesh.

Tidal Forests are found in deltas of Ganga, Mahanadi and Godavari. Trees called Sundari or Mangrove are found in these areas. These are short dense trees that tolerate and adapt themselves well to both saline and fresh water and grow in coastal areas. The Gangetic Sunderbans is the largest mangrove area in India.

Alpine Forest—Moist alpines are found all along the Himalayas and on the higher hills near the Myanmar border. It has a low scrub, dense evergreen

Mangrove Forests.

forest, consisting mainly of rhododendron and birch. Mosses and ferns cover the ground in patches. This region receives heavy snowfall. Dry alpines are found from about 3000 meters to about 4900 meters. Dwarf plants mainly the black juniper, the drooping juniper, honeysuckle, and willow predominate in these areas.

Snow-covered Forest Region.

The Importance of Forests in Our Lives

Forests play a major role in terms of climatic control, pollution abatement, and wildlife maintenance. The forest is also vital as a watershed. In addition, the forest provides shelter for wildlife, recreation and aesthetic renewal for people, and irreplaceable supplies of oxygen and soil nutrients.

Deforestation (Cutting and felling of trees in the forests), particularly in the tropical rain forests, has become a major environmental concern all over the world, as it can destabilise the earth's temperature, humidity, and carbon dioxide (CO_2) levels.

Due to huge increase in world population, and massive deforestation (cutting or felling of trees) to provide for various human needs, the CO_2 levels of our atmosphere had increased sharply during the past few decades. This has caused *Global Warming* phenomena, already experienced by the inhabitants of this planet, Earth. This is a matter of serious concern to everybody. International meetings, conferences, seminars on *Global Change* are being held from time to time all the world over to discuss the situation now and what kind of measures that each country should follow to contain their Carbon emission. It has become very evident now that Forest trees are important links to maintain the earth's geological, chemical, and hydrological cycles by a variety of means that can be described as follows: (1) It takes in CO_2 and releases oxygen; (2) Forests release carbon and mineral elements such as nitrogen and phosphorus as trees decay; (3) It absorbs moisture for growth and releases it as vapor through transpiration; (4) Forests prevent erosion by reducing the force of rainfall at the soil surface and by intercepting and absorbing water, rather than allowing it to run off directly; (5) Our forests harbor a diversity of wildlife; (6) Forests act as windbreakers; and (7) Forests serve as an agent for percolation and retention of after.

Forests are responsible for rainfall and for maintaining water cycle. The leaves transpire leading to cloud formation and thus result in rain. Because of the thick humus layer, loose soil, and soil-retaining powers of the trees' long roots, forests are vitally important for preserving adequate water supplies. Rain water also gets absorbed by the soil and goes down by gravitational pull through percolation. The percolated water gets accumulated over the rock-bed forming water table. In this way the water table in maintained. Water in river and streams also seeps through their sides and bottom adjoining ground. This is also how the level in the ground water is maintained. The streamside forests act as filter and help prevent ground water contamination by intercepting and absorbing excess nutrients and other pollutants. Thus our Forests regulate earth's temperature regime.

Forests Prevents soil erosion : The roots of trees bind to the soil and prevent erosion by not allowing the soil to run away with rainwater or blow away with storm. Vegetation cover slows down the run-off on soil surface checking soil erosion, silting and landslides, reducing the danger of flood.

Forests are the habitat for plants and animals: Forests provide home and shelter to a large number of wild animals protecting them against strong winds and solar radiation. The number of wildlife is decreasing sharply as many of them are hunted and killed by human beings, hunters and poachers for some ill motives. This has led to extinction of some species already and many animals are now endangered. Some of these animals are–Royal Bengal Tiger, Elephants, Peacocks, pigeons, some exotic birds etc.

Forest Products

Forests and forest resources play a significant role in the state's or country's economy. A large number of people are employed in the forest products' industry. Forests provide us with firewood, timber, cane, bamboos, resins, fruits etc. Forest animals provide us with honey, meat, ivory, hide, skin, lac etc. The trees provide us with essential oils that are used in medicine. Wood has various domestic and industrial applications. It provides raw material for pulp, paper, composite wood, rayon, boat building, and match industries.

Recreation

Forests provide unique recreational opportunities, which not only serve to refresh the city-worn soul, but benefit the economy through the money spent by tourists traveling in the state in pursuit of outdoor activities associated with forested areas.

Cultural Values

The variety of cultural values and symbolic functions ascribed to the forests are numerous and diverse. It varies from country to country. Physically and mystically forests have defined the environment of communities in the region throughout time. Forest trees may house the spirits of ancestors as well as those of the newborn. Sometimes forests are viewed in both positive and negative lights as sources of evil as well as power and munificence, as providers for, and hindrances to our development. The mystical qualities of specific forest resources often play a crucial role in traditional healing practices. Forests provide the venue for religious, social, and healing ceremonies. Forest products such as tam-tams and forest foods such as palm wine are used in many ceremonies.

Man and his destructive influence on our Environment :

1. Man and his Environment–How Our Environment is being Destroyed by Man and his Activities?

In this Chapter we will discuss the following:

(a) Response of living beings to changes in environment–adaptation in plants and animals,

(b) Modification of environment by human beings to protect themselves against changes and to meet their needs,

(c) Effect of human activities and population growth on agriculture, harnessing of energy, housing, industrial development and other areas of consumption and social activities (an elementary idea)

(d) Consequences of human activities–stress on land use, water sources, energy and mineral resources, forests, ocean life, environmental degradation,

(e) Role of individuals in maintaining peace, harmony and equity in nature, good neighbourly behaviour, use and misuse of common property resources.

(A) Adaptations to Environmental Changes

Adaptation of Plants and Animals

The special characteristics that enable plants and animals to be successful to survive in a particular environment are called Adaptation. The most striking fact in nature is this adaptation phenomenon of organisms to their environment. Every organism seems to have been survived on Earth's surface after they could develop mechanisms as to how to tolerate the changing environmental conditions and situations; select that can be consumed and reject all those which are harmful to our systems. After an ideal plan for that were specially designed within the plants and animals, they became fit to survive in that place in nature which they fill.

Desert Adaptations of Plants

Cactus can Survive with Limited Water in Deserts.

How Does Desert Plants Store their Water?

Many desert and arid plants have evolved ways and means to capture and store water so that during the rare times when it rains in the desert, they can take up as much water as possible and store some for subsequent needs. Cactuses, many palms, agaves and euphorbs (cactus-like desert plants) do this. These plants store water in their stems, leaves or trunks. Some desert plants, such as the barrel cactus, have expandable stems for storing water. Many of these plants also keep their stomata closed during the day to prevent too much water loss in the hot dry sun and open them instead at night. Other plants have developed 'Adaptations' that reduce water loss from their leaves-the part of a plant through which most of the water is lost. Still others have a waxy coating on the leaves, or have small leaves, that reduce the surface area exposed to the drying elements. In many cases, desert plants have no leaves at all.

Photosynthesis, which normally occurs in green leaves, is carried out in the stems, which are themselves green containing the pigment 'chlorophyll'. These types of plants that grow in dry conditions are called *xerophytes.*

Aquatic Adaptations : (A) Submerged Plants shown below

Totally submerged plants are the true water plants or *hydrophytes.* These plants are truly aquatic. They have the greatest number of adaptations

to life in water. These include–(i) The presence of little or no mechanical strengthening tissue in stems and leaf petioles. If these plants are removed from the water, they hang simply, (ii) Submerged plants lack the external protective tissues required by land plants to limit water loss. All the surface cells of these plants appear to be able to absorb water, nutrients and dissolved gases directly from the surrounding water. As a result, the internal system of tubes (xylem), which normally transports water from the roots to all parts of the plant is often greatly reduced, if not absent. Thus, if these plants are removed from the water, they wilt very quickly; (iii) There are also no stomata (breathing pores) on the leaves of these plants; (iv) Roots are often reduced and their main function is anchorage. The root hairs, which function in the absorption process, are often absent. (v) The submerged leaves are often highly dissected or divided. This has the advantage of creating a very large surface area for absorption and photosynthesis.

(B) Floating Plants

Floating plants are of two types: 1. Those which are rooted with floating leaves (e.g. Water Lily) and 2. Those which are not rooted in the sediment,

Water-lily (A floating Plant).

just float on the surface (e.g. Duckweed). Floating leaves are generally tough because they have to withstand the rough weather conditions and water movement. The green pigment-containing chloroplasts, important for photosynthesis, are restricted to the upper surface of the leaves, which are the only surface to be well lit. Stomata are also found only on the upper surface of the leaf.

(C) Swamp Plants

These are emergent plants with the lower parts often submerged. They are typically tall and narrow-leaved plants, which offer little resistance to

Reedmace.

fluctuating water levels or high winds. Their height means that they are unlikely to ever be completely submerged during flooding. The stems have tough internal fibers and a hollow structure. This allows them to withstand severe winds without damage. Reedmace has noticeably narrow aerofoil shaped leaves, presumably for this reason.

Adaptation in Animals

Desert Adaptations

Desert animals like camel have many adaptations to help them survive in the extremely high temperature of the desert. Many are nocturnal, meaning active during the cool night rather than the hot daylight hours. Surprisingly, the kangaroo rat conserves water by excreting a solid urine rather than liquid. Protection of the eye, ear and nostril against the sand is an important adaptation that the desert animals have to adopt. Camels known as the "Ship of the Desert" has its eyes well protected by long eye lashes and are kept high above the ground by long neck. The ear openings are also well protected by hair or scales. A camel can tolerate a greater degree of water

Camel known as Ship of the Desert.

depletion of the body and when water is available it may drink more than one third of its body weight and store it. Further adaptations to desert life are splayed hooves, which are ideal for walking on sand and the hump that stores fat to provide for energy.

Aquatic Adaptations

Some of the important adaptations in animals living in water include those like the following – (i) presence of respiratory organs that can take in dissolved oxygen from water, e.g., gills in fishes, (ii) presence of tail and fins to help in changing directions and paddle through water, (iii) Streamlined body which helps to move through water.

Fish can live in water because it possesses the above characteristics: Many deep sea animals produce their own light by means of luminous organs, e.g., lantern fish. The light is used for attracting and baiting the prey. Another interesting adaptation is the enormous mouth enabling them to swallow such prey which are larger than themselves, e.g., gulper and Whale fish.

Lantern Fish.

Gulper.

Terrestrial Adaptations

Terrestrial animals such as mammals have lungs for breathing. The foot is suitably modified for walking and running. Terrestrial vertebrates have in place of fins legs for walking and creeping upon dry land. For the purpose of capture of their prey, most carnivorous animals are provided with strong claws, sharp teeth, hooked beaks and other structures as are usually seen in the lion, tiger, dog, cat, owl and eagle.

The ant-eater has a long sticky tongue which it thrusts forth from its cylindrical snout deep into the recesses of the ant-hill, bringing it out with its surface covered with ants. Animals which feed on nuts are fitted with strong teeth or beaks for cracking them.

Those mammals like the horse and cow, which feed on plants, have usually broad chisel-like incisor teeth for cutting off the foliage. Molar teeth are used when it is necessary that the food should be crushed or chewed, and the sharp canine teeth go with a flesh diet.

The long neck of the giraffe enables it to browse on the foliage of trees in grassless regions. The tree frogs or tree toads have the tips of the toes swollen, forming little pads by which they cling to the bark of trees. The hooked claws of the bat hold on to rocks, the bricks of chimneys or to the surface of hollow trees, where the bat sleeps through the day.

Aerial Adaptations

We all know that birds fly. Do we know how do they fly? Here are the answers. Birds have wings constructed most fittingly with which their light bodies, supported by bones containing air, soar through the air so perfectly

These animals have adapted Terrestrial Environment.

that imitation of them is difficult. The entire body of birds is covered with feathers which are light, elastic and water proof. The bones are hallowing

Birds have Wings to Fly.

filled with air making the body light and buoyant. The bodies are streamlined to allow swift passage through the air.

Seeing birds flying in the sky, men dreamt of the ideas how can they fly in the sky. So they tried to build something like aero plane for flying in he sky. Amasingly, the design of planes is almost like the birds, so it can fly easily.

Other Adaptations

The adaptations discussed above are all adaptations to specific climatic conditions, but various organisms have also developed adaptations to other aspects of their environment. Some animals have adapted to eat a certain type of food; others have adapted to avoid being eaten themselves. Most animals have behavioral adaptations, which help them attract a mate. In the plant world, many flowers have evolved specific structures that help ensure pollination by the insects they attract.

In addition to the general adaptations, fishes living in caverns have in addition to the general adaptations certain special adaptive modifications in accordance with their special environment, especially in the eyes, which are profoundly modified in accordance with a life spent habitually in darkness. Likewise all plants living on land have a general adaptation to terrestrial life, but in addition many have special adaptations. All plants which have green leaves use them for starch (food) formation under the action of sunlight, but special adaptations fit certain species to different degrees of light intensity, and as a result one plant may be fitted to grow in open fields while another will grow in shaded places.

Camouflage, as in a toad's ability to blend in with its surroundings, is a common example of an adaptation. The combination of bright orange and black on a monarch butterfly is an adaptation to warn potential predators that the butterfly is poisonous and prevent it from being eaten. These special features have evolved over long periods of time, through the process of natural selection. Adaptations afford the organism a better chance to survive in its surroundings.

Modification of Our Environment by Human Beings

It is said that we the human beings are the most intelligent of all living creatures. It may be true. But human greed has gone so high that they have started destroying the quality of the same environment that they live in, and in a variety of ways. Modification/alteration of the environment by the human beings, either to protect themselves against the changing environment and/or to meet their growing needs, are causing regular damages to the very environment. It has now made many people most concerned all over the world.

High-rise housing complex is coming up to accommodate people, but at the cost of what? Much of Environmental degradation has taken place for

random housing projects here and there, Agricultural lands had to be compromised to provide for space for these housing. Besides, more people brought more of pollution burden in our environment. As has been dais above, because of population pressure there has been increasing need for housing; but it has been encroaching upon the agricultural land in many places (see Picture above).

Nature has given man everything they need—life, food, and shelter. However, the selfish man is completely depleting nature for his own purpose. Man has been using the natural resources injudiciously causing an imbalance in nature. As a result of which air, water, forests and soil are getting modified. The damage caused has become almost irreparable. This is causing an ecological imbalance. He is extracting fossil fuels and minerals in the name of power generation, industrialisation, urbanisation and civilisation, Thus, these activities are pushing several thousands of biological species into extinction in the long run. Already man is running short of essential environmental components such as safe drinking water, coal and petroleum, which can at the most last for only another few hundred years.

Enormous growth of population, massive industrialisation and urbanisation are aggravating environmental conditions side by side, causing massive degradation of our environment. Common social facilities and civic services like absence of safe drinking water, clean air, proper waste disposal systems and sewage problems are increasing day by day. Severe health problems like bronchial diseases, asthma, allergy, arsenic infestation in drinking water causing severe toxicity, gastrointestinal diseases, heart diseases, cancer, neurological disorders, etc., are going on increasing. There is no second opinion that over-population brings about environmental degradation that led to climatic changes, atmospheric pollution, water changes and energy shortage. Many unplanned slums are coming up here and there which lacks proper disposal of wastes and sewages. As a result, different kinds of diseases are spreading out and sometimes lead to an Epidemic disease as well. Even the holy river Ganges has become highly polluted carrying the loads of untreated human and industrial wastes.

Forests

Forests are an important and renewable national resource and also help for maintaining the ecological order. Not only they supply wood for cooking, timber for construction work, cellulose and pulp for production of paper, etc., but it also influences the wind movement, temperature, humidity, soil and water retention. Because of human pressure, unfortunately our areas under forests have been declining steadily and are gradually shrinking due to diversion of the forest for non forest purposes, such as agriculture, construction of roads, canals, railway lines, power transmission lines, river valley projects, railway lines, mining industries, urbanisation and other developmental activities.

Deforestation

Severe deforestation is also caused by illegal logging, mining, collection of firewood, forest fire and famine. For life purposes, people use it for

cooking, warming, housing, furniture making, and many other purposes. Deforestation has also led to adverse climatic changes, erratic weather and more frequent droughts and disastrous flood. This has led to loss of biodiversity and wildlife has also been threatened.

Soil

Soil is an indispensable gift of nature. Lying over the rocky core of the earth at different depths. This complex mixture of animal, vegetable and mineral matter is one of the four requisites for life. Along with sunlight, air and water, soil nourishes micro-organisms, all plant life, and most animal life and also supports human life. Numerous insects and burrowing animals live in soil. Soil is mostly polluted in places where oil refineries, oil storage depots, nuclear power stations, pulp and paper mills, sugar mills, iron and steel plants, plastic and rubber producing factories, gas works, and chemical factories have been built. Refuse dumps from domestic and industrial wastes are deposited in the land causing soil pollution. Unburnt materials from industrial furnaces known as fly-ash are the major cause of soil pollution. Household garbage consisting of spoiled groceries, food scraps, vegetable remains, packing materials, cans, cardboard cartons, cloths, paper, ash, worn-out furniture, metals, bone of dead animals, plastics, polythene bags, broken glass pieces, leathers and rubber materials, etc., contribute a large amount to soil pollution. Besides, in rural areas and villages many people go to the open for easing out: Such fecal matter of human origin including sewage from household pollutes the soil. Soil pollution occurs in agricultural land also where modern farming methods have been practiced. Use or misuse of chemical "aids" such as fertilisers and pesticides pollute the soil. Pesticides (insecticides, rodenticides, weedicides, fungicides, herbicides) are synthetic chemicals used for pest weed, and rodent control, e.g., DDT, Malathion, carbaryl, aldrine, paraquat, etc.

Population Pressure

It is unfortunate that our open land areas are diminishing rapidly because of population pressure. Present population of the World is about 7,000,000,000 (Seven Billion), and increasing. India's population alone is about 1,240,000,000. India is the second largest populous country in the world. China being the First in this regard. More population brings in more demand for everything and obviously on our Environment. We should do everything possible to see that the population growth is restricted with our modern knowledge of Science, Medicine and Technology Special social and Educational campaign should be launched by the Government, social organisations, NGOs, local clubs and others educating people for population control. Government may offer special incentives for population control to motivate people for self-restricting, planning and controlling the number of children that they give birth to. Otherwise it may pose great risks for the nation itself. Its progress and development might get stalled someday.

A picture of Population Explosion is shown below:

With population explosion comes production of increased order of Domestic wastes as well, as is shown below in the picture.

Domestic Wastes

We have discussed earlier that due to increasing commercial values of land in cities, open land is diminishing, even though green spaces are the lungs of the city. But who cares! Not only is land disappearing due to construction of concrete buildings and tar roads, but good agricultural land is also being used up to produce bricks for building, sky scrappers, Factories and more of civic amenities.

It has been estimated that the brick work for a modest house for a family of five in an urban area would require about 120 tonnes of soil, mostly top soil. There is very little space left to create parks and playgrounds for the children and elders in the cities. Furthermore, the aggressive attitudes of Man swallows even the already existing green and open areas like parks, ponds, lakes and others. This is very unfortunate!

Waste Water

As has been said earlier water is essential for sustenance of all living organisms including animals, plants and human beings. It is one of the most abundantly available nature's gifts to us. However, the usable quantity of water resources, like any other natural resources, is finite and is likely to be exhausted within a century or two. Although earth has its 2/3 full of water. the utilisable quantity of water for our drinking and also for irrigational purposes are already in short supply. Water is distributed in nature in different forms, such as rainwater, river water, spring water, sea water and mineral water. Precious water gets polluted again by human activities of different kinds.

Picture shows that Industrial Liquid wastes are being dumped in our water bodies to pollute them Pollution of our water sources.

The water sources are getting polluted by man made activities and have become unfit for use sooner than expected. We all know now that human activities contribute to a great extent the pollution of water, in the form of industrial and domestic wastes such as detergents, waste foods and excreted materials, agricultural discharges in the form of fertilisers, pesticides, industrial wastes such as toxic metals, salts, oils and grease and other contaminations. As a result, there is shortage of safe drinking water and water for other household applications. The underground drinking water sources especially in the outskirts of cities and villages are getting rapidly polluted. Situation of water supply in a city, particularly in the slums where half of the city's population lives, is extremely poor. Lack of good quality of drinking water has caused high rate of infant mortality in the slums and in villages. Moreover, lack of proper drinking water and unhygienic use of pond or well water have increased the mortality during the last few decades.

Ocean cover more than two thirds of the earth's surface and they play a crucial role in the chemical and biological balance of life on the planet. Ocean water is unfit for human consumption and industrial purposes because of its high salt content. The ocean is being polluted by petroleum and its products released from water vehicles. Transporting them from one place to another.

Radioactive pollutants also enter into the water steams from various sources such as nuclear power plants and nuclear reactors. Thus the discharges from the industries and nearby cities are causing an imbalance in the Ecology of the marine life.

Air: We already know that Air is essential for life. Even though the air is abundantly available over the surface of the earth, it contains lot of impurities. Various types of contaminants are entering into the earth's atmosphere by natural and man—made activities described earlier.

Toxic gases from Industrial Chimneys pollute our aerial environment.

Air gets polluted by industrial emissions (seen above).

Man made activities that are responsible for the pollution of air can be classified as:

(i) Domestic pollution–the use of insecticides in our homes for cleaning, burning of fuels for cooking purposes, release of chloroflurocarbons (CFCs) from refrigerators and other cooling agents, aero plane propellers, sprayers, etc., cause air pollution.

(ii) Industrial pollution–Release of gases like oxides of sulfur, nitrogen and carbon, carbon particles from different chemical industries, dusts from cement plants and various mines, liquid wastes from paper mills, sugar mills, breweries, chloro-alkali industries, thermal power stations, paint and varnish industries, iron and steel plants, tanneries and many other industries pollute our aerial environment. Pollutants particularly from Thermal power plants, cement industries and mines cause serious air pollution.

(iii) Vehicular pollution—Release of huge quantities of harmful gases like carbon monoxide, carbon dioxide, sulfur dioxide, nitrogen dioxide, formaldehyde from automobile exhausts, trains and aero planes are responsible to contribute to major air pollution.

Effects of Air Pollutants

The various air pollutants can cause allergy, bronchial problems, asthma, breathing difficulties, heart problems and many other diseases including eye problems.

Various air pollutants are also responsible for the Green house effects, warming of surface temperatures, weather changes etc. Some of them are responsible for creating the "Ozone hole", which allows harmful UV-radiation from the sun to come all the way to the earth's surface. Normally the thick OZONE layer protects us from the UV radiation. However if you are exposed too much in the sun, as when people take sun bath in the beach of the ocean, you may get exposed to high dose UV radiation. Such longer exposure can cause skin diseases like cancer, keratitis, dermatitis etc.

(C) Effect of Human Activities and Population Growth on Environmental Pollution

Effect of human activities and population growth on agriculture, harnessing of energy, housing, industrial development and other areas of consumption and social activities have been partially discussed above. More of that is being discussed now.

Enormous growth of population, massive industrialisation and unplanned urbanisation are aggravating our environmental sanctity and causing a great damage in our environmental quality. Increased urbanisation can result in increased consumption of natural resources such as trees for lumber and fresh drinking water; more pollution resulting out of that can affect air and water quality and can have a negative effect on health conditions, wildlife, and vegetation; more "crowding"; and fewer "green spaces". Common social facilities and civic services like absence of drinking water and clean air, waste disposal and sewage problems are increasing day by day. Severe problems like asthma, allergy, arsenic infestation in drinking water, etc., are going on increasing. Over-population brings about environmental problems that lead to climatic changes, atmospheric pollution, and water and energy scarcity. Many unplanned slums are coming up which lacks proper disposal of wastes and sewage. As a result, different kinds of diseases are spreading out, sometimes even taking the shape of an epidemic. Even the holy river Ganges has become highly polluted these days.

Effect of Agriculture

Nature has given man everything-life, food, and shelter. However, man is completely depleting this un-replenishable nature' gift.

Soil degradation, including nutrient depletion, erosion, and salinisation, is widespread. 20 to 30 per cent of the world's forests areas have been converted to agriculture, resulting in extensive species and habitat loss. Agriculture is encroaching on many national parks and other protected areas. In the process there is a depletion of wildlife resources. Deforestation has also led to adverse climatic changes, erratic weather and more frequent droughts and disastrous flood. The main cause of such ecological disaster is population explosion.

Agriculture consumes 70 per cent of the freshwater withdrawn annually by humans. Irrigation is draining more water than is being replenished by rainfall, causing water tables to fall. Moreover, many water sources are being polluted by excessive use of fertilisers and pesticides. Agricultural wastes are sources of soil and water pollution.

Harnessing of Energy

Resources like forests, rivers, wind power, solar energy are available forever and called renewable sources of energy, while other sources like coal, petroleum, natural gas, etc., on which we depend very heavily, are termed as non-renewable sources of energy. Their availability is limited, and once consumed it cannot be generated again. Man is extracting fossil fuels and minerals in the name of power generation, industrialisation, urbanisation and for our civilisation to advance further. These activities would become the root cause of extinction of several thousands of biological species in the long run. Today man is already running short of essential environmental components such as coal, which can at the most last for only another 600 years and minerals like aluminum, magnesium, etc., for only 100 years. Excessive use of coal and petroleum for vehicles and domestic purposes has increased the level of carbon-dioxide in the atmosphere, nitrogen dioxide and sulfur-dioxide in the air. Burning of coal for the generation of energy produces large amounts of fly-ash as waste, which causes soil and water pollution.

Expanding urbanisation is the main cause for increased pollution of land, air and water. The population of the third world cities has been doubling every 10-15 years. This situation overwhelms the Government's efforts to provide houses, clean transport facility and other basic services such as schools, colleges, restaurants, parks, recreation facilities etc. As a result, a large members of the urban people is forced to live in the unhygienic conditions of the living environment of slum and squatter settlements as drinking water, proper sewage disposal system, not adequate.

Effect of Urbanisation on Environmental Degradation

Over population has created shortage of open space in the cities. Due to increasing commercial values of land in cities, open land is diminishing, even though green spaces are the lungs of a city. Not only is land disappearing

(See the picture above how new cities are being developed to accommodate the human needs – housing, roads, office buildings, spacious divided streets, regulated traffic system, Banks, Restaurants etc.).

under concrete buildings and tar road, but good agricultural land is also being used to produce bricks. There is very little space left to create parks and playgrounds for the children and elders in the cities. Situation of water supply in a city particularly in the slums where half of the city's population live is extremely poor and below standard. Lack of good quality of drinking water has caused high rate of infant mortality in the villages and slums. It takes many lives every year in our country. One thing that we all can do is to make others aware about the danger of drinking polluted water and that at least the villagers can boil their water before drinking. This is a must.

We have tremendous water shortages (almost everywhere). A very common picture is shown above.

The bulk of the rural people live in extremely bad conditions under leaky roofs. Due to acute poverty proper houses could not be made by the villagers. Moreover, lack of proper drinking water and unhygienic use of pond or well water have increased the mortality during the last few decades.

Effects of Industrial Development

Industries require constant supply of various resources, such as water, energy and transport facilities for efficient functioning. Besides, resources they need are land, water and minerals etc. However, these natural resources are polluted by both industrial and human activities. Huge amounts of domestic and industrial waste generated causes environmental degradation.

In developed countries, most industrial wastes are either sent to landfills, incinerated or discharged to rivers. Hazardous and non-hazardous wastes as well as liquid, solid and sludge wastes are mixed together with one another and dump them with domestic wastes at the disposal sites. This contributes to problems of groundwater pollution. Waste waters from industrial sources can result in the production of certain hazardous wastes such as sludge containing heavy metals, some of which are very toxic.

Effect of Social Activities

Population Growth Rate (PGR) is the increase in a country's population during a period of time, usually one year, and is expressed as a percentage of the population at the start of that period. It reflects the number of births and deaths during a period and the number of people migrating to and from a country. Increase in population results in poverty and unemployment. This leads to violence, corruption, mental tension, etc., resulting in law and order problems. As population increases the average age of the population rises and eventually the proportion of elderly, non-working people increase. This can put great pressure on a country's pension, health care, and social security systems. Population growth can make it more difficult to raise standards of living in some countries and can put pressure on the environment at large. Slower population growth might allow a country to implement suitable environmental policies to check pollution, and develop such institutions which can help protect the environment.

(D) Consequences of Human Activities

We the human beings are the greatest polluters of all. His realisations are now quite clear to everybody. Instead, we are continually polluting our environment. Consequences of human activities include–stress on land use, water sources, energy use and uses of mineral products, widespread use of forest resources, massive use of ocean for trade and commerce and marine products. All these directly or indirectly are responsible for environmental degradation.

Nature and mankind are an inseparable part of life that includes land, water, air, space, energy, flora and fauna. These are interconnected, interrelated and interdependent. There are unlimited forms of life on earth in various shape and size. There exists a great degree of competition among various species, primarily to meet their needs for survival. Man is one among the many species competing with all others also for survival. Due to excessive uses of the natural resources, there is ecological imbalance. It is to be appreciated that Land, Air and Water are complex interrelated systems. Even if one is affected/altered, the effects are reflected on the others, and their constituents.

Land Use: Due to exploding number of population, more and more agricultural land is being sacrificed for providing them housing and other civic facilities. This poses a major threat to our food production. Misuse of land is making this indispensable life-supporting system unavailable. Land use for habitation purposes has increased from 4.09 per cent to 6.2 per cent in the past 30 years. Moreover, *Urbanisation and Industrialisation* along with construction of roads, highways, etc., have subjected in loss of land resources. Dumping of solid wastes from industries, huge amount of municipal wastes and fly-ash from thermal power stations has caused massive soil pollution.

Livestock (cattle, buffaloes, goats, and sheep) wealth plays a crucial role to provide protein food to all mankind. It is a major resource for livelihood in rural life–it is a major source of fuel and draught power, of nutrition and of raw materials for rural industries. However, the permanent *grasing of lands* which were used to be available for the livestock are now insufficient. This has resulted in overgrasing and deterioration of the quality of our landmass. Overgrasing of animals has made the soil hard, impermeable, and reduced the organic matter of the soil.

Water Sources

The *major uses* of water for various human activities include: (i) Municipal water supply, (ii) Industrial water supply, (iii) Recreational uses such as swimming, boating, (iv) Agriculture and fisheries, and (v) To maintain Ecological balance. However, rivers and lakes have been used for a long time as the dumping grounds for human sewage and industrial wastes. In villages men take bath and wash clothes and utensils in the ponds and lakes making them polluted.

Water is *polluted by*:

(a) Sewage and Domestic Wastes
(b) Pesticides
(c) Detergents and Synthetic Fertilisers
(d) Toxic metals and pollutants
(e) Oil, grease and other chemicals
(f) Acid deposition
(g) Suspended solids
(h) Thermal pollution
(i) Pathogenic (disease producing) microorganisms
(j) Radioactive substances.

The effects of water pollution are very many. They include: poisonous drinking water, poisonous food animals (due to bioaccumulation of various toxins from the environment over their life spans), unbalanced river and lake ecosystems that can no longer support full biological diversity, deforestation from acid rain, and many other effects. Some of the major human activities that cause water pollution are mentioned below in some detail:

(1) Industrial Wastes: In urban cities, industry is the greatest source of water pollution, accounting for more than half the volume of all water pollution sources and for the most deadly pollutants. The industrial waste-bearing water or effluent (wastes products in a liquid form) from industries is discharged into streams without any treatment to reduce the burden of pollutants. These are also dumped into lakes, or oceans, which becomes too polluted to provide for supply of drinking water, fishing, and swimming. In addition, numerous manufacturing plants pour-off undiluted/untreated corrosives, poisons, and other noxious byproducts from various industrial activities. The construction industry discharges metals and poisonous solvents.

(2) Thermal Wastes: Hot water discharged by factories and power plants cause thermal pollution by increasing water temperatures. As you may already know that living species have a specific thermo-tolerance mechanism. It has to maintain certain specific temperature to control and regulate its biological systems. Any change in the temperature of its surrounding environment may disrupt the internal thermo-regulatory balance causing different types of health problems. Such dumping of warm/hot water wastes directly into water bodies disrupts the water's ecological balance, killing off some aquatic plant and animal species while encouraging the overgrowth of others. Such outgrowth may cause water pollution again.

(3) Agricultural Wastes: Fertilisers, pesticides and herbicides, weedicides etc., used in the field for agricultural practices eventually accumulate in the lakes, ponds and other water bodies along with flowing rain water and/or agricultural run-off. These chemicals are harmful to fish and other aquatic plants and animals. Some chemicals accumulate in the tissues of aquatic organisms (e.g. fishes) through bioconcentration and biomagnification and in turn enter into human body when consumed.

(4) Domestic Wastes: Along with domestic wastes from towns and municipalities, sewage carries industrial contaminants and a growing tonnage of pharmaceutical, paper and plastic refuse as well. Excreted drugs and household chemicals also contaminate the water sources. Sewage wastes contain pathogenic (that causes disease) bacteria and viruses to cause diseases like typhoid, cholera, paratyphoid, bacillary dysentery, amoebic dysentery, polio and hepatitis.

Energy and Mineral Sources

Mineral resources are natural resources found in rocks underlying the earth surface, e.g., coal, iron, copper, gold, silver etc. Mineral oil is a dark and thick liquid found deep inside the earth. This is refined to make petrol, diesel, kerosene etc. Natural gas is found with mineral oil in some oilfields. Mineral resources are very precious as they take millions of years to form. However, with increasing population load and urbanisation, the demand for these minerals is increasing. Thus these resources are getting depleted.

What is more worrisome is that the non-renewable energy is widely used for domestic and industrial purposes. It includes coal, petroleum (petrol, diesel, and kerosene), etc. The extraction, production and use of these resources have resulted in the destruction of the environment through pollution. The consumption rate of these resources is twice their production and all of them are available for only a finite period, after which we have to depend on alternatives. Already search for finding alternatives are on. The alternative or the renewable energy sources include: solar, wind, tidal and geothermal energy. These non-conventional energy sources are perennial and eco-friendly. Non-conventional energy sources would help in reducing pollution. It is very unfortunate that there exists now the MAFIA groups which are illegally stealing our mineral resources to make money.

Deforestation

Every year at least 2000,000 sq. km. of tropical forests are cleared from the world for farming, settlement, mining, plantation, industry, timber and fuel. We already know that our forest plays a vital role in regulating climate, controlling runoff, purifying air, providing shelter for wildlife and producing valuable food and other products such as wood, paper and medicine. Forest trees use carbon dioxide from the atmosphere and produce biomass releasing oxygen. This maintains a balance of these two gases in the atmosphere such that both are getting benefited.

The effects of deforestation include: (i) leaching of soil and loss of soil fertility due to washing out of nutrient rich top soil, (ii) Loss of biodiversity with extinction of some species of plants and animals and (iii) change in climate-increase of carbon dioxide in the atmosphere resulting in warming of the earth.

Ocean Life

Large and small craft significantly pollute both inland and coastal waters by dumping their untreated sewage. Oil spilled accidentally or flushed from tankers and offshore rigs sullies beaches and smothers bird, fish, and plant life. Moreover, garbage, solid industrial wastes, and sludge formed in sewage treatment, all commonly dumped into oceans, are other marine pollutants found worldwide, especially along coastal areas.

To summarise the consequences of human activities that causes environmental degradation include:

- Erosion of land
- Deforestation and desertification
- Pollution of water sources
- Depletion of natural resources
- Loss of biodiversity

Most of the Governments in different countries have enacted a law which is binding for any industry or housing project or any other major construction project, that they will have to conduct an EIA (Environmental Impact Assessment Study), prepare an EMP (Environmental Management Plan) and also a DMP (Disaster management Plan) before they start their project work and get them approved by the Ministry. to obtain a clearance certificate. Unfortunately it is often found ignored. This important part is very often neglected; careful attention is needed in this regard by the concerned authorities and also by the general public such that this essential requirement is not by-passed.

(III) How to take Proper Care to Protect the Environment around us (Our Surroundings): Personal and Community Measures as well as Legislative Measures

So long we have discussed what causes pollution, what are the sources of pollution, what kind of pollutants cause air, water and soil pollution etc. We will now learn how to combat pollution and what we can do by ourselves. It is now widely believed that if we fail to protect our environment, we will cause tremendous damage to it that itself might bring in our destruction. It is so essential !

1. Proper Care and Protection of Our Environment

All the objects of our environment, such as air, water, lakes, rivers, oceans, forests, plants, animals and soil have to be protected and conserved by us. These are Nature's Gift to us. We will not be able to survive without them. We have major responsibilities to protect them not only for us, but also for our generations to come.

The quality of air, water, food and soil should be protected at all costs and by all means. We all must give proper attention in this regard. The legislative authorities, both at local, state and central Government level must look into this matter. The polluters must be punished. "Polluters must pay" should not only be just a slogan, it must be introduced as a part of the punishment given to all the polluters. And that law should be strictly implemented. The corrupt people associated with flouting the pollution control laws should be taken to task by everybody.

All State pollution control Boards should take pro-active measures against all those who are habitual polluters. Proper Technologies available in the World must be introduced to contain pollutants at all levels. Mass awareness programmes should be launched from time to time in all the states, towns and villages so that at the citizen's level there is more consciousness regarding the reasons as to why they should not pollute the environment around them. NGOs and local Clubs can be activated to take measures at the local level.

Our forest cover, our animals, plants, etc., are to be protected from getting extinct. Due to various man-made activities the quality of these Environmental objects, also called 'Ecological partners', are getting worse day by day. It is a question of survival that everybody must know.

We have already learnt that an increase in Industrial and Agricultural activities, associated with a rapid increase in our Population have caused a serious problem of Pollution in our immediate environment. Of course population pressure necessitated Urban and /City expansion programme to accommodate people in new high-rise buildings which mostly had come up in places occupying agricultural land. It has also increased the pollution levels around us. We also see an increase in consumerism, increasing loss of our Forest cover and agricultural lands as has been said earlier. New Industries have further occupied both agricultural lands and forest areas posing a great threat to our Environment and Ecology. Although there is rapid economic growth in our country, we had to sacrifice a great deal for that. The greatest damage that has been caused is on our Environment. We need a balance between the two since we cannot ignore either side of it. Otherwise it will cause us great harm in course of time.

Development without an appropriate plan is only going to harm us and our environment. It may adversely affect us and our future generations. We should be very careful about it. With every developmental plan there should be a plan for pollution control, and side by side a plan to replenish the loss of all that has been lost due to the developmental reasons. With the progress and development of the nation, we see that the number of cars in the country is increasing everyday. So an increasing amount of car exhausts are mixing up in the air polluting it profusely. The Government should strictly regulate such emission problems by asking the car makers to install emission control device in every cars, before they are sent to their show rooms. It must be a mandatory measure that the Government should implement strictly. Gaseous emissions from the industrial chimneys are also polluting our environment. Liquid wastes from industrial plants, thermal power stations, agricultural activities, household wastes, municipal and hospital wastes etc., are polluting both our air and water in an increasing manner. Law must be enacted that at the source all wastes are treated adequately using the modern technology, before their release. Industrial and other gaseous emissions contain harmful chemicals, such as carbon monoxides, carbon dioxides, various hydrocarbons, nitrogenous oxides, sulphur dioxides, methane and different types of organic solvents, hydrogen sulphides, fats and grease, and various cancer causing chemicals (benzo-alpha-pyrene, heavy metals etc.). Those agents may cause bronchitis, asthma, lung diseases including lung cancer, neurological disorders, immunological malfunctions, allergy etc. These toxic and harmful chemicals and gases should be contained by using appropriate technologies.

All solid and liquid wastes are either dumped spoiling agricultural lands or in river waters respectively. Very small portions are incinerated (burnt). We all know that the Wastes are the breeding ground of germs and also contain various types of toxic chemicals. They are the root-cause of various diseases, such as cholera, various diarrheal diseases, gastroenteritis, typhoid, hepatitis, polio etc. So proper care and attention are needed to dispose these types of wastes.

What is the Solution?

In fact, there is no perfect solution! It may sound a little awkward, but it is true. However, we can do a great deal if we all work together and keep our vigilance about pollution-causing areas. Without waiting always for the Government to come and do various things, we must also be aware and conscious about it and help the Government to control and implement various measures. We have to be more cautious that we ourselves are not responsible to cause any pollution. We and our activities should not contribute to our increasing order of pollution burden. We have to keep in mind that most of the pollution is caused by MAN. So both the Government agencies in one hand and the people on the other have to work together, hand in hand, to control pollution. The Government has to bring in stricter legislations and implement them strictly without any failure. Bureaucratic measures should not be allowed to impede or delay in implementing the laws of the land.

Due to rampant corruption, the Government policies and programmes are sometimes not implemented. An industry often violates rules and regulations. This should not be tolerated. All the violators should be punished! Unfortunately, some of the times it is observed that they remain scot-free.

Industries should be asked to recycle the pollutants they generate. Only "Zero Pollution" technology should be encouraged for their use. At our individual level, we have to be more conscious to keep our immediate environment and surroundings clean.

Since we know that all pollution problems arise out of human activities, the responsibility is now bestowed on the human beings, who should come forward to restrict it. Therefore, we need more awareness among the people about the potential cause and effect of pollution.

So it is quite evident that to reduce the pollution burden, we have to take care of our environment. We have to keep our surroundings clean first. We need to follow certain practices to keep our surroundings clean and beautiful. We need to add more green plants as well as flowering plants wherever possible.

We should not allow our trees to die as shown below:

Nature's Beautiful Creation. Let's Save It.

Felling of Trees should be Restricted

Picture below shows what acute Water shortages are there in our Villages, Hilly regions and Remote areas of our country.

As a part of creating Environmental Awareness, Please Mark and Remember some days in your calendar and Organise meetings, Debates, Morning Parades with festoons, banners on various aspects of our changing environment, environmental decay, what we need to do, what we should not do and the like.

(A) Observe June 5 as the World Environment Day and highlight the various aspects of our environment and how to protect it. World Environment Day is celebrated every year to create mass awareness regarding the necessity of protection of our environment, to highlight what has gone wrong already and what we can do about it.

(B) Organise Earth Day Celebration on March 21 every year.

On Earth Day every year, observe this day to organise various programmes to highlight what we all should do to protect our earth.

Earth day is a day that is intended to inspire awareness and appreciation for the Earth's natural environment. The name and concept of Earth Day was allegedly pioneered by John McConnell in 1969 at a UNESCO Conference in San Francisco. The first Proclamation of Earth Day was by San Francisco, the City of Saint Francis, patron saint of Ecology. Earth Day was first observed in San Francisco and other cities on March 21, 1970, the first day of spring.

(C) Organise Ban Mahotsova every year.

On the day of Ban—Mahotsova, plant trees on road sides, in parks, in our Gardens etc. Van Mahotsava is an annual pan-Indian tree planting festival, celebrated on 5 June and even in the first week of July. During this event, millions of trees are planted. Van Mahotsava was launched in the year 1950 by Shri Kanhaiyalal.

Mr. M. Munshi, the then Union Minister for Agriculture and Food, started this campaign in order to create an enthusiasm in the popular mind for the preservation of forest primarily and also for encouraging people for planting of trees. The movement was launched as "trees mean water, water means bread and bread is life"–that was the message the campaign wanted to spread out. It was also hoped that it would create tree consciousness among the people.

Ban Mahotsava, a week long festival of tree planting is organised every year in the month of July all across India and lakhs of trees are planted. The planting of trees during Van Mahatsova was to serve the following purposes:

1. To provide fuel and fodder and thus release cow dung for use as manure.
2. To increase production of fruits and add to the potential food resources of the country.
3. To help creation of shelterbelts around agricultural fields to increase their productivity.
4. To provide fodder leaves for cattle to relieve intensity of grasing over reserved forests.
5. To provide shade and ornamental trees for the landscape.
6. To provide small poles and timber for agricultural implements, house construction and fencing.
7. To help conservation of soil and further deterioration of soil fertility.
8. To inculcate tree consciousness and love of trees amongst the people; and
9. To popularise the planting and tending of trees in farms, villages, municipal and public lands for their aesthetic, economic and protective needs.

From the above, it is quite clear that it is one of the best ways of preventing earth from the adverse effects of global warming phenomena.

In order to protect our environment, we need to ensure the safety and protection of the following:

(A) Save our Ecological Partners: Love thy Nature! It can be the slogan of the Twenty-first century. Man and his environment have to co-exist and have to live in peace and harmony. We have to learn how to take care of our Ecological surroundings; our plants and animals, our parks and ponds, our monuments and mountains, our buildings, roads and houses, our schools and gardens, our religious places, our water bodies and all other things around us. In fact, all of our ecological partners should also be protected. We need to have our love, sympathy and affection towards them. They need us and we need them. One is supplementary and complementary to each other. We need all of them for maintaining the Ecological Balance.

Population Explosion (see above Picture)

An overwhelming Population increase is the root cause of increasing order of population to day. We all know that the world population is increasing sharply. In the year 2012, we are about 7,000,000,000 and increasing. Therefore, the greatest challenge before us is how to balance our population growth with that of life supporting materials including our food, water, air, and place for our agriculture, our housing, our industries and all our civic amenities along with. An Ecological balance has become necessary in every respect. Can we do it? Perhaps we can, if we want it. We have to devise ways and means as to how we can make it happen for our survival and the survival of the generations to come.

(B) Prey and Predator Relationship: Our evolution progressed thus far in a manner that followed the tune of nature. In nature, there is a Prey and Predator relationship, such that each one is dependant on the other. This maintains the balance in Nature. It does not allow any one type of animals /plants to increase in an abrupt manner. Nature always tries to maintain its own harmony! But it can do it up to certain limit! Beyond that it fails. Whenever an imbalance is created, hundreds and thousands of organisms get extinct. History of Evolution tells us about that. Only some selected species could survive and thrive. Those which could withstand the brunt of Nature's rage by developing adaptation mechanisms could survive, others got extinct.

(C) Our Ecology and Environment: We now know that both Animals and Plants are essential for us. Man cannot live by bread alone! It needs the aesthetics, decency, love, affection, kindness and feelings for others.

One important aspect of mother nature's unique balance is that it has also created some animals that provide us with a rich source of Protein food. Animals provide us with protein food and fat also. Animals also provide milk, eggs as well. On the other hand, the plant kingdom provides us with various fruits and vegetables, carbohydrates, fibers, oils, minerals and vitamins. Animals cannot make their own food, but plants can. Therefore animals also depend on plants for their food. Some large animals of course kill smaller animals for their food. If plants are destroyed, the animals will get destroyed too.

Above is an ORCHID (Nature's Beautiful Piece of Art).

The beautiful orchids grow in humid and moist weather of the hills. In regions with higher temperatures they normally do not grow. There are many different types of orchids with exotic colors, shape and size. Further, plants are essential to maintain our environment with less of carbon dioxide load as plants absorb carbon dioxide (CO_2) from the air and release oxygen in return. This oxygen we breathe in. Thus plant purifies air in addition to its other beneficial functions to protect us. Remember, we take oxygen to maintain our life, Sustainability of human beings, therefore, depends entirely on, our environmental partners, the animals and plants together. Besides food, the plants also provide us with various medicinal compounds. It's a good source of our medicines from ancient times. Therefore, we have to save plants for our own survival. Plants also provide us with cotton, with which we make different types of our clothes. Vegetable colours are often used for various purposes, such as food colour, dying etc.

Picture of a Beautiful Flower is shown above. We need them all.

Grazing animals can destroy Nature's vegetation, but it is also essential to think that such areas are also needed for grazing animals. For them proper grazing area must be identified, since they need their food also for survival.

Do not cut trees! If trees have to be cut for some other valid reasons, grow five times as many trees as are cut. We should save endangered Species of both Plants and Animals.

Several species of plants and animals have been termed as endangered. They are usually protected by LAW now-a-days. We should ensure that in all of our activities we do not disturb them or waste them.

(D) Mining and Minerals: We should not exhaust our mineral resources. They are also our Nature's gift. Minerals are available deep inside the earth and are mixed with rocks, sands etc. These are known as "Ores". Many ores, such as iron ores, copper ores, zinc ores, gold ores, aluminum, lead ores, etc., are of very importance to humans. Mother earth has only limited amount of minerals. In India, we have very rich mineral resources. We should use them cautiously.

Coal is already getting exhausted. These are taken out by "Mining" and then purified from unwanted materials. Mining operations cause lot of pollution. Huge amount of dusts are produced. Those dusts also contain heavy metals and various chemicals. Toxic gas emissions also take place. Mining operations pollute both of our air and water bodies. All these cause major health hazards—such as bronchitis, lung fibrosis, tuberculosis/silicosis/pneumoconiosis/black lung disease (among the coal miners)/cancer and many other diseases. Proper precautions like wearing face-masks, head gear/gum boots/aprons/gloves, etc., are required for all those working in the mining environment.

Apart from electricity, our major energy source is Petroleum and Diesels. It is available underneath the earth. Many useful materials come from Crude petroleum, such as petrol or diesel, tar, kerosene, lubricating oil, fuel oils etc. These are nature's gift to us. We should use them with proper attention and care. Once exhausted, it can not be replenished. Drilling of oils and petroleum gas pollutes our natural environment of sea water and its ecology. Often we see huge oil spillage that affects our water animals and also phytoplanktons (water plants)

(E) Concept of Zero Pollution: As said above, we should not allow our surroundings and our environment to get polluted and exhausted. Wherever needed, legislative measures are to be applied. Industrial, Municipal and Hospital wastes are to be treated first and then released. Zero Pollution technology should be used wherever possible. Eco-Week may be organised very year both in your school and in your locality to make the people aware about the danger of pollution. People should be made conscious regarding the protection and conservation of our environment.

4

Effect of Environmental Pollution on Human Health

(A) What is Pollution?

(B) Why does the pollutant pose dangers?

(C) Is it that we hear about pollution only recently?

(D) What can we do about it?

(E) Legislative measures

From the above discussion, we have learnt about our galaxies, our planet Earth, Evolution of plants and animals, modern humans; our culture, our family, our food and many others.

We have also learnt— (a) what causes pollution, (b) wherefrom they originate, (c) what are the nature of those pollutants, (d) what we should do about it, (e) how to keep our environment clean etc.

(A) What is Pollution?

Pollution is caused by the addition of harmful contaminants into our Natural Environment. These pollutants are mainly Man-made chemicals, throw-away and used materials of different kinds (plastics, broken materials, glasses, oily and greasy substances etc.), toxic gases emanating from industrial chimneys, burning of fossil fuels, waste waters and dusts, hydrocarbons etc.

(B) Why does the Pollutant Pose Dangers to Life Systems?

It is because the pollutants cause an alteration of the Ecosystem by causing major disorders, harmful actions and destruction of the natural balance of our Ecosystem; both physical systems and/or living organisms. Apart from those large number of materials causing pollution, pollution is also caused by Energy, such as heat, light, radiation, noise etc. Many naturally occurring substances when exceed their natural levels may become responsible for contaminating or polluting our environment. Pollution may arise from two different sources—a point source or a nonpoint source. Some of the major polluting countries of the world are USA, China, India, Russia, Azerbaijan, Peru, Ukraine and Zambia according to some world report.

(C) Is it that we Hear about Pollution only Recently?

The answer is "Not at all". Observations about pollution were recorded long ago. But it is true that it did not occur in the manner and intensity as it is today. Air pollution has always been with us. *S*oot was found on the ceilings of prehistoric caves. Such observations provided ample evidence of the high levels of pollution that was associated with inadequate ventilation of open fires. Large scale uses of metals, burning of coal, fossils, etc., also caused Air pollution. It seems that air pollution would continue to be a problem especially because of Industrial Revolution and inc easing population loads. The emergence of large number of big industries and cònsumption of immense quantities of coal and other fossil fuels gave rise to an unprecedented amount of Air Pollution these days. Large volume of untreated industrial chemical discharges added to the growing load of untreated human, industrial and agricultural wastes have engulfed our environment in a manner that our life is now threatened to its extreme point. It is serious enough that we need to take some serious measures to plug all sorts of pollution causing sources.

(D) What can we do about it?

It appears that the present generation is extinguishing the various life-forms in a rather expeditious manner through several of its activities. We have become somewhat rich and affluent. We buy more and we eat more. We already suffer more also. There is an increasing order of Heart Diseases, Cancer, Diabetes, Neurological ailments, various Infectious diseases, Gastrointestinal disorders etc. We have become more fashionable. We decorate our houses with Tiger skin, there had been an increasing demand for coral to decorate house aquaria, we are using more of leather garments, fur coats, etc., in the past several years. Such casual attitudes towards the environment will have rather serious consequences. So much so, that these species together with many others will rapidly vanish from our midst. A typical example is provided by the cone snails which are decimated by habitat destruction (coral reefs are destroyed by human activity also), overexploitation and trade (millions of cone snails are now killed annually for their shells). All this happens in spite of the fact that the snails are famous for containing toxins which is used as drugs like analgesics to treat chronic pain, cancer, heart irregularities, and many other disorders. Although the tropical cone snails may contain the largest and most important pharmacopoeia of any genus in nature, they could rapidly become extinct if urgent measures are not taken to protect them. This is particularly urgent, because to date only 100 out of a potential 50,000 conotoxins have been extracted and analysed. Some claim that we are causing species extinction at such a rate that it might bring an end to the present world. While such a picture of the critical state of our environment has induced pessimism among many and denials among others. There is no doubt that human activities and decision-making in the future will be crucial for the survival of many life forms on earth. Political, economic, social and religious leaders of our society need to sit down and discuss about the potential measures to save at least the presently available species such that they do not disappear from our planet.

If we are sincere, we can do a lot. First thing that we all can do is to increase our awareness regarding our pollution problems. Secondly, we must know what causes pollution. Thirdly, we have to plug all the sources where they come from or originate. It is true that our knowledge about pollution has increased because of the various programmes launched by both the Government and by various non-government and social organisations in recent times. It has become a popular issue after the World War II. It was primarily due to the very serious damaging effects of radioactive fallouts from atomic warfare (Hiroshima and Nagasaki atomic Bomb Blasts) and testing of atomic devices by USA and USSR, joined later by UK, France, Germany etc.

It was observed by the entire world that the great smog of 1952 in London killed about 4000 people. To what extent, Environmental pollution can cause havocs was realised by the World population. Such observations prompted various countries of the world to bring in various pollution control legislations to reduce the burden of pollutants in the environment. Unfortunately these laws are often found violated. Unless the citizens of the world communities together keep a constant vigil about this, and also continuously monitor the situations and raise their voices and demand appropriate pollution control measures, the situation is not going to be improved.

(E) Legislative Measures

People gradually realised that organising any number of debates, conducting conferences and awareness programmes on Pollution problems are not going to be able to control pollution problems entirely. What is needed is to have strict legislations and its implementation sincerely and effectively. There are such examples at hand. Between the period of mid-1950s and early 1970s, the United States Congress had to pass a number of legislative measures to control pollution. These were: The National Environmental Policy Act, the Clean Air Act, the Clean Water Act and the Noise Control Act.

It was a National news of USA in 1978 which drew the International attention regarding Dioxin (a pesticide) contamination at Love Canal. The entire World was stunned by the gravity of the news.

People were exposed to this toxin (Dioxin) continuously from 1947 onwards. The people who were exposed started developing a variety of disorders, malfunctions and health problems. News media jumped upon this issue of health damage due to toxic exposure to a pesticide.

This news led to the creation of a Superfund legislation in 1980. DDT (an Organochlorinated Pesticide) which was being used for quite sometime was actually banned in most of the developed world after the publication of Rachel Carson's Book "*Silent Spring" (it is a must for each and every person loving and having interests in the Environmental pollution problems and issues related to it)*. It created a sensation in the World. People around the Globe came to know the horrific effects of man-made chemicals on human health, especially on babies, aged, pregnant women etc. It cautioned the entire world that Pollution is not just a simple Word; it has far-reaching impacts on human health. It should now be realised that many pollutants can pass on its adverse effects through generations (genetic effect).

Pollution caused by Nuclear establishments, Nuclear arsenals, Radioactive emissions, etc., have been gradually realised with the progress of Nuclear Science and some of the Nuclear disasters that the world have witnessed during the past decades.

As the use of radio isotopes in medical diagnosis and treatments and in Biomedical Research increased, it provided information how exposures to even low dose radiation could cause major health hazards, including the development of anemia, cancer, neurological damage, abortion, birth defects etc. Introduction of radioactive contaminants in our environment may take place in a variety of ways—direct exposure to those who work in Nuclear establishments and nuclear arsenal manufacturing companies, those who work with radioisotopes, X-rays, scanning equipments etc. Radioactive contaminants are dangerous in that it can remain lethally radioactive for hundreds of thousands of years. It is a silent "KILLER". The World Watch Institute termed "Lake Karachay", as the "most polluted spot" on earth. It served as a radioactive disposal site for the Soviet Union throughout the 1950s and 1960s. Second place goes to Chernobyl in U.S.S.R. It is considered as the "Most polluted place on our planet.

Nuclear weapons continued to be tested during the Cold War period when the two superpowers, USA and USSR, competed for more and more sophisticated arsenal development. Although extreme care is practiced in nuclear establishments under the supervision of the an International Body, IAEA (International Atomic Energy Establishment) of the UN, normally, the potential for disaster suggested by various incidents such as those happened at Three Miles Island in USA and Chernobyl in Russia, and now in 2011 in the Fukushima island in Japan, stunned the entire world about the potential threat that the nuclear establishments might pose to mankind and his environment.

Some of the Pictures below show some of the infamous disasters that were caused in somė nuclear establishments around the World. Three miles island nuclear disaster (USA).

Three Miles Island Nuclear Plant Disaster in USA releasing Radioactive Gases threatened the entire State of Pennsylvania so much so that the Author himself and his family who were staying at Philadelphia at that time was seriously preparing themselves whether to flee in another place or not. Fortunately, the problems were quickly brought under control before it could spread far and beyond. Three plants had to be closed and only one is in operation now. People living near-by had to be evacuated to safer places. Being scared, many fled from the city and never returned.

Fukoshima Island Nuclear Disaster (Japan). The above is a picture of Fukoshima Island Nuclear Plant Disaster (in JAPAN) held recently in 2011. This was caused by severe earthquakes posing a major threat to the people of the adjacent cities, who had to be evacuated. The plant had to be closed later.

Chernobyl Nuclear Plant Disaster (in Former USSR).

It (radioactive fumes) engulfed the entire skyline of Europe with radioactive gases, with fall—outs in various countries of Europe and adjacent nations, contaminating water, air and food materials, such as Animal meat, milk including poultry, eggs, butter, vegetables, various water bodies and air environment etc.

(F) Indian Awareness

In India, our environmental consciousness received a momentum after 1972. It was primarily due to the efforts and initiative of late Prime Minister, Mrs. Indira Gandhi. She represented India in the First World Conference on Environment held ay Stockholm, Sweden. After her return to India, she created the Ministry of Environment and Forests under the Central Government and instructed all the State Governments to create its counterpart at the State Government level to take the initiative to impose Pollution control Laws at all levels and to initiate pollution control initiaves and awareness campaign among the people. The department has been mandated also to initiate research to develop the necessary technology in our country for pollution control. Several legislations were enacted side by side. Pollution control Boards were set up both centrally and at the State Government levels. Awareness programmes were also launched actively.

Bhopal Chemical Disaster in India

The worst ever Chemical Disaster that the World had witnessed was in the city of BHOPAL, India. This infamous incident took place on the night of December 2-3, 1984, at the Union Carbide Factory at Bhopal, India, when people were sleeping in their own homes and huts. A storage tank containing very lethal Methyl isocyanite (MIC) exploded, letting out the lethal MIC gas in the air. The people in sleep died in large numbers who were living in the vicinity of the factory in slums and also whose houses were in the direction of the wind carrying the lethal gas. The incident had taken lives of several thousands of innocent people, The incident had created history as Bhopal disaster, which not only killed several thousand people just overnight, it made more than 20,000 people suffer from various ailments and disorders, now for more than 20 years.

More than 10,000 animals died just overnight. Even the leaves of trees got severely burnt and many of those trees could not survive. The water of nearby lakes and ponds got contaminated and the aquatic lives got killed. The incident proved that such incidents can happen anywhere in the world. Since people were asleep at night, most people could not even realise what was happening there on that night and became victims inhaling the toxic gas. Several thousands got exposed while running out from their homes and fleeing from the city to various amount of that toxic MIC gas. Many died on the road side. Many are suffering from various types of ailments, such as heart and lung problems, eye problems, immunological problems, metabolic problems and genetic disorders. Pregnant women who were exposed gave birth to blue babies, there were miscarriages, and abnormal child birth also. Neurological disorders were also noted among many.

(G) Global Warming

Recently, Global Warming phenomena has attracted the attention of the world because of its serious repercussions already being experienced by the people of the entire world, in different forms and formats. Growing evidences and experiences of local and global pollution effects and an increasingly informed public at this time have given rise to environmentalism and the environmental movement all over the world, which generally seek to limit human impact on the environment.

(H) Environmental Issues in India–Human Concern

A satellite picture, taken in 2004, shows thick haze and smoke along the Ganges Basin in Northern India. Major sources of aerosols observed in the satellite picture in this area are believed to be primarily from smoke resulted from biomass burning in the northwest part of India, and air pollution from large cities in Northern India. Dust from deserts in Pakistan and the Middle East may also contribute to the mix of that aerosols.

Environmental issues in India are many. Air pollution, water pollution, garbage induced pollution and wildlife natural habitat pollution. All these have thrown many challenges to the citizens of India. The situation was worse between 1947 through 1995. According to data collection and environmental assessment studies done by the World Bank experts, between 1995 through 2010, India has made one of the fastest progresses in this regard in the world, in addressing its environmental issues and improving its environmental quality. Still, India has a long way to go to reach environmental quality similar to those enjoyed in developed economies. Pollution remains a major challenge and opportunity for India.

Recent rapid development and economic progress and its impact on our environment.

Some believe economic development is leading to environmental issues in India. Others believe economic development is the key to improving India's environmental management and preventing pollution in India. As the country becomes richer and richer in coming years, it will have to spend more towards this direction of pollution control and management. Some suggest India's growing population is the primary cause of India's environmental degradation. Systematic studies challenge this theory. Empirical evidence from countries such as Japan, England and Singapore, each with population density similar or higher than India, yet each enjoying environmental quality vastly superior to India, suggests population density may not be the only factor affecting India's environmental issues.

Major environmental issues are—forest and agricultural degradation of land, resource depletion (water, mineral, forest, sand, rocks etc.), environmental degradation, public health problems, loss of biodiversity, loss of resilience in ecosystems, livelihood and the security for the poor. The major sources of pollution in India include the rampant burning of firewood and biomass such as dried wastes from livestock. These materials are used as the primary sources of energy, lack of organised garbage and waste removal services, lack of sewage treatment operations, lack of flood control and monsoon water drainage system, diversion of consumer wastes directly into rivers, cremation practices near major rivers, use of highly polluting old public transport, and continued operation by Indian government of government owned, high emission plants built between 1950 to 1980.

- India's water supply and sanitation problems are related to many environmental issues. Environmental issues are one of the primary causes of disease, various forms of health issues and long term livelihood impact for India and similar such countries of the world.

History

(a) Religious Dictum and Early Practices to Protect the Environment

Ashoka Pillar Edicts were one of earliest efforts in India focused on respecting and preserving environment, forests and wildlife.

Yajnavalkya Smriti, a historic Indian text on statecraft and jurisprudence, suggested to have been written before 5th century AD, prohibited the cutting of trees and prescribed punishment for such acts.

Kautalya's Arthashastra, written in India's Mauryan period, emphasised the need for forest administration. Ashoka went further, and his Pillar Edicts expressed his view about the welfare of environment and biodiversity. "Happiness in this world and the next is difficult to obtain without much love for the dharma, much self-examination, much respect, much fear of evil, and much enthusiasm. Beloved-of-the-Gods, King Piyadasi (Ashoka), speaks thus: Animals were declared to be protected–parrots, mainas, aruna, geese, wild ducks, nandimukhas, gelatas, bats, queen ants, terrapins, boneless fish, vedareyaka, gangapuputaka, sankiya fish, tortoises, porcupines, squirrels, deer, bulls, okapinda, wild asses, wild pigeons, domestic pigeons and all four-footed creatures that are neither useful nor edible. Also protected were nanny goats, ewes and sows which are giving milk to their young. Cocks are not to be caponised, husks hiding living beings are not to be burnt, and forests are not to be burnt either without reason or to kill creatures. One animal is not to be fed to another.

(b) British India Efforts to Protect the Environment

British rule of India saw several laws related to environmental protection. Amongst the earliest ones was Shore Nuisance (Bombay and Kolaba) Act of 1853 and the Oriental Gas Company Act of 1857. The Indian Penal Code of 1860 imposed a fine on anyone who voluntarily fouls the water of any public spring or reservoir. In addition, the Code penalised negligent acts.

British India also enacted laws aimed at controlling air pollution. Prominent amongst these were the Bengal Smoke Nuisance Act of 1905 and the Bombay Smoke Nuisance Act of 1912. While these laws failed in having the intended effect, British-enacted legislations pioneered the growth of environmental regulations in India.

(c) Independent India Legislations for Environmental Protection

Upon independence from Britain in 1947, India adopted a constitution and numerous British-enacted laws, without any specific constitutional provision on protecting environment. India amended its constitution in 1976. Article 48(A) of Part IV of the amended constitution read: The State shall endeavour to protect and improve the environment and to safeguard the forests and wildlife of the country. Article 51A (g) imposed additional environmental mandates on the Indian state. Other Indian laws from recent history include the Water (Prevention and Control of Pollution) Act of 1974, the Forest (Conservation) Act of 1980, and the Air (Prevention and Control of Pollution) Act of 1981. The Air Act was inspired by the decisions made at Stockholm Conference. The Bhopal gas tragedy triggered the Government of India to enact the Environment (Protection) Act of 1986. India has also enacted a set of Noise Pollution (Regulation and Control) Rules in 2000. In 1985, Indian government created the Ministry of Environment and Forests. This ministry is the central administrative organisation in India for regulating and ensuring environmental protection. Despite active passage of laws by the Central Government of India, the reality of environmental quality mostly worsened between 1947 and 1990. Most of Indian economy was nationalised and owned by India, and regulations were mostly ignored by state run enterprises. Rural poor had no choice, but to sustain life in whatever way possible. The state governments of India often regarded environmental laws enacted by the central government as a mere paperwork formality. Air emissions increased, water pollution worsened, forest cover decreased. Starting in 1990s, reforms were introduced. Since then, for the first time in Indian history, major air pollutant concentrations have dropped in every five year period. During 1992 to 2010, satellite data confirms India's forest coverage which has increased for the first time by over 4 million hectares, a seven per cent increase.

2. Major Issues before India

Floods are a significant environmental issue for India. Almost every year India faces flood related environmental problems. Flood causes soil erosion, destruction of wetlands and wide migration of solid wastes.

Air pollution, poor management of wastes, growing drinking water scarcity, falling down groundwater tables, increasing water pollution, rapid degradation in the efforts of preservation and maintenance of the quality of forests, biodiversity loss, and land/soil degradation are some of the major environmental issues India faces today.

One important cause of growing environmental degradation in India is India's massive population growth. It added pressure to environmental issues and its resources.

Environmental issues in India include various natural hazards, particularly cyclones and annual monsoon floods. An estimated 60 per cent of cultivated land suffers from soil erosion, water logging, and salinity. It is also estimated that between 4.7 and 12 billion tons of topsoil are lost annually from soil erosion. The Indian Agricultural Research Institute of Parvati has estimated that a 3°C rise in temperature will result in a 15 to 20 per cent loss in annual wheat yields. These are substantial problems for a nation with such a large population, depending on the productivity of primary resources and whose economic growth relies heavily on industrial growth. Civil conflicts involving natural resources—most notably forests and arable land—have occurred in eastern and northeastern states already. It is a major danger signal for a country harboring 1.24 Billion people already in 2012.

Population Growth and Environmental Quality

There is a long history of study and debate about the interactions between population growth and the environment all over the world. According to the British thinker Malthus, for example, a growing population exerts pressure on agricultural land, causing environmental degradation, and forcing the cultivation of land of poorer and poorer quality. This environmental degradation ultimately reduces agricultural yields and food availability, causes famines and diseases and death of people, thereby reducing the rate of population growth, because it can place increased pressure on the assimilative capacity of the environment, is also seen as a major cause of air, water, and solid-waste pollution. The result, Malthus theorised, is an equilibrium population that enjoys low levels of both income and environmental quality. Malthus suggested positive and preventative forced control of human population, along with abolition of poor laws, although many different opinions about it exist today. An increase in human knowledge, rapid increases in productivity, innovation and application of knowledge, general improvements in farming methods (industrial agriculture), mechanisation of work (tractors), the introduction of high-yield varieties of wheat and other plants (Green Revolution), the use of pesticides to control crop pests, etc., helped in the sustenance of the human race thus far.

More recent scholarly articles concede that while there is no question that population growth may contribute to environmental degradation, its effects can be modified by economic growth and modern technology. Research in environmental economics has uncovered a relationship between environmental quality, measured by ambient concentrations of air pollutants and per capita income. This so-called environmental Kuznets curve shows environmental quality worsening up until about $5,000 of per capita income on purchasing parity basis, and improving thereafter. The key requirement, for this to be true, is continued adoption of technology and scientific management of resources, continued increases in productivity in every economic sector, entrepreneurial innovation and economic expansion.

Other data suggests that population density has little correlation to environmental quality and human quality of life. India's population density, in 2011, was about 368 human beings per square kilometer. Many countries with population density similar to or higher than India enjoy environmental quality as well as human quality of life far superior than India. For example: Singapore (7148/km^2), Hong Kong-China (6349/km^2), South Korea (487/km^2), Netherlands (403/km^2), Belgium (355/km^2), Japan (337/km^2), England (395/km^2), the state of Florida (353/km^2), the state of New York (412/km^2), the state of Massachusetts (840/km^2), the state of North Rhine-Westphalia (523/km^2), the region of Île-de-France (974/km^2), and the region of Lombardy (417/km^2).

3. Pollution of Environment

Water Pollution

As has been said earlier, from several drainage canal passes contaminated water direct to the Ganges at Howrah, West Bengal. Sewage and drainage canals like this are the dominant cause of water pollution in India. A 2007 study finds that discharge of untreated sewage is the single most important cause for pollution of surface and ground water in India. There is a large gap between generation and treatment of domestic wastewater in India. The problem is not only that India lacks sufficient treatment capacity but also that the sewage treatment plants that exist do not operate fully and are not maintained properly. Majority of the government-owned sewage treatment plants remain closed most of the time due to improper design or poor maintenance or lack of reliable electricity supply to operate the plants, together with absentee of employees and poor management. The wastewater generated in these areas normally percolates in the soil or evaporates. The uncollected wastes accumulate in the urban areas cause unhygienic conditions and release pollutants that leach to surface and groundwater.

A 1992 World Health Organisation (WHO) study is claimed to have reported that out of India's 3,119 towns and cities, just 209 have partial sewage treatment facilities, and only 8 have full wastewater treatment facilities. Downstream, the untreated water is used for drinking, bathing, and washing. A 1995 report claimed 114 Indian cities were dumping untreated sewage and partially cremated bodies directly into the Ganges River. Open defecation is widespread even in urban areas of India. This situation is typical of India as well as other developing countries although in India now have come up many "Sulabh SAUCHALAYA", where people can go and use it for urination and defecation.

According to another 2005 report, sewage discharged from cities and towns is the predominant cause of water pollution in India. Investment is needed to bridge the gap between 29000 million litres per day of sewage India generates, and a treatment capacity of mere 6000 million litres per day. A large number of Indian rivers are severely polluted as a result of discharge of domestic sewage.

The Central Pollution Control Board, a Ministry of Environment and Forests, Government of India entity, has established a National Water Quality Monitoring Network comprising 1429 monitoring stations in 27 states and 6 in Union Territories on various rivers and water bodies across the country. This effort monitors water quality year round. The monitoring network covers 293 rivers, 94 lakes, nine tanks, 41 ponds, eight creeks, 23 canals, 18 drains and 411 wells distributed across India. Water samples are routinely analysed for 28 pollution related parameters including dissolved oxygen, bacteriological and other internationally established parameters for determining the water quality. Additionally, nine trace metals and 28 pesticide residues are also analysed. Biomonitoring is also carried out on specific locations. The scientific analysis of water samples from 1995 to 2008 indicates that the organic and bacterial contamination is severe in water bodies of India. This is mainly due to discharge of domestic wastewater in an untreated form, mostly from the urban centers of India. In 2008, the water quality monitoring found almost all rivers with high levels of BOD (Biological Oxygen Demand). The worst pollution, in decreasing order, were found in river Markanda (590 mg O/l), followed by river Kali (364), river Amlakhadi (353), Yamuna canal (247), river Yamuna at Delhi (70) and river Betwa (58). For context, a water sample with a five day BOD between one and two mg O/L indicates a very clean water, three to eight mg O/L indicates a moderately clean water, eight to 20 indicates borderline water, and greater than 20 mg O/L indicates ecologically-unsafe polluted water. Studies have found that the Mithi River, which flows through the city of Mumbai, is heavily polluted. Total coliform and fecal coliform counts in the rivers of India range between 500 to 100,000 MPN/100 ml. The presence of coliform suggests that the water is being contaminated with the fecal material of humans, livestock's, pets and other animals. Major Rivers, such as Yamuna, Ganga, Gomti, Ghaggar, Chambal, Mahi, Vardha are amongst the other most coliform polluted water bodies in India. For example, coliform counts must be below 104 MPN/100 ml, preferably absent from water for it to be considered safe for general human use, and for irrigation where coliform may cause disease outbreak from the use of contaminated-water in agriculture. In 2006, 47 per cent of water quality monitoring stations in India reported total average annual coliform levels above 500 MPN/100 ml. During 2008, 33 per cent of all water quality monitoring stations reported total coliform levels exceeding those levels, suggesting recent effort to add pollution control infrastructure and upgrade treatment plants in India, may be reversing the water pollution trend.

Recent Trends

Treatment of domestic sewage and subsequent utilisation of treated sewage for irrigation can prevent pollution of water bodies, reduce the demand for fresh water in irrigation sector and become a resource for irrigation. Since 2005, Indian wastewater treatment plant market has been growing annually at the rate of 10 to 12 per cent. The United States is the largest supplier of treatment equipment and supplies to India, with 40 per cent market share of new installation. At this rate of expansion, and assuming the government of India continues on its path of reform, major investments in sewage treatment plants and electricity infrastructure development, India will nearly triple its water treatment capacity by 2015, and treatment capacity supply will match India's daily sewage water treatment requirements by about 2020.

Water resources have not been linked to either domestic or international violent conflict as was previously anticipated by some observers. Possible exceptions, notes a 2004 report, include some communal violence related to distribution of water from the Kaveri River and political tensions surrounding actual and potential population displacements by dam projects, particularly on the Narmada River.

A 1997 article claimed Punjab is another hotbed of pollution, for example, Buddha Nullah, a rivulet which run through Malwa region of Punjab, India, and after passing through highly populated Ludhiana district, before draining into Sutlej River, a tributary of the Indus river, is today an important case point in the recent studies, which suggest this as another Bhopal in the making. A joint study by PGIMER and Punjab Pollution Control Board in 2008, revealed that in villages along the Nullah, calcium, magnesium, fluoride, mercury, beta-endosulphan and heptachlor pesticides were more than permissible limit (MPL) in ground and tap waters. Plus the water had high concentration of COD and BOD (chemical and biochemical oxygen demand), ammonia, phosphate, chloride, chromium, arsenic and chlorpyrifos pesticide. The ground water also contains nickel and selenium, while the tap water has high concentration of lead, nickel and cadmium. The Hindon River, which flows through the city of Ghaziabad, highly polluted and groundwater of this city has colored and poisoned by industrial effluents, Hindon Vahini is strongly opposing of water pollution activities.

Flooding during monsoons worsens India's water pollution problem, as it washes and moves all sorts of solid garbage and contaminated soils into its rivers and wetlands.The annual average precipitation in India is about 4000 billion cubic metres. From this, with the state of Indian infrastructure in 2005, the available water resource through the rivers is about 1869 billion cubic meters. Accounting to uneven distribution of rain over the country each year, water resources available for utilisation, including ground water, is claimed to be about 1122 billion cubic meters. Much of this water is unsafe, because pollution degrades water quality. Water pollution severely limits the amount of water available to Indian consumer, its industry and its agriculture.

The Holy River Ganges

To know why 1,000 Indian children die of diarrhoeal sickness every day, take a wary stroll along the Ganges in Varanasi. As it enters the city, Hinduism's sacred river contains 60,000 faecal coliform bacteria per 100 millilitres, 120 times more than is considered safe for bathing. Four miles downstream, with inputs from 24 gushing sewers and 60,000 pilgrim-bathers, the concentration is 3,000 times over the safety limit. In places, the Ganges becomes black and septic; corpses of semi-cremated adults or enshrouded babies drift slowly by.

More than 400 million people live alongside the river Ganges. An estimated 2,000,000 persons ritually bathe daily in the river, which is considered holy by the Hindus. In the Hindu religion, it is said to flow from the lotus feet of Vishnu (for Vaisnava devotees) or the hair of Shiva (for Saivites). The spiritual and religious significance could be compared to what the Nile River meant to the ancient Egyptians. While the Ganges may be considered holy, there are some problems associated with the ecology of this river. Unfortunately, it is filled with chemical wastes, sewage and even the remains of human and animal corpses which carry major health risks by either direct bathing in the water, or by drinking (the Fecal-oral route). The Government should take adequate measures to purify the Ganges water.

The Yamuna

The popular US news media NewsWeek described Delhi's sacred Yamuna River as "a putrid ribbon of black sludge" where fecal bacteria is 10,000 over safety limits despite a 15-year programme to address the problem. Cholera epidemics are not unknown. NewsWeek observed Indian Government was particularly ill equipped to handle the conflicting pressures of rapid growth and poverty going side by side. Even though India revised its national water policy in 2002 to encourage community participation and decentralise water management practices, the country's Byzantine bureaucracy ensures that it remains a "mere statement of intent." Responsibility for managing water issues is fragmented among a dozen different ministries and departments without any coordination. The government bureaucracy and state-run project department has failed to solve the problem, despite having spent many years and $500 million on this project.

(i) Recent Efforts to Address Water Issues

The government of India envisions a US$100 billion project to interlink all major river networks in India. This initiative would connect water-deficient areas to water-abundant ones by interlinking 37 Indian rivers. One of the largest projects anywhere in the world, it would transfer water through 30 links across 9,600 kilometers. It would connect 32 dams and use 56 million tons of cement and two million tons of steel. The project aims a transformation of India's water treatment, management, transmission and distribution.

The Indian government has proposed reforms to attract investment and privatisation of its water networks. Water companies from all over the world have established a presence in India to pursue an estimated 70 projects worth several billion dollars in 20 Indian cities. India is debating the social and environmental impact of this project. One of the first projects under consideration is the linking of Ken and Betwa rivers in northern India.

Air Pollution

Cooking fuel in rural India is prepared from a wet mix of dried grass, fuel wood pieces, hay, leaves and mostly cow/livestock dung. This mix is patted down into disc-shaped cakes, dried, and then used as fuel in stoves. When it burns, it produces smoke and numerous indoor air pollutants at concentrations five times higher than coal.

A rural stove using biomass cakes, fuel wood and trash as cooking fuel. Surveys suggest over 100 million households in India use such stoves (chullahs) every day, two-three times a day. Clean burning fuels and electricity are unavailable in rural parts and small towns of India because of poor rural highways and limited energy generation infrastructure.

Traffic congestion on inadequate road infrastructure is a daily reality of India's urban centers. Slow speeds and idling vehicles produce, per trip, four to eight times more pollutants and consume more carbon footprint fuels, than free flowing traffic.

(J) Fuel Wood and Biomass Burning

Fuel wood and biomass burning is the primary reason for near-permanent haze and smoke observed above rural and urban India, and in satellite pictures of the country. Fuel wood and biomass cakes are used for cooking and general heating needs. These are burnt in cook stoves known as *chullah* or *chulha* in some parts of India. These cook stoves are present in over 100 million Indian households, and are used two to three times a day, daily. As of 2009, majority of Indians still use traditional fuels such as dried cow dung, agricultural wastes, and firewood as cooking fuel. This form of fuel is inefficient source of energy, its burning releases high levels of smoke, PM10 particulate matter, NOX (Nitrogen Oxides), SOX (Sulphur Oxides), PAHs (Polyaromatic Hydrocarbons), other polyaromatics, formaldehyde, carbon monoxide and various other air pollutants. Some reports, including one by the World Health Organisation (WHO), claim that 300,000 to 400,000 people die of indoor air pollution and carbon monoxide poisoning in India because of biomass burning and use of chullahs. Burning of biomass and firewood will not stop, unless electricity or clean burning fuel and combustion technologies become reliably available and widely adopted in rural and urban India.

India is the world's largest consumer of fuel wood, agricultural waste and biomass for energy purposes. From the most recent available nationwide study, India used 148.7 million tones coal replacement worth of fuel wood and biomass annually for domestic energy use. India's national average annual per capita consumption of fuel wood, agri-waste and biomass cakes was 206 kilogram coal equivalent. In 2010 terms, with India's population increased to about 1.2 billion, the country burns over 200 million tonnes of coal replacement worth of fuel wood and biomass every year to meet its energy need for cooking and other domestic use. The study found that the households consumed around 95 million tonnes of fuelwood, one-third of which was logs and the rest was twigs. Twigs were mostly consumed in the villages, and logs were more popular in cities and towns of India. The overall contribution of fuel wood, including sawdust and wood waste, was about 46 per cent of the total, the rest being agri-waste and biomass dung cakes. Traditional fuel (fuel wood, crop residue and dung cake) dominates domestic energy use in rural India and accounts for about 90 per cent of the total. In urban areas, this traditional fuel constitutes about 24 per cent of the total.

Fuel wood, agri-waste and biomass cake burning releases over 165 million tonnes of combustion products into India's indoor and outdoor air every year. To place this volume of emission in proper context, the Environmental Protection Agency (EPA) of the United States estimates that fire wood smoke contributes over 420,000 tonnes of fine particles throughout the United States–mostly during the winter months. United States consumes about one-tenth of fuel-wood consumed by India, and mostly for fire place and home heating purposes. EPA estimates that residential wood combustion in the USA accounts for 44 per cent of total organic matter emissions and 62 per cent of the PAH, which are probable human carcinogens and are of great concern to EPA. The fuel-wood sourced residential wood smoke makes up over 50 per cent of the wintertime particle pollution problem in California. In 2010, the state of California had about the same number of vehicles as all of India.

India burns tenfold more fuel-wood every year than the United States; the fuel-wood quality in India is different than the dry firewood of the United States. The Indian stoves in use are less efficient thereby producing more smoke and air pollutants per kilogram equivalent. India has less land area and less emission air space than the United States. In summary, the impact on indoor and outdoor air pollution by fuel-wood and biomass cake burning is contributing in a major way so far as Air pollution is concerned.

A United Nations study finds firewood and biomass stoves can be made more efficient in India. Animal dung, now used in inefficient stoves, could be used to produce biogas, a cleaner fuel with higher utilisation efficiency. In addition, an excellent fertiliser can be produced from the slurry from biogas plants. Switching to gaseous fuels would bring the greatest gains in terms of both thermal efficiency and reduction in air pollution, but would require more investment. A combination of technologies may be the best way forward.

Between 2001 and 2010, India has made progress in adding electrical power generation capacity, bringing electricity to rural areas, and reforming market to improve availability and distribution of liquefied cleaner burning fuels in urban and rural areas. Over the same period, scientific data collection and analysis show improvement in India's air quality, with some regions witnessing 30 to 65 per cent reduction in NOx, SOx and suspended particulate matter. Even at these lower levels, the emissions are higher than those recommended by the World Health Organisation. Continued progress in the area of clean energy production is necessary.

Scientific studies conclude that biomass combustion in India is the country's dominant source of carbonaceous aerosols, emitting 0.25 teragram per year of black carbon into air, 0.94 teragram per year of organic matter, and 2.04 teragram per year of small particulates with diameter less than 2.5 microns. Biomass burning, as domestic fuel in India, accounts for about three times as much black carbon air pollution as all other sources combined, including vehicles and industrial sources.

Vehicular Emissions

Other sources of pollution in Indian cities are vehicles and emissions from industry. Until 1992, India protected its automobile industry using license raj. Many two wheel, three wheel and four wheel vehicles lacked catalytic converters. Per vehicle emissions were amongst the highest in the world. The refining of oil and supply of fuel was owned, regulated and run by the government.

In 2005, India adopted emission standard of Bharat Stage IV for vehicles, which is equivalent to Euro IV European standards for vehicle emissions. Nevertheless, the old pre-2005 vehicles, and even pre-1992 vehicles are still on Indian streets. Strict regulatory measures are necessary.

(K) Fuel Adulteration

Some Indian taxis and auto-rickshaws run on adulterated fuel blends. Adulteration of gasoline and diesel with lower-priced fuels is common in South Asia, including India. Some adulterants increase emissions of harmful pollutants from vehicles, worsening urban air pollution. Financial incentives arising from differential taxes are generally the primary cause of fuel adulteration. In India and other developing countries, gasoline carries a much higher tax than diesel, which in turn is taxed more than kerosene meant as a cooking fuel, while some solvents and lubricants carry little or no tax. As fuel prices rise, the public transport driver cuts costs by blending the cheaper hydrocarbon into highly taxed hydrocarbon. The blending may be as much as 20-30 per cent. For a low wage driver, the adulteration can yield short term savings that are significant over the month. The consequences to long term air pollution, quality of life and effect on health are simply ignored. Also ignored are the reduced life of vehicle engine and higher maintenance costs, particularly if the taxi, auto-rickshaw or truck is being rented for a daily fee.

Adulterated fuel increases tailpipe emissions of hydrocarbons (HC), carbon monoxide (CO), oxides of nitrogen (NOx) and particulate matter (PM). Air toxin emissions—which fall into the category of unregulated emissions—of primary concern is benzene and polyaromatic hydrocarbons (PAHs), both well known carcinogens.

Kerosene is more difficult to burn than gasoline; its addition results in higher levels of HC, CO, and PM emissions even from catalyst-equipped cars. The higher sulfur level of kerosene is another issue. The permissible level of fuel sulfur in India, in 2002, was 0.25 per cent by weight as against 0.10 per cent for gasoline. The higher levels of sulfur can deactivate the catalyst. Once the catalyst becomes deactivated, the amount of pollution from the vehicle dramatically increases. Fuel adulteration is essentially an unintended consequence of tax policies and the attempt to control fuel prices, in the name of fairness. Air pollution is the ultimate result. This problem is not unique to India, but prevalent in many developing countries including those outside of south Asia. This problem is largely absent in economies that do not regulate the ability of fuel producers to innovate or price based on market demand.

(L) Traffic Congestion

Traffic congestion is severe in India's cities and towns. Traffic congestion is caused for several reasons, some of which are: increase in number of vehicles per kilometer of available road, a lack of intra-city divided-lane highways and intra-city expressways networks, lack of inter-city expressways, traffic accidents and chaos from poor enforcement of traffic laws.

Traffic congestion reduces average traffic speed. At low speeds, scientific studies reveal, vehicles burn fuel inefficiently and pollute more per trip. For example, a study in the United States found that for the same trip, cars consumed more fuel and polluted more if the traffic was congested, than when traffic flowed freely. At average trip speeds between 20 to 40 kilometers per hour, the cars pollutant emission was twice as much as when the average speed was 55 to 75 kilometers per hour. At average trip speeds between five to 20 kilometers per hour, the cars pollutant emissions were four to eight times as much as when the average speed was 55 to 70 kilometers per hour. Fuel efficiencies similarly were much worse with traffic congestion.

Traffic gridlock in Delhi and other India cities is extreme. The average trip speed on many Indian city roads is less than 20 kilometers per hour; a 10 kilometer trip can take 30 minutes, or more. At such speeds, vehicles in India emit air pollutants four to eight times more than they would with less traffic congestion; Indian vehicles also consume a lot more carbon footprint fuel per trip, than they would if the traffic congestion was less.

In cities like Bangalore, around 50 per cent of children suffer from asthma.

(M) Recent Trends in India's Air Quality

With the last 15 years of economic development and regulatory reforms, India has made progress in improving its air quality. The table presents the average emissions sampled at many locations, over time, and data analysed by scientific methods, by multiple agencies, including The World Bank. For context and comparison, the table also includes average values for Sweden in 2008, observed and analysed by same methods. By 1995–2008, average nationwide levels of major air pollutants have dropped by between 25–45 per cent in India.

Air Quality, Trends over 1995-2008, Averaged for India

Air quality Indicator	*India 1995*	*India 2005*	*India 2008*	*Sweden 2008*
Pollutant, PM10 (Micrograms per cubic meter)	109	67	59	11
Pollutant, CO_2 emissions (kg per 2005 PPP$ of GDP)	0.7	0.6	0.5	0.2
Health, mortality rate (under 5, per 1000)	100	73	67	3
Pollutant, methane, Agriculture emissions (per cent total)	68.8	64.4	n.a.	28.1
Pollutant, nitrous oxide, Agriculture emissions (per cent total)	75.2	73.4	n.a.	60.2

India's Central Pollution Control Board now routinely monitors four air pollutants namely sulphur dioxide (SO_2), oxides of nitrogen (NOx), suspended particulate matter (SPM) and respirable particulate matter (PM10). These are the target air pollutants for regular monitoring at 308 operating stations in 115 cities/towns in 25 states and 4 Union Territories of India. The monitoring of meteorological parameters such as wind speed and direction, relative humidity and temperature has also been integrated with the monitoring of air quality. The monitoring of these pollutants is carried out for 24 hours (four-hourly sampling for gaseous pollutants and eight-hourly sampling for particulate matter) with a frequency of twice a week, to yield 104 observations in a year.

For 2010, the key findings of India's central pollution control board are:

- Most Indian cities continue to violate India's and world air quality PM10 targets. Respirable particulate matter pollution remains a key challenge for India. Despite the general non-attainment, some cities showed far more improvement than others. A decreasing trend has been observed in PM10 levels in cities like Solapur and Ahmedabad over the last few years. This improvement may be due to local measures taken to reduce sulphur in diesel and stringent enforcement by Gujarat government.
- A decreasing trend has been observed in sulphur dioxide levels in residential areas of many cities such as Delhi, Mumbai, Lucknow and Bhopal during the last few years. The decreasing trend in sulphur dioxide levels may be due to recently introduced clean fuel standards, and the increasing use of LPG as domestic fuel instead of coal or fuel-wood, and the use of LPG instead of diesel in certain vehicles.
- A decreasing trend has been observed in nitrogen dioxide levels in residential areas of some cities such as Bhopal and Solapur during last

few years. The decreasing trend in sulphur dioxide levels may be due to recently introduced vehicle emission standards, and the increasing use of LPG as domestic fuel instead of coal or fuel-wood.

- Most Indian cities greatly exceed acceptable levels of suspended particulate matter. This may be because of refuse and biomass burning, vehicles, power plant emissions, industrial sources.
- The Indian air quality monitoring stations reported lower levels of PM10 and suspended particulate matter during monsoon months possibly due to wet deposition and air scrubbing by rainfall. Higher levels of particulates were observed during winter months possibly due to lower mixing heights and more calm conditions. In other words, India's air quality worsens in winter months, and improves with the onset of monsoon season.

For its 2008 annual report, Central Pollution Control Board used 346 operating Air Quality Monitoring Stations, covering 130 cities / towns in 26 States and four Union Territories. With the weekly data collected and then averaged over the year, Central Pollution Control Board reported the following annual trends from 1998 to 2008: The average annual SOx and NOx emissions level and periodic violations in industrial areas of India were significantly and surprisingly lower than the emission and violations in residential areas of India.

- The 24-hour average PM10 and suspended particulate matter emissions and violations in almost all areas of India violated India's and WHO targets. The PM10 and suspended particulate matter concentrations, in industrial areas of India were, however, lower than those in residential areas of India. Residential areas of India were the source of over 90 per cent of the most serious and repeated violations in particulate air pollution.
- Of the four major Indian cities, air pollution was consistently worst in Delhi, every year over five year period (2004–2008). Kolkata (previously known as Calcutta) was a close second, followed by Mumbai. Chennai air pollution which were the least of the four.
- The states of Kerala and Meghalaya, relative to other Indian states, experienced on average some of lowest air pollution levels. The cities of Thiruvananthapuram, Kottayam and Shillong, relative to other Indian cities and towns, experienced some of lowest air pollution levels.
- Air Quality data collected from the monitoring station at Taj Mahal, Agra since year 1991 to 2008, suggests that both particulate and acid rain pollutants at Taj Mahal have been declining over the years. The 2008 average annual air pollutant concentrations were between 38 to 67 per cent lower than those in 1991.

(N) Solid Waste Pollution

Trash and garbage is a common sight in urban and rural areas of India. It is a major source of pollution. Indian cities alone generate more than 100 million tons of solid waste a year. Street corners are piled with trash. Public places and sidewalks are despoiled with filth and litter, rivers and canals act as garbage dumps. In part, India's garbage crisis is from rising consumption. India's waste problem also points to a stunning failure of governance. In 2000, India's Supreme Court directed all Indian cities to implement a comprehensive waste-management programme that would include household collection of segregated waste, recycling and composting. These directions have simply been ignored. No major city runs a comprehensive program of the kind envisioned by the Supreme Court. Indeed, forget waste segregation and recycling directive of the India's Supreme Court, the Organisation for Economic Cooperation and Development estimates that up to 40 per cent of municipal waste in India remains simply uncollected. Even medical waste, theoretically controlled by stringent rules that require hospitals to operate incinerators, is routinely dumped with regular municipal garbage. A recent study found that about half of India's medical waste is improperly disposed of. Municipalities in Indian cities and towns have waste collection employees. However, these are unionised government workers and their work performance is neither measured nor monitored. Some of the few solid waste landfills India has, near its major cities, are overflowing and poorly managed. They have become significant sources of greenhouse emissions and breeding sites for disease vectors such as flies, mosquitoes, cockroaches, rats, and other pests.

In 2011, several Indian cities embarked on waste-to-energy projects of the type in use in Germany, Switserland and Japan. For example, New Delhi is implementing two incinerator projects aimed at turning the city's trash problem into electricity resource. These plants are being welcomed for addressing the city's chronic problems of excess untreated waste and a shortage of electric power. They are also being welcomed by those who seek to prevent water pollution, hygiene problems, and eliminate rotting trash that produces potent greenhouse gas methane. The projects are being opposed by waste collection workers and local unions who fear changing technology may deprive them of their livelihood and way of life. Along with waste-to-energy projects, some cities and towns such as Pune, Maharashtra is introducing competition and the privatisation of solid waste collection, street cleaning operations and bio-mining to dispose the waste. A scientific study suggests public private partnership is, in Indian context, more useful in solid waste management. According to this study, government and municipal corporations must encourage PPP-based local management through collection, transport and segregation and disposal of solid waste.

(O) Noise Pollution

The Supreme Court of India gave a significant verdict on noise pollution in 2005. Unnecessary honking of vehicles makes for a high decibel level of noise in cities. The use of loudspeakers for political purposes and by temples and mosques make for noise pollution in residential areas because using more speakers in a program the level of noise pollution increases. In January 2010, Government of India published norms of permissible noise levels in urban and rural areas.

(P) Land Pollution

In March 2009, the issue of Uranium poisoning in Punjab came into light, caused by fly ash ponds of thermal power stations, which reportedly lead to severe birth defects in children in the Faridkot and Bhatinda districts of Punjab.

(Q) Greenhouse Gas Emissions

India was the third largest emitter of Carbon dioxide in 2009 at 1.65 Gt per year, after China (6.9 Gt per year) and the United States (5.2 Gt per year). With 17 per cent of world population, India contributed some five per cent of human-sourced carbon dioxide emission; compared to China's 24 per cent share. On per capita basis, India emitted about 1.4 tons of carbon dioxide per person, in comparison to the United States' 17 tons per person, and a world average of 5.3 tons per person. About 65 per cent of India's carbon dioxide emissions in 2009 was from heating, domestic uses and power sector. About nine per cent of India's emissions were from transportation (cars, trains, two wheelers, airplanes, others). India's coal-fired, oil-fired and natural gas-fired thermal power plants are inefficient and offer significant potential for CO_2 emission reduction through better technology. Compared to the average emissions from coal-fired, oil-fired and natural gas-fired thermal power plants in European Union (EU-27) countries, India's thermal power plants emit 50 to 120 per cent more CO_2 per kWh produced. Between1990 and 2009, India's carbon dioxide emissions per GDP purchasing power parity basis have decreased by over 10 per cent, a trend similar to China. Meanwhile, between 1990 and 2009, Russia's carbon dioxide emissions per GDP purchasing power parity basis have increased by 40 per cent. India has one of the better records in the world, of an economy that is growing efficiently on CO_2 emissions basis. In other words, over the last 20 years, India has reduced CO_2 emissions with each unit of GDP increase. India aims to further reduce emissions intensity of its growing GDP by 20 to 25 per cent before 2020, with technology transfer and international cooperation. Nevertheless, it is expected, that like China, India's absolute carbon dioxide emissions will rise in years ahead, even as International Energy Agency's Annex I countries expect their absolute CO_2 emissions to drop. A significant source of greenhouse emissions from India is from black carbon, NOx, methane and other air pollutants. These pollutants are emitted in large quantities in India every day from incomplete and inefficient combustion of biomass. A majority of Indian population lacks access to clean burning fuels, and uses biomass combustion as cooking fuel. India's poorly managed solid wastes, inadequate sewage treatment plants, water pollution and agriculture are other source of greenhouse gas emissions.

(R) Environmental Issues and Indian Laws

Since about late 1980s, the Supreme Court of India has been pro-actively engaged in India's environmental issues. In most countries, it is the executive and the legislative branches of the government that plan, implement and address environmental issues; the Indian experience is different. The Supreme Court of India has been engaged in interpreting and introducing new changes in the environmental jurisprudence directly. The Court has laid down new principles to protect the environment, re-interpreted environmental laws, created new institutions and structures, and conferred additional powers on the existing ones through a series of directions and judgments. The Court's directions on environmental issues go beyond the general questions of law, as is usually expected from the highest Court of a democratic country. The Supreme Court of India, in its order, includes executive actions and technical details of environmental actions to be implemented. Indeed, some critics of India's Supreme Court describe the Court as the *Lords of Green Bench* or *Garbage Supervisor*. Supporters of India's Supreme Court term these orders and the Indian bench as pioneering, both in terms of laying down new principles of law, and in delivering environmental justice.

The reasons for the increasing interjection of India's Supreme Court in governance arenas are, experts claim, complex. A key factor has been the failure of government agencies and the state owned enterprises in discharging their Constitutional and Statutory duties. This has prompted civil society groups to file public interest complaints with the Courts, particularly the Supreme Court, for suitable remedies. Public interest litigation and judicial activism on environmental issues extends beyond India's Supreme Court. It includes the High Courts of individual states. India's judicial activism on environmental issues has, some suggest, delivered positive effects to the Indian experience. The Supreme Court has, through intense judicial activism, the proponents claim, become a symbol of hope for the people of India. As a result of judicial activism, India's Supreme Court has delivered a new normative regime of rights and insisted that the Indian state cannot act arbitrarily but must act reasonably and in public interest on pain of its action being invalidated by judicial intervention.

Even after a stay related to an infrastructure project is vacated, or a court order gives a green light to certain project, new issues become grounds for court notices and new public interest litigation. Judicial activism in India has, in several key cases, found state-directed economic development ineffective and a failure, then interpreted laws and issued directives that encourage greater competition and free market to reduce environmental pollution. In other cases, the interpretations and directives have preserved industry protection, labor practices and highly polluting state-owned companies detrimental to environmental quality of India.

Wildlife in India

Ecological issues are an integral and important part of environmental issues challenging India. Poor air quality, water pollution and garbage pollution–all affect the food and environment quality necessary for ecosystems.

India is a large and diverse country. Its land area includes regions with some of the world's highest rainfall to very dry deserts, coast line to alpine regions, river deltas to tropical islands. The variety and distribution of forest vegetation is large. India is one of the 12 mega biodiverse regions of the world.

Indian forest types include tropical evergreens, tropical deciduous, swamps, mangroves, sub-tropical, montane, scrub, sub-alpine and alpine forests. These forests support a variety of ecosystems with diverse flora and fauna.

Until recently, India lacked an objective way to determine the quantity of forests it had, and the quality of forests it had.

Forest Cover Measurement Methods

In the 1980s, space satellites were deployed for remote sensing of real forest cover. Standards were introduced to classify India's forests into the following categories:

- **Very Dense Forest:** All lands, with a forest cover with canopy density of 70 per cent and above.
- **Moderately Dense Forest:** All lands, with a forest cover with canopy density of 40-70 per cent.
- **Open Forest:** All lands, with forest cover with canopy density of 10 to 40 per cent.
- **Mangrove Cover:** Mangrove forest is salt tolerant forest ecosystem found mainly in tropical and sub-tropical coastal and/or inter-tidal regions. Mangrove cover is the area covered under mangrove vegetation as interpreted digitally from remote sensing data.

- **Non Forest Land:** defined as lands without any forest cover.
    - **Scrub Cover:** All lands, generally in and around forest areas, having bushes and or poor tree growth, chiefly small or stunted trees with canopy density less than 10 per cent.
    - **Tree Cover:** Land with tree patches (blocks and linear) outside the recorded forest area exclusive of forest cover and less than the minimum mapable area of one hectare.
    - **Trees Outside Forests:** Trees growing outside Recorded Forest Areas.

The first satellite recorded forest coverage data for India became available in 1987. India and the United States cooperated in 2001, using Landsat MSS with spatial resolution of 80 meters, to get accurate Indian forest distribution data. India thereafter switched to digital image and advanced satellites with 23 meters resolution and software processing of images to get more refined data on forest quantity and forest quality. The 2007 forest census data thus obtained and published by the Government of India suggests the five states with largest area under forest cover as the following: Madhya Pradesh: 7.64 million hectares:

- Arunachal Pradesh: 6.8 million hectares
- Chhattisgarh: 5.6 million hectares
- Orissa: 4.83 million hectares
- Maharashtra: 4.68 million hectares.

India hosts significant biodiversity; it is home to 7.6 per cent of all mammalian, 12.6 per cent of avian, 6.2 per cent of reptilian, and 6.0 per cent of flowering plant species.

In recent decades, human encroachment has posed a threat to India's wildlife; in response, a system of national parks and protected areas, first established in 1935, was substantially expanded. In 1972, India enacted the Wildlife Protection Act and Project Tiger to safeguard crucial habitat; further federal protections were promulgated in the 1980s. Along with over 500 wildlife sanctuaries, India now hosts 14 biosphere reserves, four of which are part of the World Network of Biosphere Reserves; 25 wetlands are registered under the Ramsar Convention.

These laws did not have the effect they intended. Over the last 20 years, India has reversed the deforestation trend. Specialists of the United Nations report India's forest as well as woodland cover has increased. A 2010 study by the Food and Agriculture Organisation ranks India amongst the 10 countries with the largest forest area coverage in the world (the other nine being Russian Federation, Brazil, Canada, United States of America, China, Democratic Republic of the Congo, Australia, Indonesia and Sudan). India is also one the top 10 countries with the largest primary forest coverage in the world, according to this study. From 1990 to 2000, FAO finds India was the fifth largest gainer in forest coverage in the world; while from 2000 to 2010, FAO considers India as the third largest gainer in forest coverage.

National Forest Commission and India's Afforestation Programme

In 2003, India set up a National Forest Commission to review and assess India's policy and law, its effect on India's forests, its impact of local forest communities, and to make recommendations to achieve sustainable forest and ecological security in India. The report made over 300 recommendations including the following:

- India must pursue rural development and animal husbandry policies to address local communities need to find affordable cattle fodder and grasing. To avoid destruction of local forest cover, fodder must reach these communities on reliable roads and other infrastructure, in all seasons year round.
- The Forest Rights Bill is likely to be harmful to forest conservation and ecological security. The Forest Rights Bill became a law since 2007.
- The government should work closely with mining companies. Revenue generated from lease of mines must be pooled into a dedicated fund to conserve and improve the quality of forests in the region where the mines are located.
- Power to declare ecologically sensitive areas must be with each Indian state.
- The mandate of State Forest Corporations and government owned monopolies must be changed.
- Government should reform regulations and laws that ban felling of trees and transit of wood within India. Sustainable agro-forestry and farm forestry must be encouraged through financial and regulatory reforms, particularly on privately owned lands.

India's national forest policy expects to invest US$ 26.7 billion by 2020, to pursue nationwide afforestation coupled with forest conservation, with the goal of increasing India's forest cover from 20 per cent to 33 per cent.

Pollution caused by Radioactive Substances

Radioactive contamination, results from nuclear power plants and nuclear weapons' research, testing, manufacture, use and their deployment . . . famous examples are: Hiroshima and Nagasaki Atomic Bomb blasts, three mile island Episodes in USA, Chernobyl Disaster in USSR, and now Fukoshima Nuclear Plant disaster in Japan.

We all know the sufferings of people in Hiroshima and Nagasaki of Japan, due to atomic Bomb blasts caused by USA.

Fukoshima Island Nuclear Disaster.

About 90,000 to 150,000 people died in Hiroshima and about 60,000 to 90,000 people died in Nagasaki islands. The incident shocked the World including those in USA.

People everywhere understood the potential dangers associated with the nuclear arsenals and later nuclear testing were banned. The two superpowers, USA and USSR came to an agreement that they would destroy their nuclear arsenals by installments. Voices were heard from every part of the planet. Against use of nuclear weapons, which are known as weapons of mass destruction (WMD).

Picture above shows the mushrooming of cloud immediately after Atomic Bomb blasts in Hiroshima and Nagasaki of Japan.

Thermal Pollution (Pollution caused by Temperature Changes of Water)

Thermal pollution is caused due to temperature change in natural water bodies. An example of this is the use of normal water as coolant in a power plant and release of hot and warm water in the water bodies after their use.

Global Warming and Weather Change phenomena are also responsible for changes in Water temperature of major water bodies of the world, threatening the lives of aquatic animals.

Pollution caused by Lights

Light pollution, includes light trespass, Watching of Television, Use of Computers, Cell phone use, exposure to over illumination and astronomical interferences, use of Microscopes, Electron Microscopes etc.

Noise Pollution

Noise pollution is caused by motor vehicle, producing about ninety per cent of all unwanted noise worldwide. Use of loud speakers in public places during functions, political rallies, social functions, etc., also cause Noise pollution.

Pollution caused by Electro Magnetic Radiation

It may be caused due to the exposure of overhead power lines, exposure to medical gadgets of various types, such as X-rays, radioisotopes, use of cell phones, i-pods, exposure to the screens of TV, Computers etc.

Pollution caused by Natural Disaster

Pollution can also be caused by various natural disasters. Hurricanes may cause water bodies to get contaminated from sewage. Petrochemical spills from ruptured boats or automobiles may cause pollution of the surrounding areas. As has been said earlier that large scale environmental damage is not uncommon when coastal oil rigs or refineries are involved in the oil spillage... oil tankers, also can produce potentially hazardous releases, causing fire, etc., when accidents occur.

Pollution from Various Sources and their Causes

Oil Pollution

Oil pollution is caused by oil spillage in the Sea due to accidents (collision) in Oil Tankers, ruptures in Pipelines digging out oil from the bottom of the sea (see picture above), major fire, explosions etc. Recently in 2011 two major Oil pollution (spillage) incidents took place-one in the Gulf of Mexico by busting an oil digging pipe and in the Indian Sea due to the collision of two oil tankers. Both causing huge loss of money, causing serious threat to aquatic lives, fishes, birds and others. Air pollution produced by ships may alter clouds, affecting global temperatures.

Thus it may be noted that air pollution may come from both natural and man made sources. It is now widely known that globally man made pollutants arises from a variety of sources—combustion, construction activities, mining, industrial activities, agriculture and warfare, etc.

Oil Pollution in the Sea.

Motor vehicle emissions are one of the leading causes of air pollution. China, United States, Russia, Mexico, Japan and India are the world leaders in emissions of air pollutants. These sources include—chemical plants, coal-fired power plants, oil refineries, petrochemical plants, steel plants, acids and alkali plants nuclear power plants, etc. Besides, incinerators, large livestock farms (dairy cows, pigs, poultry farms), plastic factories, metals production factories, and other heavy industries. Agricultural air pollution are caused from felling and burning of natural vegetation as well as spraying of pesticides and herbicides.

Global Change and Global Warming

An estimated amount of about 400 million metric tons of hazardous wastes are generated each year around the years. The United States alone produces about 250 million metric tons of it. Americans constitute less than five per cent of the world's population, but produce roughly 25 per cent of the world's CO_2, and generate approximately 30 per cent of world's waste. In 2007, China has overtaken the United States as the world's largest producer of CO_2.

In February 2007, a report by the Intergovernmental Panel on Climate Change (IPCC), illustrated that human activities had been the primary cause of Global Warming It has been indicated that human activities are basically responsible for the generation of greenhouse gas emissions ; if desired they can cut it (down) down also to avoid the consequences of Global Warming phenomena. The Global Change phenomena have already impacted the World Climate causing more floods, hurricanes, earthquakes, Tsunamies etc.

So large number of countries of the world led by UN's Intergovernmental Panel on Climate Change (IPCC), had gathered together again and again to make rules and regulation regarding the control of Carbon-emissions, after ascertaining which country emits how much at the present. It has been realised that to control carbon emissions, there has to be a transition from fossil fuels like coal and oil uses. It has to be cut down within the next decades.

Pollutant Effects on Human Health

An overview of main health effects on humans from some common types of pollution.

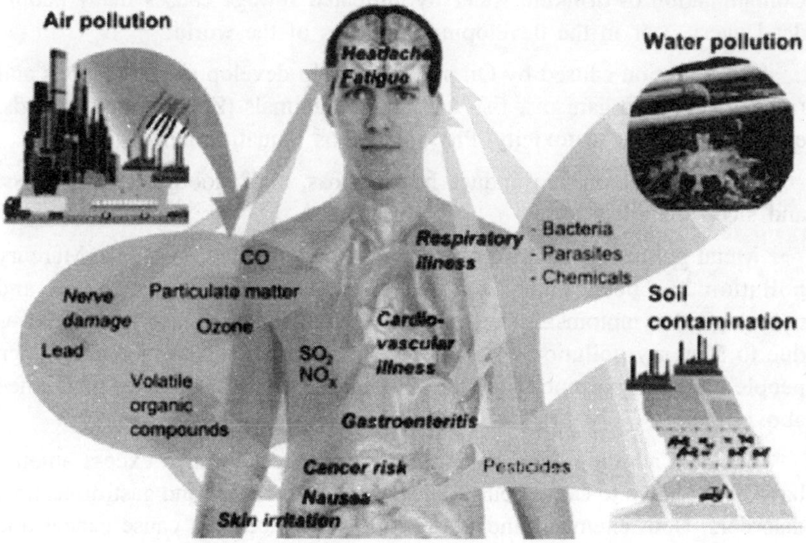

It has been observed that different types of pollutants may cause different types of disorders and/or diseases. In an atmosphere of polluted air many organisms may be killed. Humans may show various kinds of sickness, health problems, malfunctions, diseases including death. Some diseases such as viral infections, chest pain, bronchitis, allergic disorders, respiratory diseases, cardiovascular disease, throat and tonsil inflammation, and congestion may be caused by polluted air and Ozone. Mainly older people, children and infants are very susceptible to diseases induced by air pollution. Those with heart or lung disorders are under additional risks. Pregnant women are vulnerable also.

In an estimate it has been shown that about 600,000 people die prematurely each year in China because of air pollution. In India, air pollution is believed to cause more than 500,000 dead every year. An estimated 50,000 people get killed annually in the US due to various pollution related diseases or disorders.

When water gets polluted, it may pose a major health problem. Contamination of drinking water by untreated sewage causes many people dead every year in the developing countries of the world. Water pollution causes approximately 14,000 deaths per day, mostly due to contamination of drinking water. An estimated 700 million Indians have no access to a proper toilet, and 1,000 Indian children die of diarrheal sickness every day.

It is very sad that quite a large number of Indians still have no access to proper toilets. As a result water gets polluted easily and many children die of when water gets polluted, it may pose a major health problem. Contamination of drinking water by untreated sewage causes many people dead every year in the developing countries of the world.

Oil pollution caused by Oil spills can help develop skin irritations and rashes. Aquatic organisms, fish and aquatic animals (Zooplanktons), birds, etc., may die due to toxicity. Phytoplanktons (aquatic plants).

Noise pollution may induce hearing loss, high blood pressure, stress, and sleep disorders.

Metal pollution may also cause many health related problems. Mercury pollution has been linked to developmental deficits in children and neurological symptoms... The infamous Mina Mata Disease in Japan was due to Mercury pollution of sea water. Fish absorbed that mercury. When people used that poisoned fish, they suffered from those diseases mentioned above.

Lead, Cadmium, Nickel, Chromium and even Iron in excess amount have been shown to cause neurological problems, cancer and gastrointestinal disorders. Both chemical and radioactive substances can cause cancer and as well as birth defects.

Environmental and Ecological Effects: Pollution has been found to be present widely in the environment. There are a number of effects reported in the literature: There can be both direct effects and indirect effects of various pollutants on our health and also on the Ecological species.

Direct Effects: The emission of Greenhouse gases leads to Global Warming phenomena, which affects our ecosystems in many different ways. Carbon dioxide emissions may cause ocean acidification. There will be a decrease in the pH (a determinant of acidity and alkalinity) of the Earth's oceans as CO_2 becomes dissolved. A pH of 7.0 is considered Normal or

Neutral pH. A pH above seven is termed as acidic and below 7.0 is taken as alkaline. Nitrogen oxides are removed from the air by rain and fertilise land which can change the species composition of the ecosystems. Sometimes excesses of Nitrogen oxides including SO_2, converted to Nitric acids and Sulfuric acids), may come down as "Acid rain" to cause harm to both plants and living organisms in the soil. This will affect our food web.

Indirect Effects

Biomagnifications describe situations where toxins (such as heavy metals) may pass through one organism to another in the food chain, becomes more and more concentrated in the process. Finally they are much more concentrated than their initial concentration. Sometimes some Invasive species can enter into an environment and overwhelms (overpowers) the native species and thus destroy or reduce biodiversity. Many invasive plants can contribute biomolecules that can alter soil and chemical compositions of an environment. This may reduce native species due to their competitiveness.

Smog and haze that we see as a result of air pollution can reduce the amount of sunlight normally received by us. This may inhibit the process of photosynthesis (to prepare food for plants); this may lead to the production of tropospheric ozone which may damage plants.

Databases on Environmental Health Information

Internationally several advanced nations have created Databases with information on toxic and harmful chemicals and their effects on human health and the health of our ecological partners. Such information is available for the use of other nations of the world as well.

The Toxicology and Environmental Health Information Programme (TEHIP) at the United States National Library of Medicine (NLM) maintains a comprehensive toxicology and environmental health web site that includes access to resources produced by TEHIP and by other government agencies and organisations. This web site includes links to databases, bibliographies, tutorials, and other scientific and consumer-oriented resources. TEHIP also is responsible for the Toxicology Data Network (TOXNET®) an integrated system of toxicology and environmental health databases that are available free of charge on the web.

TOXMAP is a Geographic Information System (GIS) that is part of TOXNET. TOXMAP uses maps of the United States to help users visually explore data from the United States Environmental Protection Agency's (EPA) Toxics Release Inventory and Superfund Basic Research Programmes. In India, Cancer Registries have been initiated in different parts of the country, wherein information about cancer incidences, its type and causes, etc., are tabulated.

Regulation and Monitoring

To protect the environment from the adverse effects of pollution, many nations worldwide have enacted legislation to regulate various types of pollution as well as to mitigate the adverse effects of pollution.

Pollution Control Technology

Apart from controlling pollution at the individual levels, there are many different forms pollution control technologies are now available. The technologies are meant for use by the Industrial operations, and Government organisations. Some pictures of such technologies are shown below:

A litter trap catches to catch floating rubbish from river water.

A dust collector that can contain dusts resulting out of industrial operations.

We have learnt from the discussion above that Pollution control is equated with proper Environmental management. This means nothing but control of emissions and effluents into air, water or soil. It is now widely

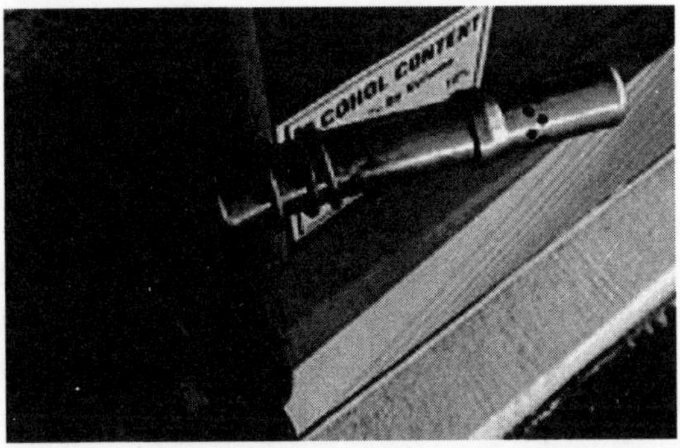

Gas Nozzle with Vapour Recovery.

appreciated that without pollution control, the waste products generated by various human activities will cause degradation to the environment. Although pollution cannot be prevented completely, still a lot can be done with respect to pollution prevention and minimisation of wastes and use of proper technology for waste treatment before their release in the environment.

Practices

Recycling of Used Material

In the area of prevention of pollution, recycling is a widely accepted procedure that can be followed. Substances that can be easily recycled are– waste papers, plastic packets, bottles and other plastic materials, broken metallic parts, broken glasses etc.

Pollution Control Devices

1. Polluted Water Treatment Processes

- Sewage treatment
    - Sedimentation (Primary treatment)
    - Activated sludge bioreactors (Secondary treatment; also used for industrial wastewater)
- Industrial waste-water treatment
    - Biofilters
    - Powdered activated carbon treatment
    - Ultrafiltration

2. Polluted Air Treatment Technology

- Dust collection systems
    - Electrostatic precipitators

- Scrubbers
    - Baffle spray scrubber
    - Mechanically aided scrubber
    - Spray tower
    - Aerated lagoons
    - Constructed wetlands (also used for urban runoff)
- Vapour recovery systems

Although various pollution control technologies are available these days, many Industries do not use them. Even if some Industries have installed air and waste water treatment plants, most of them are lying unused or inoperable. Strict measures are needed from the concerned Departments of the Government.

What are we Learning?

All life forms generate wastes, which is a natural process. During the early stage of our development, there are many reports that many life forms got extinct from Earth. It is quite possible that those which could not adapt to that environment of pollutants lying around got killed, and others survived, Adaptation to the changing environment was a requirement of early survival that supports the Natural Selection hypothesis.

As men became more and more modern and knowledgeable, it started recognising that to survive for a long time good health is required. So they started recognising the harmful substances that can cause harm to their health. Side by side they also devised instruments for quantitative measurements of pollutants to learn how is tolerable and what and how much can cause harm. Thus they developed the LD50 (A dose in which 50 per cent animals would die in the laboratory experiments). Many-fold lower than that dose they labeled as Minimum Acceptable dose for humans.

Carbon Dioxide Menace

Carbon Dioxide, although is essential for the Photosynthesis of plants has been regarded as a most dangerous substance that is responsible for Global Change phenomena. including the Earth's Climate Change phenomena. It has been investigated as to what is the potential for long-term rising levels of atmospheric carbon dioxide. An increase in carbon dioxide levels may cause an increase in the acidity of Ocean water, and thus pose life-threatening effects on marine plants and animals. So there is now world-wide concern regarding the control of carbondioxide emissions (popularly called carbon emissions) from all known sources to save the World from the serious threat it has already advanced.

Some Suggested list of activities for environmental conservation and protection:

The following activities are only suggestive and not exhaustive. Teachers may innovate and design activities suitable to their own conditions/ surroundings/resources and the level and interest of the children. Outdoor

Let us continue to enjoy the Green above

activities are encouraged. Summer camp, tours to Zoo gardens, Museums, Aquariums, Planetariums, Boat trips, forest tours, village fairs, etc., are suggested.

Teachers/Elders: Some may use their own discretion to organise activities in the village schools depending on resource availability to:

1. Provide experiences to observe beauty, symmetry, rhythm and variety of nature.
2. Encourage observation of plants, animals, objects, sites, situations, happenings and occurrences.
3. Encourage collection of different types of objects from the surroundings and their preservation.
4. Conduct activities for comparison and classification of objects based on simple physical characteristics.
5. Conduct Nature walks. Celebrate Nature week.
6. Narrate stories and real life incidents.
7. Promote collection, preparation and use of charts, posters, pictures, puzzles and cut-outs.
8. Organise picnics and visits to different places (local sites, museums, historical monuments, parks, orchards, firms, gardens) and follow them with discussions.
9. Encourage care and adoption of plants and animals.

10. Encourage participation in activities like clay modeling, making masks, puppetry, paper cutting and folding.
11. Involve children in drawing and painting of objects and pictures.
12. Help children in taking care of self and in maintaining cleanliness.
13. Organise dramas, role plays and simulations.
14. Guide children in developing proper healthy habits and strengthening them periodically through follow-up.
15. Share children's experiences through simple discussions.
16. Help children maintain a garden or take care of plants in the school and at school. Let them adopt at least one plant each and take care of it.
17. Involve children in planting and taking care of trees.
18. Guide observations regarding level of cleanliness of different sites and in labeling them as clean or dirty, hygienic or unhygienic and polluted or unpolluted.
19. Organise individual and group activities for maintaining cleanliness in school and classroom.
20. Promote proper ways of waste disposal at home, in school and in the neighborhood. Observe cleanliness week.
21. Make use of dry leaves, flowers and waste materials and natural products in decoration of school and at home.
22. Involve children in activities through eco-clubs, school, health clubs, and eco-corners.
23. Conduct nature and environment related games.
24. Organise recitation of songs and poems.

Teaching and Learning Strategies

At the primary stage, strategies of teaching-learning of Environmental Science would vary from school to school and the teachers will have to select the most appropriate ones according to the needs of the students' resource availability and others. Some of the suggested strategies are given below:

1. Providing direct experiences through field visits and interactions.
2. Encouraging students' participation in joyful activities utilising local resources.
3. Providing opportunities for observation of natural phenomena and helping students to appreciate them.
4. Creating curiosity among students through teacher demonstrations.
5. Helping students acquire interpersonal and social skills through group activities.

Index